Franz Ahn

Ahn's Short Latin Course

Vol. 1

Franz Ahn

Ahn's Short Latin Course
Vol. 1

ISBN/EAN: 9783337302894

Printed in Europe, USA, Canada, Australia, Japan

Cover: Foto ©Paul-Georg Meister /pixelio.de

More available books at **www.hansebooks.com**

STEIGER'S Latin Series.

AHN'S
SHORT LATIN COURSE.

BY

Dr. P. HENN.

I. ESSENTIALS OF LATIN GRAMMAR.
II. PARALLEL EXERCISES FOR TRANSLATION.
III. READING LESSONS WITH VOCABULARY.

NUMBER TWO.

NEW YORK:
E. STEIGER & CO.
1883.

PREFACE.

The present volume, **Number Two** of *AHN'S Short Latin Course,* continues, carefully and on the same plan, the instruction in Latin commenced in **Number One**. It is divided into three Parts.

Part First exhibits, besides a review of the Declensions, the chief grammatical forms of Conjugation, and an explanation of the most important rules of Syntax. The Exercises in **Part Second** are intended to furnish to the teacher the opportunity of drilling his pupils in the practical application of the rules *while they are learning them.* As the pupil is expected to learn by heart the Vocabulary belonging to each lesson, words once given are not repeated; it should, however, be borne in mind that any word whose meaning cannot be recalled, may be looked up in the **Vocabularies** to the Exercises, which contain every word and idiom in the text.

The subject of Conjugation having been finished (**Part First**, 93), all the forms and constructions needed as a preparation for easy reading are given, and may be followed directly by the earlier **Reading Lessons** in **Part Third**, while, at the same time, the more important constructions of Syntax (**Part First**, 94 and after) may be taken up and exemplified by exercises upon each construction. It must, however, be left to the teacher's judgment and experience whether to follow this practice, or to postpone the Reading Lessons until the pupil has finished the systematic study of Syntax. In the separate **Vocabulary** to Part Third it has been the aim to give to each word the particular meanings which occur in the Reading Lessons without, however, omitting its leading signification.

In preparing the *Short Latin Course* it has been the author's intention *to save unnecessary work.* But it must not be thought that this book does away with the necessity of honest work altogether. There is no more pernicious idea than that of learning a language "in six easy lessons". All the work, however, that is done, should have the one aim in view, viz.: to conduct the pupil by the *shortest and easiest road* to a sound and practical knowledge of Latin.

TABLE OF CONTENTS.

PART I. — ESSENTIALS OF LATIN GRAMMAR.
ETYMOLOGY (continued).

Sections		Page
1. 2.	Peculiarities of Declension	1
3—10.	Greek Nouns	1
11—22.	Irregular Nouns	2
23—25.	Verbs of the First Conjugation	4
26—35.	Verbs of the Second Conjugation	5
36—62.	Verbs of the Third Conjugation	7
36. 37.	Verbs in ŭō, vō	7
38. 39.	Verbs in Iō	7
40—44.	Verbs in dō, tō	8
45. 46.	Verbs in bō, pō	9
47—54.	Verbs in cō, gō (gŭō), quō, hō, ctō	10
55—59.	Verbs in lō, mō, nō, rō	12
60—62.	Verbs in sō, xō, scō	13
63. 64.	Verbs of the Fourth Conjugation	13
65—68.	Deponent Verbs	14
69—71.	Semi-Deponents and Neutral Passives	15
72—77.	Derivative Verbs	16
78—87.	Irregular Verbs	17
88—91.	Defective Verbs	22
92. 93.	Impersonal Verbs	23

CONSTRUCTIONS OF SYNTAX.

94—102.	Agreement of the Predicate	24
103. 104.	Agreement of Attribute and Apposition	25
105. 106.	Agreement of Pronouns	25
107—111.	Questions	26
112—164.	Uses of Cases	26
112—115.	Cases with Prepositions	26
116—118.	Cases with Adjectives	28
119—145.	Cases with Verbs	29
146—157.	Relations of Time, Space and Place	34
158—164.	Ablative in Special Constructions	36
165—170.	Use of Tenses	37

Sections		Page
171—174.	*Sequence of Tenses*	37
175—177.	*Imperative*	38
178. 179.	*Infinitive*	39
180.	*Gerund*	39
181.	*Gerundive*	40
182—186.	*Accusative with the Infinitive*	40
187—189.	*Participles*	41
190—192.	*Periphrastic Conjugation*	42
193. 194.	*Ablative Absolute*	42
195—198.	*The Supine and its Equivalents*	43
199—208.	*Subjunctive after Conjunctions*	44
209.	*Subjunctive after Relatives*	46
210.	*Subjunctive in Indirect Questions*	47

PART II. — PARALLEL EXERCISES.

ETYMOLOGY (continued).

1. 2.	*Declension* (Gr. 1—22)	48
3. 4.	*First Conjugation* (Gr. 23—25)	48
5. 6.	*Second Conjugation* (Gr. 26—35)	49
7. 8.	*Third Conjugation.* Verbs in **ŭō, vŏ** (Gr. 36. 37)	49
9. 10.	Verbs in **ĭŏ** (Gr. 38. 39)	50
11—14.	Verbs in **dŏ, tŏ** (Gr. 40—44)	50
15. 16.	Verbs in **bŏ, pŏ** (Gr. 45. 46)	51
17—20.	Verbs in **cŏ, gŏ (gŭŏ), quŏ, hŏ, ctŏ** (Gr. 47—54)	52
21—24.	Verbs in **lŏ, mŏ, nŏ, rŏ** (Gr. 55—59)	52
25. 26.	Verbs in **sŏ, xŏ, scŏ** (Gr. 60—62)	53
27. 28.	*Fourth Conjugation* (Gr. 63. 64)	54
29. 30.	*Deponent Verbs* (Gr. 65—68)	54
31. 32.	*Semi-Deponents and Derivatives* (Gr. 69—77)	55
33. 34.	*Irregular Verbs:* ĕdĕrĕ, vellĕ, nollĕ, mallĕ, īrĕ — (Gr. 78—82)	55
35. 36.	quīrĕ, nequīrĕ, ferrĕ, fĭĕrī (Gr. 83—87)	56
37. 38.	*Defective and Impersonal Verbs* (Gr. 88—93)	56

CONSTRUCTIONS OF SYNTAX.

39—42.	*Agreement of the Predicate. Questions* (Gr. 94—111).	57
43—46.	*Cases with Prepositions* (Gr. 112—115)	58
47. 48.	*Cases with Adjectives* (Gr. 116—118)	59
49. 50.	*Cases with Verbs.* — *Genitive* (Gr. 119—128)	59
51. 52.	*Dative* (Gr. 129—132)	60
53. 54.	*Accusative* (Gr. 133—139)	60
55. 56.	*Ablative* (Gr. 140—145)	60

Sections		Page
57—60.	*Relations of Time, Space, and Place* (Gr. 146—157)...	61
61 62	*Ablative in Special Constructions* (Gr. 158—164)	62
63. 64	*Use of Tenses* (Gr. 165—170)	63
65 66.	*Sequence of Tenses* (Gr. 171—174)	63
67 68.	*Imperative, Infinitive* (Gr. 175—179)	64
69 70.	*Gerund, Gerundive* (Gr. 180—181)	64
71. 72.	*Accusative with the Infinitive* (Gr. 182—186)	65
73 74.	*Participles* (Gr. 187—189)	65
75. 76.	*Periphrastic Conjugation* (Gr. 190—192)	66
77. 78.	*Ablative Absolute* (Gr. 193. 194)	66
79. 80.	*Supines* (Gr. 195—198)	67
81—84.	*Subjunctive after Conjunctions* (Gr. 199—208)	68
85. 86.	*Subjunctive after Relatives* (Gr. 209)	69
87. 88.	*Subjunctive in Indirect Questions* (Gr. 210. 211)	69
	VOCABULARY: 1. *Latin and English*	71
	2. *English and Latin*	93

PART III. — READING LESSONS.

1. Daedălus ... 110
2. Judicium Parĭdis ... 110
3. Bellum Trojānum ... 111
4. Ulixes in specu Polyphēmi ... 112
5. Darēus et Scythae ... 114
6. Romŭlus ... 114
7. Sabinōrum virgĭnes rapiuntur ... 114
8. Tarquinĭus Superbus ... 115
9. Horatĭus Cocles ... 115
10. Mucĭus Scaevola ... 115
11. Pyrrhus ... 116
12. Arminĭus ... 117
13. De morte Epaminondae ... 118
14. De Romanōrum disciplīna militāri ... 118
15. De Apelle ... 119
16. Senes et mors ... 119
17. Judicĭum Philippi ... 119
18. De Socrăte ... 119
19. De Mida ... 120
20. Agricŏlae Lyciae in ranas mutantur ... 120
21. De Tantălo ... 121
22. De Thesĕo ... 121
23. De Iphigenĭa ... 121
24. De Codro ... 122

Sections	Page
25. De libris Sibyllīnis	122
26. De Cyro et Tomȳri	123
27. De Marcio Coriolāno	123
28. De Herostrăto	124
29. De Stilpōne philosŏpho	124
30. De amicitia Orestis et Pyladis	124
31. De Solōne et Croeso	124
32. De Amāsi et Polycrate	126
33. Quomŏdo Croesus, Lydiae rex, a Cyro, Persărum rege, victus sit	128
34. De Cyro puĕro	132
35. Quomódo Cyrus Persărum regnum condidĕrit	136
VOCABULARY: *Latin and English*	139

PART FIRST.

ESSENTIALS OF LATIN GRAMMAR.

ETYMOLOGY (continued).

PECULIARITIES OF DECLENSION.

1. In composition with pătĕr, mātĕr, fīlĭŭs, fīlĭă, the word fămĭlĭă has in the **Genitive Singular** fămĭlĭās, *e. g.*, pāterfămĭlĭās, *the father of a fami'y.*

2. In the **Genitive Plural** of the **Second Declension ŭm** is often found for **ōrŭm**, especially in certain words denoting money, measure, or weight, as: nummŭm for nummōrŭm, *of moneys,* also in a few other words, as: dĕŭm for dĕōrŭm, lībĕrŭm for lībĕrōrŭm.

Greek Nouns.

3. Review the Greek forms of the **First Declension** I. 18.

4. A few **Greek Nouns** of the **Second Declension** end in **ŏs, ŏn**, instead of **ŭs, ŭm**. Greek Nouns ending in **eŭs** (like Orpheŭs) are thus declined:

| Nom. Or' pheŭs | Dat. Or' phĕ ō | Voc. Or' pheŭ |
| Gen. Or' phĕ ī | Acc. Or' phĕ ŭm | Abl. Or' phĕ ō |

5. The greater number of **Greek Nouns** belong to the **Third Declension**. In the **Dative** and **Ablative Plural**, Neuters in **mă** have commonly **īs** instead of **ĭbŭs**; thus: pŏēmătĭs, instead of pŏēmătĭbŭs.

6. Several feminine nouns in **ō** have **Genitive Sing. ŭs**, all the other cases ending in **ō**, as: ĕchō, Gen. ĕchūs, Dat. ĕchō, *an echo.*

7. Many Greek nouns have **Genitive ŏs**, as: lampăs, lampădŏs, *a lamp* — and **Accusative ă**, as: Sălămĭs, Acc. Sălămīnă, *Salamis;* āĕr, Acc. āĕră, *air;* aethēr, Acc. aethĕră, *ether.*

8. The **Vocative Sing.** drops s in nouns in **eŭs, ĭs, ўs**, and **ās** (**antĭs**), as: Daphnĭs, Voc. Daphnī, *Daphnis;* Orpheŭs, Voc. Orpheŭ, *Orpheus;* Atlās, Voc. Atlă, *Atlas.*

9. The ending **ōn** occurs in the **Genitive Plur.** of a few titles of books, as: Mĕtămorphōsēs, -ĕōn.

10. Many Greek nouns have **Plural Nom. ĕs**, as: lampăs, lampădĕs — and **Accus. ăs**, as: Ărabs, Ărăbăs, *Arabian;* Cyclops, Cyclōpăs, *a Cyclops.*

Irregular Nouns.

11. Some Nouns are **Defective in Case**, i. e., they want one or more cases. The **Nominative** is wanting in (frux) *fruit*, frūgĭs; (ops) *help*, ŏpĭs; (dĭcĭŏ) *dominion*, dĭcĭōnĭs.

12. The **Genitive** and **Dative** of vis, *force*, are wanting.

13. nĭhĭl, *nothing*, and părŭm, *too little*, can only be used as **Nominatives** or **Accusatives**.

14. The **Genitive** and **Ablative** of nēmŏ, *nobody*, are wanting, and supplied by nullīus, nullo.

15. The **Genitive Plural** is wanting in cŏr, *the heart;* ōs, *the mouth;* pax, *peace*, and some others.

16. Several nouns occur only in the **Ablative Singular**; such are:

sponte, *freely, of one's own accord*   nātū, *by birth*   noctū, *at night*
jussū, *by order*   interdĭū, *in day-time*

17. Defective in Number are those which want either the **Singular** or the **Plural**.

18. Nouns used in the **Singular** only: **Singularĭa tantum.** Some nouns, from the nature of the things meant, have no Plural, as: justĭtĭă, *justice;* fāmēs, *hunger;* aurŭm, *gold.* There are also other nouns which lack the Plural, without any obvious reason, as: spĕcĭmĕn, *a sample;* vespĕr, *evening;* mĕrīdĭēs, *mid-day;* vēr, *spring.*

19. Nouns used in the **Plural** only: **Pluralĭa tantum.** The commonest of them are:

First Declension.

dēlĭcĭae, -**ārŭm**, *delight*   insĭdĭae, -**ārŭm**, *an ambush*
dīvĭtĭae, -**ārŭm**, *riches*   nundĭnae, -**ārŭm**, *market-day*
exsĕquĭae, -**ārŭm**, *a funeral*   nuptĭae, -**ārŭm**, *a wedding*
fĕrĭae, -**ārŭm**, *holidays*   tĕnĕbrae, -**ārŭm**, *darkness*
indūtĭae, -**ārŭm**, *a truce*   Athēnae, -**ārŭm**, *Athens*

Second Declension.

armă, -**ōrŭm**, *arms, weapons*   lĭbĕrī, -**ōrŭm**, *children*
fastī, -**ōrŭm**, *an almanac*   postĕrī, -**ōrŭm**, *descendants*
gĕmĭnī, -**ōrŭm**, *twins*   Delphī, -**ōrŭm**, *Delphi*

Third Declension.

Alpēs, -īum, *the Alps*
mājōrēs, -ūm, *ancestors*
faucēs, -īum, *the throat*
mānēs, -īum, *the shades of the dead*

20. Some words have besides their **general** meaning a **special** meaning in the **Plural**:

Singular.	Plural.
aedēs, -ĭs, *a temple*	aedēs, -īum, *a house*
ăquă, -ae, *water*	ăquae, -ārŭm, *medicinal springs*
auxĭlĭŭm, -ī, *help*	auxĭlĭă, -ōrŭm, *auxiliary troops*
castrŭm, -ī, *a fort*	castră, -ōrŭm, *a camp*
cōpĭă, -ae, *abundance*	cōpĭae, -ārŭm, *troops*
littĕră, -ae, *a letter (of the alphabet)*	littĕrae, -ārŭm, *an epistle; learning, literature*
impĕdīmentŭm, -ī, *a hindrance*	impĕdīmentă, -ōrŭm, *baggage*
rostrŭm, -ī, *a beak*	rostră, -ōrŭm, *speaker's platform*
sāl, sălĭs, *salt*	sălēs, -īum, *witticisms*

21. Redundant nouns are those which are found of **Different Genders** in the same Declension; as:

Singular.	Plural.
jŏcŭs, -ī, *a joke, jest*	jŏcī, -ōrŭm, & jŏcă, -ōrŭm, *jokes*
lŏcŭs, -ī, *a place*	{ lŏcī, -ōrŭm, *passages (in books)* { lŏcă, -ōrŭm, *places*
caelŭm, -ī, *heaven*	caelī, -ōrŭm, *heavens*
frēnŭm, -ī, *a bridle*	frēnī, -ōrŭm, & frēnă, -ōrŭm, *a bit*

or of **Different Declensions**; as:

luxŭrĭă, -ae	luxŭrĭēs, -ēī, *luxury*
mātĕrĭă, -ae	mātĕrĭēs, -ēī, *matter*
segnĭtĭă, -ae	segnĭtĭēs, -ēī, *slothfulness*
ĕlĕphantŭs, -ī	ĕlĕphās, -antĭs, *an elephant*
plēbs, -ĭs	plēbēs, -ēī, *the common people*

22. The Latin has only a few **Indeclinable Nouns**; viz.:

făs, *right*
nĕfăs, *wrong*
instăr, *an image, kind*
nĕcessĕ, *necessary*
mānĕ, *morning*
nĭhĭl, *nothing*
pondō, (lit. *in weight*), *pounds*
ŏpŭs, *need*

besides the names of the Latin and Greek letters, as: A, D, alphă, deltă, and some foreign words, as: sĭnăpĭ, *mustard*.

(See *Exercises 1, 2*, page 48.)

Verbs of the First Conjugation.

23. Most of the Verbs of the **First Conjugation** form their **Perfect** and **Supine** in -āvī, -ātŭm, like ămō. Only a few deviate from the regular formation. Mark the following:

Perfect in ŭī, Supine in ĭtŭm (tŭm).

crĕpō, -ārĕ, *to creak*	crĕpŭī	crĕpĭtŭm
cŭbō, -ārĕ, *to lie down*	cŭbŭī	cŭbĭtŭm
dŏmō, -ārĕ, *to tame*	dŏmŭī	dŏmĭtŭm
sŏnō, -ārĕ, *to sound*	sŏnŭī	sŏnĭtŭm, sŏnātūrŭs
tŏnō, -ārĕ, *to thunder*	tŏnŭī	tŏnĭtŭm
vĕtō, -ārĕ, *to forbid, prohibit*	vĕtŭī	vĕtĭtŭm
frĭcō, -ārĕ, *to rub*	frĭcŭī	frĭcātŭm, frictŭm
mĭcō, -ārĕ, *to shine*	mĭcŭī	*(wanting)*
sĕcō, -ārĕ, *to cut*	sĕcŭī	sectŭm, sĕcātūrŭs

Compounds of the obsolete plĭcō have both ŭī, ĭtŭm and āvī, ātŭm, thus:

applĭcō, -ārĕ, *to apply*	applĭcāvī / applĭcŭī	applĭcātŭm / applĭcĭtŭm
explĭcō, -ārĕ, *to unfold*	explĭcāvī / explĭcŭī	explĭcātŭm / explĭcĭtŭm
implĭcō, -ārĕ, *to involve*	implĭcāvī / implĭcŭī	implĭcātŭm / implĭcĭtŭm
pōtō, -ārĕ, *to drink*	pōtāvī	pōtŭm
ĕnĕcō, -ārĕ, *to slay*	ĕnĕcāvī(ŭī)	ĕnĕcātŭm(tŭm)

24. Perfect in I, Supine in tŭm,
with lengthened stem-vowel.

jŭvō, -ārĕ } *to assist*	jūvī	jūtŭm
adjŭvō, -ārĕ	adjūvī	adjūtŭm

Fut. Participle: jŭvātūrŭs, *but* adjūtūrŭs *or* adjŭvātūrŭs

lăvō, -ārĕ, *to wash*	lăvī	lăvātŭm (lautŭm, lōtŭm)

25. With Reduplicated Perfect.

Some Verbs of the *First*, *Second* and *Third Conjugations* repeat in the *Perfect* the initial consonant of the stem with the vowel following it, or with ĕ. Compound Verbs omit the reduplication, but Compounds of dō, *I give;* stō, *I stand;* discō, *I learn;* poscō, *I demand,* and some Compounds of currō, *I run,* retain it.

dō, -ārĕ, *to give*	dĕdī	dătŭm
circumdō, -ārĕ, *to surround*	circumdĕdī	circumdătŭm

Like **dŏ**, are conjugated the Compounds with words of *two* syllables, as: circumdŏ, *I surround*. The Compounds with words of *one* syllable pass over into the 3d Conjugation. a in dărĕ is everywhere short, except in **dās**, *thou givest;* **dā**, *give thou*.

stŏ, stārĕ, *to stand*   stĕtī   stătŭm
circumstŏ,-ārĕ, *to stand around*   circumstĕtī   *(wanting)*
praestŏ, -ārĕ, *to afford*   praestĭtī   *(wanting)*

Like **circumstŏ**, all Compounds of **stārĕ** with Prepositions of *two* syllables have **stĕtī** in the Perfect, but no Supine. Those compounded with Prepositions of *one* syllable have **stĭtī** in the Perfect, and likewise **no Supine**.

(See *Exercises 3, 4*, p. 48.)

Verbs of the Second Conjugation.

26. Most Verbs of the **Second Conjugation** have **ŭī** in the **Perfect** and **ĭtŭm** in the **Supine**, and this is considered the regular formation. Many Verbs however, with a regular Perfect in **ŭī** want the Supine, as: tĭmĕŏ, -ĕrĕ, *to fear;* arcĕŏ, -ĕrĕ, *to keep off*, &c. Others want both, Perfect and Supine, as: immĭnĕŏ, -ĕrĕ, *to threaten*.

27. A great many Verbs of the Second Conjugation deviate from the regular formation mentioned above.

28. Perfect in ēvī, Supine in ētŭm (ĭtŭm, tŭm).

delĕŏ, -ĕrĕ, *to destroy*   delēvī   delētŭm
flĕŏ, -ĕrĕ, *to weep*   flēvī   flētŭm
nĕŏ, ĕrĕ, *to spin*   nēvī   nētŭm
[plĕŏ, *I fill*]*
implĕŏ, -ĕrĕ, *to fill (up)*   implēvī   implētŭm
[ŏlĕŏ, *I grow*]
ăbŏlĕŏ, -ĕrĕ, *to abolish*   ăbŏlēvī   ăbŏlĭtŭm

29.   Perfect in ī, Supine in tŭm.

căvĕŏ, -ĕrĕ, *to be on one's guard*   căvī   cautŭm
făvĕŏ, -ĕrĕ, *to favor*   făvī   fautŭm
fŏvĕŏ, -ĕrĕ, *to cherish*   fŏvī   fŏtŭm
mŏvĕŏ, -ĕrĕ, *to move, trouble*   mōvī   mōtŭm
vŏvĕŏ, -ĕrĕ, *to vow, devote*   vōvī   vōtŭm
păvĕŏ, -ĕrĕ, *to quake for fear*   păvī   *(wanting)*
fervĕŏ, -ĕrĕ, *to glow*   fervī, ferbŭī *(wanting)*
cōnīvĕŏ, -ĕrĕ, *to shut the eyes*   cōnīvī, cōnixī *(wanting)*

---

* Obsolete forms are enclosed within brackets [ ].

30. Dropping the I of the Supine.

dŏcĕō, -ērĕ, to teach	dŏcŭī	doctŭm
tĕnĕō, -ērĕ, to hold	tĕnŭī	(tentŭm)
miscĕō, -ērĕ, to mix, mingle	miscŭī	mixtŭm, mistŭm
torrĕō, -ērĕ, to roast	torrŭī	tostŭm
censĕō, -ērĕ, to value, think	censŭī	censŭm

31. Perfect in sī, Supine in tŭm.

augĕō, -ērĕ, to increase	auxī	auctŭm
indulgĕō, -ērĕ, to indulge	indulsī	indultŭm
torquĕō, -ērĕ, to torture	torsī	tortŭm
lūcĕō, -ērĕ, to shine	luxī	(wanting)
lūgĕō, -ērĕ, to mourn	luxī	(wanting)
frīgĕō, -ērĕ, to be cold	(frixī)	(wanting)

32. Perfect in sī, Supine in sŭm.

ardĕō, -ērĕ, to burn	arsī	arsŭm
haerĕō, -ērĕ, to hang	haesī	haesŭm
jŭbĕō, -ērĕ, to order	jussī	jussŭm
mănĕō, -ērĕ, to stay, remain	mansī	mansŭm
mulcĕō, -ērĕ, to soothe	mulsī	mulsŭm
mulgĕō, -ērĕ, to milk	mulsī	mulsŭm
rīdĕō, -ērĕ, to laugh	risī	risŭm
suādĕō, -ērĕ, to advise	suāsī	suāsŭm
tergĕō, -ērĕ / tergō, -ĕrĕ } to wipe	tersī	tersŭm
algĕō, -ērĕ, to be cold	alsī	(wanting)
fulgĕō, -ērĕ, to shine	fulsī	(wanting)
turgĕō, -ērĕ, to swell	tursī	(wanting)
urgĕō, -ērĕ, to urge	ursī	(wanting)

33. Perfect in ī, Supine in sŭm.

prandĕō, -ērĕ, to breakfast	prandī	pransŭm

Participle pransŭs, in an active sense, *having breakfasted*

sĕdĕō, -ērĕ, to sit	sēdī	sessŭm
vĭdĕō, -ērĕ, to see	vīdī	visŭm

34. With Reduplication:

mordĕō, -ērĕ, to bite	mŏmordī	morsŭm
pendĕō, -ērĕ, to hang	pĕpendī	pensŭm
spondĕō, -ērĕ, to pledge	spŏpondī	sponsŭm
tondĕō, -ērĕ, to shear	tŏtondī	tonsŭm

35. Mark the solitary Verb:
ciĕō, -ĕrĕ } *to rouse*   cīvī   cĭtŭm (cītŭm)
ciō, -īrĕ

(See *Exercises 5, 6*, p. 49.)

Verbs of the Third Conjugation.

VERBS ending in ŭō, vō.

36. Perfect in ī, Supine in tŭm.

ăcŭō, -ĕrĕ, *to sharpen, whet*   ăcŭī   ăcūtŭm
   Perf. Part. wanting; ăcūtŭs, *sharp*, is Adjective only.

argŭō, -ĕrĕ, *to accuse*   argŭī   (argūtŭm)
imbŭō, -ĕrĕ, *to dip, dye*   imbŭī   imbūtŭm
indŭō, -ĕrĕ, *to put on*   indŭī   indūtŭm
exŭō, -ĕrĕ, *to put off*   exŭī   exūtŭm
lŭō, -ĕrĕ, *to atone for*   lŭī   (lŭĭtŭm)
lŭō, -ĕrĕ, *to wash*   lŭī   lūtŭm
mĭnŭō, -ĕrĕ, *to lessen*   mĭnŭī   mĭnūtŭm
rŭō, -ĕrĕ, *to rush forth*   rŭī   rŭtŭm
spŭō, -ĕrĕ, *to spit*   spŭī   spūtŭm
stătŭō, -ĕrĕ, *to set, place*   stătŭī   stătūtŭm
sŭō, -ĕrĕ, *to sew*   sŭī   sūtŭm
trĭbŭō, -ĕrĕ, *to give, confer on* trĭbŭī   trĭbūtŭm
solvō, -ĕrĕ, *to (dis)solve*   solvī   sŏlūtŭm
volvō, -ĕrĕ, *to roll, turn*   volvī   vŏlūtŭm
congrŭō, -ĕrĕ, *to agree*   congrŭī   (wanting)
mĕtŭō, -ĕrĕ, *to fear*   mĕtŭī   (wanting)
plŭō, -ĕrĕ, *to rain*   plŭī (plŭvī) (wanting)
sternŭō, -ĕrĕ, *to sneeze*   sternŭī   (wanting)

37. The following Verbs form their *Perfect* and *Supine* differently:

vīvō, -ĕrĕ, *to live*   vixī   victŭm
strŭō, -ĕrĕ, *to build*   struxī structŭm
flŭō, -ĕrĕ, *to flow*   fluxī   fluxŭm

(See *Exercises 7, 8*, p. 49.)

VERBS ending in IŌ.

38. Some Verbs of the **Third Conjugation** insert **ĭ** before the ending of the **Present**, as: căpĕrĕ, *to take;* căpĭō, *I take.* This **ĭ** appears likewise in all the other forms derived from the Present, but not before another **ĭ** or **ĕ**, except in the third person of the Future Active: capĭĕt, *he will take* (see I. *142*).

căpĭō, -ĕrĕ, *to take*	cēpī	captŭm
făcĭō, -ĕrĕ, *to do, make*	fēcī	factŭm
jăcĭō, -ĕrĕ, *to throw, cast*	jēcī	jactŭm
[lăcĭō, *I entice*]		
allĭcĭō, -ĕrĕ, *to allure*	allexī	(allectŭm)
[spĕcĭō, *I see*]		
aspĭcĭō, -ĕrĕ, *to look*	aspexī	aspectŭm
cŭpĭō, -ĕrĕ, *to wish, desire*	cŭpīvī	cŭpītŭm
fŏdĭō, -ĕrĕ, *to dig*	fōdī	fossŭm
fŭgĭō, -ĕrĕ, *to flee or fly*	fūgī	(fŭgĭtŭm)
părĭō, -ĕrĕ, *to bring forth*	pĕpĕrī	partŭm
	Fut. Part.	părĭtūrŭs
quătĭō, -ĕrĕ, *to shake*	*(wanting)*	quassŭm
răpĭō, -ĕrĕ, *to snatch away*	răpŭī	raptŭm
săpĭō, -ĕrĕ, *to be wise*	săpīvī, săpŭī	*(wanting)*

39. The Verb **făcĕrĕ**, *to do, make*, has for its **Passive** fīō, factŭs sŭm, fĭĕrī, *to be made, become* (see *86*). Its **Imperative** is făc, *do*.

The same rule applies to those Compounds of făcĭō which retain **ă**, as: pătĕfăcĭō, *I open;* **Pass.** pătĕfīō, *I am opened;* **Imperat.** pătĕfăc, *open*. The Compounds of făcĭō with **Prepositions** change **ă** to **ĭ**, and form the **Passive** and the **Imperative** regularly, as: interfĭcĭō, *I kill;* **Pass.** interfĭcĭŏr; **Imperat.** interfĭcĕ.

(See *Exercises 9, 10*, p. 50.)

Verbs ending in dō, tō.
40.   Perfect in sī, Supine in sŭm.

claudō, -ĕrĕ, *to shut, close*	clausī	clausŭm]
dīvĭdō, -ĕrĕ, *to divide, separate*	dīvīsī	dīvīsŭm
laedō, -ĕrĕ, *to violate, hurt*	laesī	laesŭm
lūdō, -ĕrĕ, *to play*	lūsī	lūsŭm
plaudō, -ĕrĕ, *to applaud*	plausī	plausŭm
rādō, -ĕrĕ, *to scrape*	rāsī	rāsŭm
rōdō, -ĕrĕ, *to gnaw*	rōsī	rōsŭm
trūdō, -ĕrĕ, *to thrust*	trūsī	trūsŭm
vādō, -ĕrĕ, *to go*	*(wanting)*	*(wanting)*

41.   With Reduplication:

cădō, -ĕrĕ, *to fall*	cĕcĭdī	cāsŭm
caedō, -ĕrĕ, *to fell*	cĕcĭdī	caesŭm
pendō, -ĕrĕ, *to weigh*	pĕpendī	pensŭm
tendō, -ĕrĕ, *to spread*	tĕtendī	tensŭm & tentŭm
tundō, -ĕrĕ, *to thump*	tŭtŭdī	tūsŭm & tunsŭm

42. Compounds of **dărĕ** with **monosyllabic** words pass over into the **Third Conjugation**.

crēdō, -ĕrĕ, *to believe*	crēdĭdī	crēdĭtŭm
vendō, -ĕrĕ, *to sell*	vendĭdī	vendĭtŭm
condō, -ĕrĕ, *to build*	condĭdī	condĭtŭm
ēdō, -ĕrĕ, *to give out, publish*	ēdĭdī	ēdĭtŭm
perdō, -ĕrĕ, *to ruin*	perdĭdī	perdĭtŭm
reddō, -ĕrĕ, *to give back, make*	reddĭdī	reddĭtŭm
trādō, -ĕrĕ, *to deliver*	trādĭdī	trādĭtŭm

(See *Exercises 11, 12*, p. 50.)

43. Perfect in ī, Supine in sŭm.

[candō, *I burn*]

accendō, -ĕrĕ, *to kindle*	accendī	accensŭm
cūdō, -ĕrĕ, *to forge*	cūdī	cūsŭm
ĕdō, -ĕrĕ, *to eat (79)*	ēdī	ēsŭm

[fendō, *I fend*]

dēfendō, -ĕrĕ, *to defend*	dēfendī	dēfensŭm
mandō, -ĕrĕ, *to chew*	mandī	mansŭm
prĕhendō, -ĕrĕ, *to seize*	prĕhendī	prĕhensŭm
scandō, -ĕrĕ, *to climb*	scandī	scansŭm
fundō, -ĕrĕ, *to pour; to rout*	fūdī	fūsŭm
vertō, -ĕrĕ, *to turn*	vertī	versŭm

44. Various Irregularities:

cēdō, -ĕrĕ, *to yield*	cessī	cessŭm
findō, -ĕrĕ, *to split, cleave*	fĭdī	fissŭm
scindō, -ĕrĕ, *to cut*	scĭdī	scissŭm
mētō, -ĕrĕ, *to reap*	messŭī	messŭm
mittō, -ĕrĕ, *to send*	mīsī	missŭm
pandō, -ĕrĕ, *to spread*	pandī	passŭm
pĕtō, -ĕrĕ, *to seek*	pĕtīvī, pĕtĭī	pĕtītŭm
sīdō, -ĕrĕ, *to sit down*	sēdī	*(wanting)*
sistō, -ĕrĕ, *to stop*	stĭtī	stătŭm

See *Exercises 13, 14,* p. 51.)

VERBS ending in **bō, pō**.

45. Verbs in **bō, pō** take **sī** in the **Perfect**, **tŭm** in the **Supine**; at the same time **b** before **s** and **t** becomes **p**, as: nūbō, nupsī, nuptŭm.

glūbō, -ĕrĕ, *to peel*	(glupsī)	gluptŭm
nūbō, -ĕrĕ, *to marry*	nupsī	nuptŭm
scrībō, -ĕrĕ, *to write*	scripsī	scriptŭm

carpō, -ĕrĕ, *to pluck, crop*	carpsī	carptŭm
rēpō, -ĕrĕ, *to creep, crawl*	repsī	reptŭm
scalpō, -ĕrĕ, *to carve*	scalpsī	scalptŭm
sculpō, -ĕrĕ, *to chisel*	sculpsī	sculptŭm
serpō, -ĕrĕ, *to creep*	serpsī	(serptŭm)

46. Irregular:

accumbō, -ĕrĕ, *to recline at table*	accŭbŭī	accŭbĭtŭm
bībō, -ĕrĕ, *to drink*	bībī	(bībĭtŭm)
rumpō, -ĕrĕ, *to break*	rūpī	ruptŭm
strĕpō, -ĕrĕ, *to make a noise*	strĕpŭī	strĕpĭtŭm
lambō, -ĕrĕ, *to lick*	lambī	(lambĭtŭm)
scăbō, -ĕrĕ, *to scratch*	scăbī	*(wanting)*

(See *Exercises 15, 16*, p. 51.)

VERBS ending in cō, gō (gŭō), quō, hō, ctō.

47. c, g, q, and h with s become x,
g, h, and q before t become c.

dūc-ō — duxī = ducsī   rĕgō — rectŭm = regtŭm
rĕg-ō — rexī = regsī   trăhō — tractŭm = trahtŭm
cōqu-ō — coxī = coqsī   cōquō — coctŭm = coqtŭm
trăh-ō — traxī = trahsī

48. Perfect in sī, Supine in tŭm.

cingō, -ĕrĕ, *to gird, surround*	cinxī	cinctŭm
[flīgō, -ĕrĕ, *to strike*	flixī	flictŭm]
afflīgō, -ĕrĕ, *to dash*	afflixī	afflictŭm
jungō, -ĕrĕ, *to join*	junxī	junctŭm
plangō, -ĕrĕ, *to beat, lament*	planxī	planctŭm
rĕgō, -ĕrĕ, *to rule, govern*	rexī	rectŭm
sūgō, -ĕrĕ, *to suck*	suxī	suctŭm
tĕgō, -ĕrĕ, *to cover*	texī	tectŭm
tingō (tingŭō), -ĕrĕ, *to stain*	tinxī	tinctŭm
ungō (ungŭō), -ĕrĕ, *to anoint*	unxī	unctŭm
[stingŭō, *I put out*]		
exstingŭō, -ĕrĕ, *to put out*	exstinxī	exstinctŭm
trăhō, -ĕrĕ, *to draw*	traxī	tractŭm
vĕhō, -ĕrĕ, *to carry*	vexī	vectŭm
dīcō, -ĕrĕ, *to say, tell, call*	dixī	dictŭm
dūcō, -ĕrĕ, *to lead*	duxī	ductŭm

The **Imperatives** of dīcĕrĕ, *to say*; dūcĕrĕ, *to lead*, are: dīc, dūc; Compounds follow the simple Verbs: ēdūc, praedīc.

cŏquō, -ĕrĕ, *to cook, bake*   coxī   coctŭm

49. The Supine is irregular:

fingō, -ĕrĕ, to fashion	finxī	fictŭm
pingō, -ĕrĕ, to paint	pinxī	pictŭm
stringō, -ĕrĕ, to bind	strinxī	strictŭm
fīgō, -ĕrĕ, to fix	fixī	fixŭm

50. Present strengthened by t:

flectō, -ĕrĕ, to bend	flexī	flexŭm
nectō, -ĕrĕ, to tie	nexī, nexŭī	nexŭm
pectō, -ĕrĕ, to comb	pexī	pexŭm
plectō, -ĕrĕ, to beat (only Passive)	(wanting)	(wanting)

51. The Supine is wanting:

angō, -ĕrĕ, to torment, vex	anxī	——
ningō, -ĕrĕ, to snow	ninxī	——
clangō, -ĕrĕ, to clang	(wanting)	——

(See *Exercises 17, 18*, p. 52.)

52. With Reduplication:

parcō, -ĕrĕ, to spare	pĕpercī	parsŭm
pungō, -ĕrĕ, to pierce, sting	pŭpŭgī	punctŭm
tangō, -ĕrĕ, to touch	tĕtĭgī	tactŭm
pangō, -ĕrĕ, to bargain	pĕpĭgī	pactŭm
pangō, -ĕrĕ, to strike, drive	panxī	panctŭm

53. With lengthened Stem-vowel.

Many Consonant-stems with short stem-syllable take ī in the Perfect, before which the stem-vowel is lengthened, and ă becomes ē.

ăgō, -ĕrĕ, to drive, do	ēgī	actŭm
frangō, -ĕrĕ, to break	frēgī	fractŭm
lĕgō, -ĕrĕ, to read	lēgī	lectŭm
collĭgō, -ĕrĕ, to collect	collēgī	collectŭm
dīlĭgō, -ĕrĕ, to love	dīlexī	dīlectŭm
intellĕgō, -ĕrĕ, to understand	intellexī	intellectŭm
neglĕgō, -ĕrĕ, to neglect	neglexī	neglectŭm
īcō, -ĕrĕ, to strike	īcī	ictŭm
vincō, -ĕrĕ, to conquer	vīcī	victŭm
linquō, -ĕrĕ, to leave	līquī	(wanting)
rēlinquō, -ĕrĕ, to leave (behind)	rēlīquī	rēlictŭm

54. Perfect in sī, Supine in sŭm.

mergō, -ĕrĕ, to dip in, plunge	mersī	mersŭm
spargō, -ĕrĕ, to scatter, sprinkle	sparsī	sparsŭm
vergō, -ĕrĕ, to verge	(wanting)	(wanting)

(See *Exercises 19, 20*, p. 52.)

Verbs ending in **lō, mō, nō, rō**.

55. Perfect in sī, Supine in tŭm.

cōmō, -ĕrĕ, *to adorn*	compsī	comptŭm
dēmō, -ĕrĕ, *to take away*	dempsī	demptŭm
prōmō, -ĕrĕ, *to take out*	prompsī	promptŭm
sūmō, -ĕrĕ, *to take*	sumpsī	sumptŭm
[temnō, *I despise*]		
contemnō, -ĕrĕ, *to despise*	contempsī	contemptŭm

56. According to the Analogy of the 2d Conjugation.

ălō, -ĕrĕ, *to nourish*	ălŭī	altŭm, ălĭtŭm
cŏlō, -ĕrĕ, *to till; worship*	cŏlŭī	cultŭm
consŭlō, -ĕrĕ, *to counsel*	consŭlŭī	consultŭm
mŏlō, -ĕrĕ, *to grind*	mŏlŭī	molĭtŭm
occŭlō, -ĕrĕ, *to conceal*	occŭlŭī	occultŭm
frĕmō, -ĕrĕ, *to growl*	frĕmŭī	frĕmĭtŭm
gĕmō, -ĕrĕ, *to groan*	gĕmŭī	gĕmĭtŭm
trĕmō, -ĕrĕ, *to tremble*	trĕmŭī	*(wanting)*
vŏmō, -ĕrĕ, *to vomit*	vŏmŭī	vŏmĭtŭm
gignō, -ĕrĕ, *to beget*	gĕnŭī	gĕnĭtŭm
pōnō, -ĕrĕ, *to place*	pŏsŭī	pŏsĭtŭm
excellō, -ĕrĕ, *to excel*	*(wanting)*	*(wanting)*

57. With Reduplication.

cănō, -ĕrĕ, *to sing*	cĕcĭnī	cantŭm
currō, -ĕrĕ, *to run*	cŭcurrī	cursŭm
fallō, -ĕrĕ, *to cheat*	fĕfellī	falsŭm
pellō, -ĕrĕ, *to drive (away)*	pĕpŭlī	pulsŭm

(See *Exercises 21, 22*, p. 52.)

58. Perfect in vī.

cernō, -ĕrĕ, *to see, discern*	(crēvī)	(crētŭm)
lĭnō, -ĕrĕ, *to smear*	lēvī (līvī)	lĭtŭm
sĭnō, -ĕrĕ, *to let*	sīvī	sĭtŭm
spernō, -ĕrĕ, *to despise*	sprēvī	sprētŭm
sternō, -ĕrĕ, *to strew*	strāvī	strātŭm
sĕrō, -ĕrĕ, *to sow, plant*	sēvī	sătŭm
sĕrō, -ĕrĕ, *to join*	sĕrŭī	sertŭm
dēsĕrō, -ĕrĕ, *to forsake*	dēsĕrŭī	dēsertŭm
tĕrō, -ĕrĕ, *to rub, wear out*	trīvī	trītŭm

59. Various Irregularities:

vellō, -ĕrĕ, *to pluck, pull*	vellī (vulsī)	vulsŭm
prĕmō, -ĕrĕ, *to press*	pressī	pressŭm

ĕmō, -ĕrĕ, to buy	ēmī	emptŭm
gĕrō, -ĕrĕ, to carry on	gessī	gestŭm
ūrō, -ĕrĕ, to burn	ussī	ustŭm
verrō, -ĕrĕ, to sweep	verrī	versŭm
quaerō, -ĕrĕ, to seek, desire	quaesīvī	quaesītŭm
acquīrō, -ĕrĕ, to acquire	acquīsīvī	acquīsītŭm
fĕrō, ferrĕ, to bear (*84*)	tŭlī	lātŭm
fŭrō, -ĕrĕ, to rage	(wanting)	(wanting)
tollō, -ĕrĕ, to lift, take away	sustŭlī	sublātŭm

(See *Exercises 23, 24*, p. 53.)

VERBS ending in sō, xō, scō.

60. vīsō, -ĕrĕ, to visit   vīsī   (wanting)
depsō, -ĕrĕ, to knead   depsŭī   depstŭm
pinsō, -ĕrĕ, to pound   pinsŭī   pinsĭtŭm
texō, -ĕrĕ, to weave   texŭī   textŭm

61. According to the Analogy of the 4th Conjugation.

arcessō, -ĕrĕ, to summon   arcessīvī   arcessītŭm
căpessō, -ĕrĕ, to lay hold of   căpessīvī   căpessītŭm
făcessō, -ĕrĕ, to accomplish   făcessīvī   făcessītŭm
lăcessō, -ĕrĕ, to excite   lăcessīvī   lăcessītŭm
incessō, -ĕrĕ, to fall upon   incessīvī (-ī)   (wanting)

62. crescō, -ĕrĕ, to grow   crēvī   crētŭm
noscō, -ĕrĕ, to (learn to) know   nōvī   nōtŭm
cognoscō, -ĕrĕ, to know   cognōvī   cognĭtŭm
pascō, -ĕrĕ, to graze   pāvī   pastŭm
quĭescō, -ĕrĕ } to rest   quĭēvī   quĭētŭm
rĕquĭescō, -ĕrĕ   rĕquĭēvī   rĕquĭētŭm
suescō, -ĕrĕ, to become used   suēvī   suētŭm
  consuescō, -ĕrĕ, to be accustomed   consuēvī   consuētŭm
compescō, -ĕrĕ, to restrain   compescŭī   (wanting)
discō, -ĕrĕ, to learn   dĭdĭcī   (wanting)
poscō, -ĕrĕ, to demand   pŏposcī   (wanting)

(See *Exercises 25, 26*, p. 53.)

Verbs of the Fourth Conjugation.

63. In the Fourth Conjugation the Regular Forms of the Principal Parts are these:

Pres. Ind. & Pres. Inf.		Perfect.	Supine.
-ĭō	-īrĕ	-īvī	-ītŭm
audĭō	audīrĕ, to hear	audīvī	audītŭm

64. The following **Verbs** of the **Fourth Conjugation** vary from the usual mode of formation:

farcĭō, -īrĕ, to stuff	farsī	fartŭm
fulcĭō, -īrĕ, to support	fulsī	fultŭm
haurĭō, -īrĕ, to draw	hausī	haustŭm
sancĭō, -īrĕ, to sanction	sanxī	sanctŭm, sancītŭm
sarcĭō, -īrĕ, to mend	sarsī	sartŭm
sentĭō, -īrĕ, to feel, perceive	sensī	sensŭm
sĕpĕlĭō, -īrĕ, to bury	sĕpĕlīvī	sĕpultŭm
vĕnĭō, -īrĕ, to come	vēnī	ventŭm
invĕnĭō, -īrĕ, to find out	invēnī	inventŭm
vincĭō, -īrĕ, to bind	vinxī	vinctŭm
saepĭō, -īrĕ, to hedge in	saepsī	saeptŭm
sălĭō, -īrĕ, to leap	sălŭī	saltŭm
ămĭcĭō, -īrĕ, to clothe	(wanting)	ămictŭm
părĭō, -ĕrĕ, to bring forth (**3d Conjugation**)		
ăpĕrĭō, -īrĕ, to open	ăpĕrŭī	ăpĕrtŭm
rĕpĕrĭō, -īrĕ, to find	reppĕrī	rĕpertŭm

(See *Exercises 27, 28*, p. 54.)

Deponent Verbs.

65. More than half of all Deponents in the language are of the FIRST CONJUGATION and all of them are regular.

66.   SECOND CONJUGATION.

Pres. Ind. & Inf.	Perfect.
fătĕŏr, -ērī, to confess	fassŭs sŭm
confĭtĕŏr, -ērī, to confess	confessŭs sŭm
diffĭtĕŏr, -ērī, to disavow	(wanting)
mĕdĕŏr, -ērī, to cure	(wanting)
mĭsĕrĕŏr, -ērī, to have pity	mĭsĕrĭtŭs, mĭsertŭs sŭm
rĕŏr, -ērī, to think	rătŭs sŭm

67.   THIRD CONJUGATION.

fruŏr, -ī, to enjoy	frŭĭtŭs & fructŭs sŭm
fungŏr, -ī, to discharge	functŭs sŭm
grădĭŏr, -ī, to step	gressŭs sŭm
lābŏr, -ī, to glide, roll on	lapsŭs sŭm
lŏquŏr, -ī, to speak	lŏcŭtŭs sŭm
mŏrĭŏr, -ī, to die	mortŭŭs sŭm—F.Part.mŏrĭtŭrŭs
nītŏr, -ī, to stay one's self on	nīsŭs & nixŭs sŭm
pătĭŏr, -ī, to suffer	passŭs sŭm

amplectŏr, -ī, *to embrace*   amplexŭs sŭm
quĕrŏr, -ī, *to complain*   questŭs sŭm
sĕquŏr, -ī, *to follow*   sĕcûtŭs sŭm
ûtŏr, -ī, *to use*   ûsŭs sŭm
rĕvertŏr, -ī, *to turn back*   rĕvertī, Active — Part. rĕversŭs
ădīpiscŏr, -ī, *to obtain*   ădcptŭs sŭm
expergiscŏr, -ī, *to awake*   experrectŭs sŭm
īrascŏr, -ī, *to grow angry*   (īrătŭs sŭm) — īrătŭs, *angry*
nanciscŏr, -ī, *to get*   nactŭs & nanctŭs sŭm
nascŏr, -ī, *to be born*   nătŭs sŭm—Fut. Part. nascītūrūs
oblīviscŏr, -ī, *to forget*   oblītŭs sŭm
păciscŏr, -ī, *to strike a bargain*   pactŭs sŭm
pascŏr, -ī, *to feed*   pastŭs sŭm
prŏfīciscŏr, -ī, *to set out, start*   prŏfectŭs sŭm
ulciscŏr, -ī, *to avenge*   ultŭs sŭm
vescŏr, -ī, *to feed upon, eat*   *(wanting)*

68.   FOURTH CONJUGATION.

assentĭŏr, -īrī, *to assent*   assensŭs sŭm
mētĭŏr, -īrī, *to measure*   mensŭs sŭm
ordĭŏr, -īrī, *to begin*   orsŭs sŭm
expĕrĭŏr, -īrī, *to try, exercise*   expertŭs sŭm
oppĕrĭŏr, -īrī, *to await*   oppertŭs sŭm
ŏrĭŏr, -īrī, *to rise, arise*   ortŭs sŭm

Pres. Ind. { ŏrĭŏr   ŏrĕrĭs   ŏrītŭr } 3d Conjugation.
          { ŏrĭmŭr   ŏrĭmĭnī   ŏrĭuntŭr }
Imperf. Subj. ŏrīrĕr or ŏrĕrĕr   **Gerundive.** ŏrĭundŭs, -ă, -ŭm
Fut. Part. orītūrŭs, -ă, -ŭm

Semi-Deponents and Neutral Passives.

69. Some Verbs which form their **Perfect** like *Deponents*, are called **Semi-Deponents**, as:

audĕō, -ĕrĕ, *to dare*   ausŭs sŭm, *I dared*
gaudĕō, -ĕrĕ, *to rejoice*   gāvīsŭs sŭm, *I rejoiced*
sŏlĕō, -ĕrĕ, *to be wont*   sŏlĭtŭs sŭm, *I was wont*
fīdō, -ĕrĕ, *to trust*   fīsŭs sŭm, *I trusted*

70. Some Active Verbs have a Perfect **Passive** Participle with **Active** meaning, viz.:

cēnō, -ārĕ, *to dine*   cēnātŭs, *having dined*
prandĕō, -ĕrĕ, *to breakfast*   pransŭs, *having breakfasted*
pōtō, -ārĕ, *to drink*   pōtŭs, *having drunk*
jūrō, -ārĕ, *to swear*   jūrātŭs, *having sworn*

71. Again, a few **Active** Verbs have a **Passive** meaning; they are sometimes called **Neutral Passives**, viz.:

văpŭlārĕ, *to be flogged;* vēnīrĕ (vēnŭm īrĕ, *to go to sale*), *to be sold.*

Derivative Verbs.

72. Inceptives (Inchoatives) end in **scō** and denote the beginning of an action. They are of the **Third Conjugation**. When formed from Verbs they are called **Verbal Inceptives**. Most of them want the Supine, but take the Perfect of their Primitives; others take the Perfect and Supine of their Primitives.

73. With the Perfect of their Primitives:

ărescō, -ĕrĕ, *to become dry*   ărŭī
ărĕō

călescō, -ĕrĕ, *to become warm*   călŭī
călĕō

sĕnescō, -ĕrĕ, *to grow old*   sĕnŭī
sĕnĕō

74. With the Perfect and Supine of their Primitives:

exardescō, -ĕrĕ, *to take fire*   exarsī   exarsŭm
ardĕō

obdormiscō, -ĕrĕ, *to fall asleep*   obdormīvī   obdormītŭm
dormīō

rĕvīviscō, -ĕrĕ, *to revive*   rĕvixī   rĕvictŭm
vīvō

75. Those Inceptives which are derived from Nouns or Adjectives are called **Denominatives**; most of them want the Perfect and Supine.

Wanting Perfect and Supine.

aegrescō, -ĕrĕ, *to fall sick*   plūmescō, -ĕrĕ, *to get feathers*
aegĕr, *sick*   plūmă, *a feather*
dītescō, -ĕrĕ, *to grow rich*   pŭĕrascō, -ĕrĕ, *to become a*
dīvĕs, *rich*   pŭĕr, *a child*   [*child*

With the Perfect in ŭī.

mătūrescō, -ĕrĕ, *to ripen* (mătūrŭs, *ripe*)   mătūrŭī
nĭgrescō, -ĕrĕ, *to become black* (nĭgĕr, *black*)   nĭgrŭī

76. Frequentatives end in **ārĕ** or **ĭtārĕ**, and denote a *forcible or repeated action;* they are derived either from **Supines** in **sŭm** or **tŭm**, as:

dīcō, *I say*   dictŭm   dictārĕ, *to dictate*
hăbĕō, *I have*   hăbĭtŭm   hăbĭtārĕ, *to have frequently*
currō, *I run*   cursŭm   cursārĕ, *to run about*

or from the **Present** of the 1st, 2d, and 3d Conjugations, as:

    clămō, *I cry*   clămārĕ   clămĭtārĕ, *to cry out aloud*
    lătĕō, *I am hid*   lătĕrĕ   lătĭtārĕ, *to lie hid*
    ăgō, *I do*   ăgĕrĕ   ăgĭtārĕ, *to drive*

77. Desideratives denote *desire* or *tendency*. They are formed by changing **ūrŭs** of the **Future Participle** into **ŭrĭō**, and are of the 4th Conjugation. Only a few are in common use:

    ēsŭrĭō, -īrĕ, *to be hungry*, from ĕdō, ēsŭrŭs
    mŏrĭtŭrĭō, -īrĕ, *to wish to die*, from mŏrĭŏr, mŏrĭtŭrŭs.
    (See *Exercises 31, 32*, p. 55.)

Irregular Conjugation.

78. A few Verbs are **Irregular** in the Conjugation of the **Present** and the forms derived from it. These are:

essĕ, *to be;* possĕ, *to be able;* ĕdĕrĕ, *to eat;* vellĕ, *to be willing, to wish;* nollĕ, *to be unwilling, not to wish;* mallĕ, *to be more willing, to prefer, have rather;* īrĕ, *to go;* quīrĕ, *to be able;* nĕquīrĕ, *not to be able;* ferrĕ, *to bear, carry, endure;* fĭĕrī, *to become, or be made, to happen.*

For the Conjugation of essĕ and possĕ see I. *113—117.*

79. ĕdŏ, -ĕrĕ, ĕdī, ĕsŭm, *to eat*, regular of the 3d Conjugation, has also some contracted forms similar to those of the corresponding tenses of the Verb essĕ, but always with **ē** long before **s**; viz.:

Present Indicative.		Imperfect Subjunctive.	
		ĕdĕrĕm	ēssĕm, *I should eat*
ĕdīs	ēs, *thou eatest*	ĕdĕrēs	ēssēs, *thou wouldst eat*
ĕdĭt	ēst, *he eats*	ĕdĕrĕt	ēssĕt, *he would eat*
		ĕdĕrēmŭs	ēssēmŭs, *we should eat*
ĕdĭtĭs	ēstĭs, *you eat*	ĕdĕrētĭs	ēssētĭs, *you would eat*
		ĕdĕrent	ēssent, *they would eat*

Imperative.

	Singular.			Plural.	
Pres.	ĕdĕ	ēs, *eat thou*	ĕdĭtĕ	ēstĕ, *eat ye*	
Fut.	ĕdĭtō	ēstō, *thou shalt eat*	ĕdĭtōtĕ	ēstōtĕ, *ye shall eat*	
	ĕdĭtō	ēstō, *he shall eat*			

Infinitive.

    ĕdĕrĕ   ēssĕ, *to eat*

Passive. ĕdĭtŭr ēstŭr, *is eaten*—ĕdĕrētŭr, ēssētŭr, *should be eaten*

80. nōlŏ is compounded of nōn and vŏlŏ, and mālŏ of măgĭs vŏlŏ. The Perfects are vŏlŭī, nōlŭī, mālŭī; the Supines are wanting; likewise, the Imperatives of vellĕ and mallĕ are wanting, and the Participle of mallĕ.

Present.

INDICATIVE.
I am willing, unwilling, more willing.

vŏ' lŏ	nō' lŏ	mă' lŏ
vīs	nōn vīs	mă' vīs
vult	nōn vult	mă' vult
vŏ' lŭ mŭs	nō' lŭ mŭs	mă' lŭ mŭs
vul' tĭs	nōn vul' tĭs	mă vul' tĭs
vŏ' lunt	nō' lunt	mă' lunt

SUBJUNCTIVE.
I may be willing, unwilling, more willing.

vĕ' lĭm	nō' lĭm	mă' lĭm
vĕ' līs	nō' līs	mă' līs
vĕ' lĭt	nō' lĭt	mă' lĭt
vĕ lī' mŭs	nō lī' mŭs	mă lī' mŭs
vĕ lī' tĭs	nō lī' tĭs	mă lī' tĭs
vĕ' lint	nō' lint	mă' lint

Imperat. Sing. nōlī, nōlītŏ
Plur. nōlītĕ, nōlītōtĕ, nōluntō

All the rest are formed regularly from the **Principal Parts**:

	INDICATIVE.	SUBJUNCTIVE.		
Imperf.	vŏlēbăm	vellĕm	Infin. Perf.	vŏlŭissĕ
	nōlēbăm	nollĕm		nōlŭissĕ
	mālēbăm	mallĕm		mālŭissĕ
Perfect.	vŏlŭī	vŏlŭĕrĭm	Part.	vŏlens
	nōlŭī	nōlŭĕrĭm		nōlens
	mālŭī	mālŭĕrĭm		
Pluperf.	vŏlŭĕrăm	vŏlŭissĕm	Gerund.	vŏlendī, vŏlendō
	nōlŭĕrăm	nōlŭissĕm		nōlendī
	mālŭĕrăm	mālŭissĕm		
Fut. Perf.	vŏlŭĕrō			
	nōlŭĕrō			
	mālŭĕrō			

81. The Verb ĭrĕ, *to go*, in most of its parts has the endings of the **Fourth Conjugation**. It deviates only in the **Present** and the forms derived from it.

Pres. Ind. & Pres. Inf.	Perfect.	Supine.
ĕō, Irĕ, *to go*	IvI	Itŭm

INDICATIVE.	SUBJUNCTIVE.

Present.

ĕ' ō, *I go*	ĕ' ăm, *I may go*
ĭs	ĕ' ās
ĭt	ĕ' ăt
I' mŭs	ĕ ā' mŭs
ĭ' tĭs	ĕ ā' tĭs
ĕ' unt	ĕ' ant

Imperfect.

I' băm, *I was going*	I' rĕm, *I should go*
I' bās	I' rēs
I' băt	I' rĕt
I bā' mŭs	I rē' mŭs
I bā' tĭs	I rē' tĭs
I' bant	I' rent

Future.

I shall go   *I may be about to go*

I' bō	I tū' rŭs,	sĭm
I' bĭs	-ă, -ŭm	sĭs
I' bĭt		sĭt
I' bī mŭs	I tū' rī,	sī' mŭs
I' bī tĭs	-ae, -ă	sī' tĭs
I' bunt		sint

IMPERATIVE.

Singular.	Plural.
Pres. I, *go*	I' tĕ, *go ye*
Fut. I' tō, *thou shalt go*	I tō' tĕ, *ye shall go*
I' tō, *he shall go*	ĕ un' tō, *they shall go*

PARTICIPLES.

Pres. I' ens, Gen. ĕ un' tĭs, *going*
Fut. I tū' rŭs, -ă, -ŭm, *being about to go*

GERUND.	SUPINE.
Gen. ĕ un' dī, *of going*	
Dat. ĕ un' dō, *for going*	
Acc. ĕ un' dŭm, *going*	I' tŭm ⎱ *to go*
Abl. ĕ un' dō, *by going*	I' tū ⎰

82. The Compounds of ĕō are conjugated in the same way. But usually they drop the **v** of the **Perfect**, as: rĕdĭī for rĕdīvī, &c., and contract the **i i** of the **Perfect Infinitive** and of the **Pluperfect Subjunctive** into **ī**, as: rĕdīssĕ for rĕdī(v)issĕ, &c. Examples are:

intĕrĕō, -īrĕ, *to perish* rĕdĕō, -īrĕ, *to return*
praetĕrĕō, -īrĕ, *to pass by* transĕō, -īrĕ, *to pass over*

(See *Exercises 33, 34,* p. 55.)

83. queō quīrĕ, *to be able* quīvī quĭtŭm
nĕqueō nĕquīrĕ, *not to be able* nĕquīvī nĕquĭtŭm

are conjugated like īrĕ, *to go (81);* they are, however, usual only in the Present Indicative and Subjunctive.

84. Pres. Ind. & Pres. Inf. Perfect. Supine.
fĕrō ferrĕ, *to bear* tŭlī lātŭm

is irregular in the following forms only:

Active.	Passive.
Present.	
fĕ' rō, *I bear*	fĕ' rŏr, *I am borne*
fers	fer' rĭs
fert	fer' tŭr
fĕ' rĭ mŭs	fĕ' rĭ mŭr
fer' tĭs	fĕ rĭ' mĭ nī
fĕ' runt	fĕ run' tŭr

IMPERATIVE.

Sing. fĕr, *bear thou* fer' rĕ, *be thou borne*
" fer' tō, *thou shalt bear* fer' tŏr, *thou shalt be borne*
" fer' tō, *he shall bear* fer' tŏr, *he shall be borne*

Plur. fer' tĕ, *bear ye* fĕ rĭ' mĭ nī, *be ye borne*
" fer tō' tĕ, *ye shall bear*
" fĕ run' tō, *they shall bear* fĕ run' tŏr, *they shall be borne*

All the rest are formed *regularly* from the **Principal Parts.**

85. **Compounds** of **fĕrō** are conjugated like the simple Verb.

adfĕrō	adferrĕ, *to afford*	attŭlī	adlātŭm
aufĕrō	auferrĕ, *to carry away*	abstŭlī	ablātŭm
confĕrō	conferrĕ, *to bring together*	contŭlī	collātŭm
diffĕrō	differrĕ, *to defer*	distŭlī	dīlātŭm
effĕrō	efferrĕ, *to carry out*	extŭlī	ēlātŭm
infĕrō	inferrĕ, *to carry into*	intŭlī	illātŭm
praefĕrō	praeferrĕ, *to prefer*	praetŭlī	praelātŭm
rĕfĕrō	rĕferrĕ, *to bring back*	rettŭlī, rĕtŭlī	rĕlātŭm

86. Pres. Ind. & Pres. Ind.　　　　Perfect.
　　fīŏ, fĭĕrī, *to become*　　　　factŭs sŭm

fīŏ is used as the **Passive** of făcĭō. The compound tenses are formed regularly from făcĭō, as: factŭs sŭm, factŭs ĕrăm, &c. The rest are as follows:

INDICATIVE.　　　　　　　SUBJUNCTIVE.

Present.

fī' ŏ, *I become*　　　　fī' ăm, *I may become*
fīs　　　　　　　　　　fī' ās
fĭt　　　　　　　　　　fī' ăt
fī' mŭs　　　　　　　　fī ā' mŭs
fī' tĭs　　　　　　　　fī ā' tĭs
fī' unt　　　　　　　　fī' ant

Imperfect.

fī ē' băm, *I became*　　fī' ĕ rĕm, *I should become*
fī ē' bās　　　　　　　fī' ĕ rēs
fī ē' băt　　　　　　　fī' ĕ rĕt
fī ĕ bā' mŭs　　　　　　fī ĕ rē' mŭs
fī ĕ bā' tĭs　　　　　　fī ĕ rē' tĭs
fī ē' bant　　　　　　　fī' ĕ rent

Future.

fī' ăm, *I shall become*　　*(wanting)*
fī' ēs
fī' ĕt
fī ē' mŭs
fī ē' tĭs
fī' ent

　　Pres. Infin.　fī' ĕ rī, *to become*

87. The Compounds of făcĭō with Prepositions change **ă** into **ĭ**, and form the Passive regularly, as:

　　interfĭcĭō, *I kill*　　　　interfĭcĭŏr, *I am killed*

But when compounded with words other than Prepositions, făcĭō retains its **ă**, and uses fīŏ as its Passive, as:

　　mansuĕfăcĭō, *I tame*　　　　mansuĕfīŏ, *I become tame*
　　līquĕfăcĭō, *I make liquid*　　līquĕfīŏ, *I melt*

The accent remains the same as in the simple Verbs, thus: mansuĕfă'cĭs, *thou tamest.*

　　　　(See *Exercises 35, 36*, p. 56.)

Defective Verbs.

88. Defective Verbs want certain parts.

coepī, *I have begun*   mĕmĭnī, *I remember*   ōdī, *I hate*

are in use only in the **Perfect** and the tenses derived from it. To coepī, *I have begun*, incĭpĭō, *I begin*, serves as a Present. mĕmĭnī, *I remember*, and ōdī, *I hate*, are Present in sense; hence in the Pluperfect and Future Perfect they have the sense of the Imperfect and Future. nōvī, *I know* (Perf. of noscō, *I learn to know*), and consuēvī, *I am wont* (Perf. of consuescō, *I accustom myself*), are also Present in sense.

INDICATIVE.

	I have begun	*I remember*	*I hate*
Perf.	coe' pī	mĕ' mĭ nī	ō' dī
	coe pi' stī	mĕ mĭ ni' stī	ō di' stī
	coe' pĭt	mĕ' mĭ nĭt	ō' dĭt
	coe' pĭ mŭs	mĕ mĭ' nĭ mŭs	ō' dĭ mŭs
	coe pi' stĭs	mĕ mĭ ni' stĭs	ō di' stĭs
	coe pē' runt	mĕ mĭ nē' runt	ō dē' runt
Pluperf.	coe' pĕ răm, &c.	mĕ mĭ' nĕ răm, &c.	ō' dĕ răm, &c.
Fut. Perf.	coe' pĕ rō, &c.	mĕ mĭ' nĕ rō, &c.	ō' dĕ rō, &c.

SUBJUNCTIVE.

Perf.	coe' pĕ rĭm, &c.	mĕ mĭ' nĕ rĭm, &c.	ō' dĕ rĭm, &c.
Pluperf.	coe pis' sĕm, &c.	mĕ mĭ nis' sĕm, &c.	ō dis' sĕm, &c.

IMPERATIVE.

	(wanting)	mĕ men' tō	*(wanting)*
		mĕ men tō' tō	

INFINITIVE.

Perf.	coe pis' sĕ	mĕ mĭ nis' sĕ	ō dis' sĕ
Fut.	coep tū rūs es' sĕ	*(wanting)*	ō sū' rūs es' sĕ

PARTICIPLES.

Perf.	coep' tŭs, -ă, -ŭm	*(wanting)*	(ō' sŭs, -ă, -ŭm)
Fut.	coep tū' rŭs, -ă, -ŭm	*(wanting)*	ō sū' rŭs, -ă, -ŭm

PASSIVE. coep' tŭs, -ă, -ŭm sŭm, *I have begun* (used with the Pass. Infinit.)

89. ăjō, *I say, say yes, affirm* — inquăm, *I say, quoth I* — fārī, *to speak*

Pres. Ind.	Pres. Subj.	Imp. Ind.	Pres. Ind.	Perf. Ind.
ă' jō	——	ă jē' băm	in' quăm	——
ă' īs	ă' jās	ă jē' bās	in' quīs	in qui' stī
ă' ĭt	ă' jăt	ă jē' băt	in' quĭt	in' quĭt
——	——	ă jē bā' mŭs	in' quī mŭs	——
——	——	ă jē bā' tĭs	in' quī tĭs	in qui' stĭs
ă' junt	ă' jant	ă jē' bant	in' quī ŭnt	——

Perf. Ind.
ă' ĭt

	Imp. Ind.	Fut. Ind.
		in' quī ēs
	in quī ē' bat	in' quī ĕt

Participle.   Imperat.
ă' jens, *affirmative*   in' quĕ, in' quī tō

inquăm, *say*, is used only in direct quotations, as the English *quoth*.

Besides the **Infinitive** fārī, *to speak*, mark:

Pres. fātŭr, *he speaks*   Imperat. fārĕ, *speak thou*
Fut. fābŏr, *I shall speak*   Gerund. fandī, *of speaking*
     fābĭtŭr, *he will speak*   fandō, *for speaking*
Perf. fātŭs sŭm, *I have spoken*, &c.   Supine. fātū, *to speak*
     Participle. (fantĭs, fantī) infans, *speechless*
     Gerundive. fandŭs, -ă, -ŭm, *to be spoken of*

90.
ă' vē	sal' vē, sal vē' bĭs, *hail thou!*	vă' lē } *fare-*
ă vē' tĕ	sal vē' tĕ, *hail ye!*	vă lē' tĕ } *well*
ă' gĕ	ă' gī tĕ, *come*	ă' pă gĕ, *be gone*
cĕ' dŏ	cet' tĕ, *give*	

91. To these may be added:

quae' sō, *I beseech*   fŏ' rĕm, *I should be*
quae' sŭ mŭs, *we beseech*   fŏ' rēs, *thou shouldst be*
                               fŏ' rĕt, *he should be*
                               fŏ' rent, *they should be*
                               fŏ' rĕ, *to be about to be*

Impersonal Verbs.

92. The following Verbs signifying *personal conditions are absolutely* impersonal:

Present.	Infinitive.	Perfect.
dĕcĕt, *it becomes*	dĕcērĕ	dĕcŭĭt
dedĕcĕt, *it is unbecoming*	dedĕcērĕ	dedĕcŭĭt
lĭbĕt, *it pleases*	lĭbērĕ	lĭbŭĭt or lĭbĭtŭm est

Present.	Infinitive.	Perfect.
lĭcĕt, *it is lawful, allowed*	lĭcērĕ	lĭcŭĭt or lĭcĭtŭm est
lĭquĕt, *it is clear*	lĭquērĕ	lĭcŭĭt
mĭsĕrĕt, *it excites pity*	mĭsĕrērĕ	mĭsĕrĭtŭm (-tŭm) est
ŏportĕt, *it is needful*	ŏportērĕ	ŏportŭĭt
pĭgĕt, *it grieves*	pĭgērĕ	pĭgŭĭt or pĭgĭtŭm est
paenĭtĕt, *it causes sorrow*	paenĭtērĕ	paenĭtŭĭt
pŭdĕt, *it shames*	pŭdērĕ	pŭdŭĭt or pŭdĭtŭm est
taedĕt, *it wearies*	taedērĕ	pertaesŭm est

93. Verbs describing *phenomena of nature* are almost invariably impersonal in virtue of their meaning:

plŭĭt, *it rains*
ningĭt, *it snows*
grandĭnăt, *it hails*
tŏnăt, *it thunders*
fulgŭrăt ⎱ *it lightens*
fulmĭnăt ⎰
lūcescĭt, *it dawns*
vespĕrascĭt, *evening comes on*

(See *Exercises 37, 38*, p. 56.)

CONSTRUCTIONS OF SYNTAX.

Agreement of the Predicate.

94. A **Sentence** is composed of **Subject and Predicate**: The Subject, a noun (or a word having the value of a noun) names that of which something is asserted; the Predicate, a verb, expresses that which is asserted of the Subject.

95. The **Subject** of the sentence is in the **Nominative Case**, as: arbor viret, *the tree is green*.

96. The **Verb** agrees in **Person** and **Number** with its Subject, as: ego valĕo, si vos valētis, *I am well if you are well*.

97. **Participles** in compound tenses agree with the Subject in **Number**, **Gender**, and **Case**, as: castra capta sunt, *the camp was taken*.

98. When the Predicate consists of the Verb sŭm with an Adjective, the Verb sŭm agrees with the Subject in **Number** and **Person**, and the Predicate Adjective in **Number**, **Gender**, and **Case**, as: verae amicitīae sempiternae sunt, *true friendships are everlasting*.

99. When the Predicate consists of the Verb sŭm with a Substantive, the **Predicate Substantive** agrees with the Subject in **Case**, and if it has different forms for different Genders, in **Gender** and **Number** also, as:

  usus est magister, *experience is a teacher*
  historĭa est magistra, *history is a teacher*

100. The Predicate of **two** or more **Subjects** is in the **Plural Number**:

  vita et mors sunt jura natūrae   *life and death are laws of nature*

101. As to the **Gender** of an **Adjective Predicate** referring to **two or more Subjects** mark the following:

When the Subjects are of the *same* Gender, the Predicate Adjective is of that Gender, as: Corinthus et Carthāgo a Romānis dirūtae sunt, *Carthage and Corinth were destroyed by the Romans.* When the Genders are *different*, the Predicate Adjective is **Masculine**, if the Subjects are things *with life;* and **Neuter**, when they are things *without life;* as: pater et mater mortŭi sunt, *father and mother are dead;* honōres et victorĭae fortuīta sunt, *honors and victories are accidental things.*

102. If the **Nominatives** are of *different* Persons, the Verb takes the first Person rather than the second, and the second rather than the third, as: tu et Tullĭa valētis, *you and Tullia are well.*

(See *Exercises 39, 40,* p. 57.)

Agreement of Attribute and Apposition.

103. The most usual **Attribute** of a Substantive is an **Adjective**; it agrees with its Substantive in **Number, Gender,** and **Case.**

104. One Substantive placed after another to explain it, is by **Apposition** in the **same Case,** and when practicable, in the **same Gender** and **Number,** as: usus, magister egregĭus, *experience, an excellent teacher;* historĭa, magistra egregĭa, *history, an excellent teacher.*

Agreement of Pronouns.

105. A **Relative** or **Demonstrative** Pronoun agrees with its Antecedent in **Gender, Number** and **Person**; but the **Case** depends on the clause in which it stands, as: arbōres serit agricŏla, quarum fructus ipse numquam adspicĭet, *the husbandman plants trees the fruit of which he himself will never see.*

106. With Antecedents of different Gender, or of different Persons, the Pronoun conforms to the rule for the Predicate (see *101, 102*), as: puĕri et mulĭĕres, qui captī erant, *the boys and women* *who had been taken prisoners;* ego et tu, qui eōdem anno natī sumus, *you and I who were born in the same year.*

Questions.

107. **Questions** in Latin are generally introduced by some interrogative word or particle.

108. The **Interrogative Particles** are:

nĕ, nŭm, nonnĕ, ŭtrŭm, ăn.

Of these **nĕ** asks merely for information; it cannot stand by itself, but is joined to any emphatic word, usually the Verb, which then comes first in the sentence; it is not translated, as:

audisne vocem patris?   *do you hear my father's voice?*

109. When a **negative answer** is expected, **nŭm** is used, which stands at the beginning of the sentence and is likewise not translated, as:

num vespertilio avis est?   *Is the bat a bird?*

110. With **nōn**, **nĕ** forms a special interrogative particle **nonnĕ**, *not;* the answer expected is *yes*, as:

nonne lectio hujus libri te delectat?   *does not the perusal of this book delight you?*

111. **Double** or **Alternative Questions** have the following forms:

ŭtrŭm, *whether*..   ăn, *or*..
——nĕ,   "   ..   ăn,   " ..
......,   "   ..   ăn,   " ..

utrum domi fuisti **an** in schola? } *have you been at home or in school?*
domĭne fuisti **an** in schola?
domi fuisti **an** in schola?

(See *Exercises* 41, 42, p. 57.)

Uses of Cases: I. As governed by Prepositions.

112. The following **Prepositions** are used with the **Accusative**:

ăd, *to, at, toward*   contrā, *against, opposite to*
adversŭs, adversŭm, *against, toward*   ergā, *toward, unto*
                                         extrā, *without, beyond*
antĕ, *before*   infrā, *under, beneath*
ăpŭd, *at, with, near*   intĕr, *between, among*
circā, circŭm, *around*   intrā, *within*
circĭtĕr, *about, near*   juxtā, *near, beside*
cĭs, cĭtrā, *on this side of*   ŏb, *for, on account of*

pĕnĕs, *in the power of*
pĕr, *through, by, during*
pōnĕ, *behind* (rare)
post, *after, behind*
praetĕr, *past, beside, except*
prŏpĕ, *near*
proptĕr, *on account of, close by*

sĕcundŭm, *after, next to, according to, along*
suprā, *above*
trans, *across, over, beyond*
ultrā, *beyond, on the further side of, past*
versŭs, *toward* (always post-[poned)

☞ *To be learned by heart.* ☜
ăd, adversŭs *and* adversŭm,
ăpŭd, antĕ, circā, circŭm,
cĭs *and* cĭtrā, circĭtĕr,
contrā, extrā, ergā, intrā,
also intĕr, juxtā, infrā,
pōst, ŏb, pĕnĕs, pōnĕ, pĕr,
praetĕr, proptĕr, prŏpĕ, suprā,
trans, sĕcundŭm, versŭs, ultrā.
(See *Exercises 43, 44*, p. 58.)

113. Prepositions which are used with the **Ablative**:

ā
ăb } *from, away from*
abs
absquĕ, *without, but for*
clăm, *without the knowledge of*
cōram, *in presence of*
cŭm, *with*

dē, *from, down from, of, about*
ē, ex, *from, out of*
prae, *for, before, in comparison with*
prō, *for, instead of*
sĭnĕ, *without*
tĕnŭs, *as far as, up to*

☞ *To be learned by heart.* ☜
ā, ăb, abs, cŭm, dē,
cōram, prō, ex, ē,
tĕnŭs, sĭnĕ, prae.

114. Prepositions with the **Accusative** and **Ablative**, but strictly with a difference of meaning:

In, *into, in;* **sŭb,** *under;* **subtĕr,** *beneath;* **sŭpĕr,** *above.*

In and **sŭb**, when followed by the **Accusative**, indicate *motion to*, when by the **Ablative** *rest in*, a place.

115. The **Genitive** is used with the **Prepositional Ablatives** causā, *on account of*, and gratiā, *for the sake of*, which commonly follow their Genitive, as: honōris gratiā, *for honor's sake*. The Possessives agree with these Ablatives, as: meā, tuā, suā, nostrā, vestrā, causā, *for my, thy, his, &c. sake.*

(See *Exercises 45, 46*, p. 58.)

Uses of Cases: 2. As governed by Adjectives.

Genitive with Adjectives.

116. **Adjectives** denoting *Desire, Knowledge, Recollection, Participation, Mastery, Fullness,* and their **Opposites,** take the **Genitive:**

cŭpĭdŭs, *eager, desirous*
stŭdĭōsŭs, *devoted to*
pĕrītŭs, *skillful in*
inscĭŭs ⎫
nescĭŭs ⎬ *ignorant*
ignārŭs ⎭
mĕmŏr, *mindful*
immĕmŏr, *unmindful*

expers, *without share in*
compŏs, *capable, master of*
impŏs, *not in possession of*
impŏtens, *unable or powerless to control*
plēnŭs, *full*
partĭceps, *sharing in, partaker of, endowed with*

ratiōnis et oratiōnis expertes, *devoid of reason and speech.*

Dative with Adjectives.

117. **Adjectives** denoting *Likeness, Fitness, Friendliness, Nearness* and the like, with their **Opposites,** take the **Dative:**

acceptŭs, *acceptable*
ămīcŭs, *friendly*
inĭmīcŭs, *unfriendly, opposed*
aptŭs, *apt, suitable*
cārŭs, *dear*
commūnĭs, *common*
dulcĭs, *agreeable*
făcĭlĭs, *easy*
diffĭcĭlĭs, *difficult*
grātŭs, *pleasing*
ingrātŭs, *unpleasant*
grăvĭs, *burdensome*

jūcundŭs, *agreeable*
injūcundŭs, *disagreeable*
mŏlestŭs, *troublesome*
nĕcessārĭŭs, *necessary*
ŏdĭōsŭs, *hateful*
păr, *equal, a match for*
dispăr, *unlike*
sălūtārĭs, *beneficial*
sĭmĭlĭs, *like*
dissĭmĭlĭs, *unlike*
turpĭs, *disgraceful*
ūtĭlĭs, *useful*

canis similis lupo est
flamma fumo est proxima

a dog is similar to a wolf
fire is next akin to smoke

Ablative with Adjectives.

118. The following **Adjectives** take the **Ablative:**

dignŭs, *worthy*
indignŭs, *unworthy*

frētŭs, *trusting, relying*
contentŭs, *satisfied*

ălĭēnŭs, *strange, foreign,* takes the **Ablative** with or without **ā, ăb.**

vir patre dignissimus
aliēnum a vita mea

a man most worthy of his father
foreign to my life

(See **Exercises 47, 48,** p. 59.)

Uses of Cases: 3. As Object of Verbs.
Genitive.

119. Verbs of *Reminding, Remembering, Forgetting* take the Genitive:

admŏnērĕ
commŏnērĕ } *to remind*
commŏnĕfăcĕrĕ

mĕmĭnissĕ
rĕmĭniscī } *to remember*
rĕcordārī

oblīviscī, *to forget*

120. Verbs of **Reminding**, with the Accusative of the *Person*, are followed by the Genitive of the *Person* or *Thing* to which the attention is called, as:

te vetĕris amicitĭae admoneō, *I remind you of our old friendship.*

121. Verbs of **Remembering** and **Forgetting** take the Genitive if a *Person*, and either the Genitive or Accusative, if a *Thing* is remembered or forgotten, as:

memĭnī vivŏrum *I am mindful of the living*
anĭmus memĭnit praeteritōrum *the mind remembers the past*
oblivisci nihil soles nisi injurĭas *you are wont to forget nothing except injuries.*

122. Verbs of *Accusing, Convicting, Condemning* and *Acquitting*, with the Accusative of the Person, take the **Genitive** of the **Charge**.

accūsārĕ
incūsārĕ
insĭmŭlārĕ } *to accuse, charge*
argŭĕrĕ

arcessĕrĕ } *to summon*
rĕum făcĕrĕ

cŏargŭĕrĕ } *to convict*
convincĕrĕ

damnārĕ } *to condemn, find*
condemnārĕ } *guilty*

absolvĕrĕ, *to acquit*

honestam famīlĭam scelĕris arguĭs *you accuse an honorable family of crime*
alĭquem levitātis convincĕre *to convict one of levity.*

123. Verbs of *Condemning* and *Acquitting* may also take the **Ablative** of the *charge* and the *punishment*, as: damnāre capĭtis or capĭte, *to condemn to death*, and always take the **Ablative** of the *fine;* multāre, *to mulct, punish*, is always construed with the **Ablative**.

Camillus decem milĭbus damnātus est *Camillus was fined 10,000*
Manlĭus virtūtem filĭi morte multāvit *Manlius punished the valor of his son with death.*

124. Verbs of *Valuing* are joined with the **Genitive** when the value is expressed in an indefinite manner, as: magni aestimāre, *to value highly;* pluris esse, *to be of more account.*

125. With the **Impersonal** intĕrest (and sometimes also with rĕfert), *it concerns, interests, it is the interest of, it is of importance for,* the **Genitive** is used to denote the **Person** or **Thing concerned.**

126. This **Genitive** seems to be governed by causā understood; hence, instead of the **Genitive** of the Personal Pronoun, the Ablative Singular feminine of the **Possessives** meā, tuā, suā, nostrā, vestrā is used with these Verbs, as: meā intĕrest, *I am concerned;* with omnĭum, however, nostrūm and vestrūm must be used: omnĭum nostrūm intĕrest, *it concerns all of us.*

127. Certain **Impersonal Verbs** take the Person who feels in the **Accusative**, and the Exciting Cause in the **Genitive**, or if a Verb, in the **Infinitive**, viz.:

mĭsĕrĕt, *it excites pity*	pŭdĕt, *it shames*
paenĭtĕt, *it causes sorrow*	taedĕt ⎫ *it wearies, tires*
pĭgĕt, *it disgusts, grieves*	pertaesŭm est ⎭

The **Persons** are expressed as follows:

mĭsĕrĕt **mē**, *I pity*	paenĭtĕt **mē**, *I am sorry, repent*
mĭsĕrĕt **tē**, *thou pitiest*	pĭgĕt **mē**, *I am grieved at, disgusted with*
mĭsĕrĕt **ĕŭm**, *he pities*	
mĭsĕrĕt **nōs**, *we pity*	pŭdĕt **mē**, *I am ashamed*
mĭsĕrĕt **vōs**, *you pity*	taedĕt **mē** ⎫ *I am weary,*
mĭsĕrĕt **ĕōs**, *they pity*	**mē** pertaesŭm est ⎭ *tired*
me stultitīae meae pudet	*I am ashamed of my folly*
non me paenĭtet vixisse	*I am not sorry for having lived.*

128. The **Genitive** may be used as a **Predicate** with the Verbs essĕ and fĭĕrī to denote that to which something belongs or to which something is peculiar. In English the words *part, property, duty, business,* are commonly supplied. Instead of the **Genitives** of Personal Pronouns the **Neuter Possessives**: meŭm, tuŭm, &c., are used.

sapientis est pauca loqui	*it is the part of a wise man to speak little*
haec domus est Caesăris	*this house is Caesar's*
mentīri non est meum	*to lie is not my way.*

(See *Exercises 49, 50*, p. 59.)

Dative.

129. Many **Intransitive Verbs** of *Advantage* or *Disadvantage*, *Pleasing* or *Displeasing*, *Bidding* or *Forbidding*, such as: prodesse, *to do good;* nocēre, *to do harm;* indulgēre, *to favor;* parēre, oboedīre, *to obey;* maledicēre, *to curse;* parcēre, *to spare;* studēre, *to devote one's self;* obtrectāre, *to decry;* invidēre, *to envy;* medēri, *to heal;* nubēre, *to marry*, take the **Dative**, thus:

   probus invidet nemīni   *the upright man envies no one*
   non parcam opěrae   *I will spare no pains.*

130. Among the most notable **Exceptions** are:
jŭvārĕ   } *to help, assist*   dēfīcĕrĕ, *to be wanting*
adjŭvārĕ }   jŭbērĕ, *to order*
aequārĕ, *to be equal*   vĕtārĕ, *to forbid*
       which govern the **Accusative**.

131. The **Dative** is used with essĕ to denote the *Possessor*, the thing possessed being the Subject.

When so used it is commonly translated by *to have;* mĭhĭ nōmĕn est, means *my name is* or *I am called;* the proper name is put either in the **Nominative** or the **Dative**, as:

   est mihi domi pater   *I have a father at home*
   puĕro nomen est Carŏlus (Carŏlo) *the boy's name is Charles.*

132. Certain **Verbs** take the **Dative** to denote the *Purpose* or *End*, as: dono dare, *to give as a present*, and often at the same time another Dative of the person **for whom** or **to whom**. Such are:

essĕ, *to be*   mittĕrĕ, *to send*   hăbērĕ, *to hold*
fĭĕrī { *to become,*   accīpĕrĕ, *to receive*   vertĕrĕ, *to interpret,*
      { *turn out*   vĕnīrĕ, *to come*   *turn (against)*
dărĕ, *to give*   rĕlinquĕrĕ, *to leave*   dūcĕrĕ, *to count*
exemplo est formīca   *the ant is (for) an example*
malo est hominĭbus avaritĭa *avarice is an evil to men.*

(See *Exercises 51, 52,* p. 60.)

Accusative.

133. The **Accusative** is used after the **Impersonals**: dĕcĕt, *it becomes;* dĕdĕcĕt, *it is unbecoming,* as: oratōrem irasci dedĕcet, *it is unbecoming in an orator to be angry.*

134. Verbs of *Naming, Making, Taking, Choosing, Showing* admit two **Accusatives** of the same person or thing. Such are:

   appellārĕ, nōmĭnārĕ, vŏcārĕ, dīcĕrĕ, *to name* or *call*
   arbĭtrārī, existĭmārĕ, hăbērĕ, pŭtārĕ, *to regard, consider, think*

jūdĭcāre, *to judge*
făcĕre, effĭcĕre, reddĕre, *to make*
creāre, ēlĭgĕre, *to elect;* dēsignāre, *to appoint*
sē praebēre, sē praestāre, *to show, offer one's self.*

 Nerōnem senātus hostem judi- *the senate declared Nero an*
  cāvit   *enemy.*

135. The **Double Accusative** is turned into the **Double Nominative** with the Passive, as: Nero a senātu hostis judicātus est.

136. dŏcēre, ēdŏcēre, *to teach;* cēlāre, *to conceal from,* take two **Accusatives**, one of the person, and the other of the thing.

 Dionysĭus Epaminondam musĭ- *Dionysius taught Epaminon-*
  cam docŭit   *das music*
 non te celāvi sermōnem   *I did not conceal from you the*
            conversation.

137. The **Passive** of dŏcēre or ēdŏcēre with the **Nominative** of the person and the **Accusative** of the thing is *almost never* used, but is replaced by discĕre ălĭquĭd ăb ălĭquō.

138. Verbs signifying *to ask, to demand, to request, to inquire* take two **Accusatives,** one of the person, and the other of the thing:

 poscĕre }   ōrāre } *to ask,* rŏgāre } *to ask,*
 flāgĭtāre } *to ask,* rŏgāre } *entreat,* interrŏgāre} *inquire*
 postŭlāre} *demand* pĕtĕre } *beseech* quaerĕre }

 posce deos venĭam   *ask favor of the gods*
 me sententĭam rogāvit   *he asked me my opinion.*

139. But to this there are many **Exceptions**. We may also say:
    poscĕre *or* flagitāre alĭquid ab alĭquo.
We always say: postulāre *or* petĕre alĭquid ab alĭquo;
    quaerĕre alĭquid ab, ex, *or* de alĭquo.
    (See *Exercises 53, 54,* p. 60.)

Ablative.

140. The **Ablative** is used with the **Deponent Verbs**:

 ūtŏr, -ī, *to use*   pŏtĭŏr, -īrī, *to make one's self*
 frŭŏr, -ī, *to enjoy*   *master of*
 fungŏr, -ī, *to discharge*   vescŏr, -ī, *to feed*

    and their **Compounds**:

 ăbūtŏr, -ī, *to abuse*   dēfungŏr, -ī, *to discharge*
 perfrŭŏr -ī, *to enjoy fully*   perfungŏr, -ī, *to fulfil*

utar vestra benignitāte, *I will avail myself of your kindness;*
vescīmur bestĭis, *we live upon animals.*

141. ŏpŭs est, *there is need, it is needful, necessary*, takes the **Dative** of the **Person** who is in want, and the **Ablative** of the **Thing** wanted (Impersonal Construction); but the Thing wanted may be the Subject and ŏpŭs est (sunt) the Predicate (Personal Construction).

opus mihi est libro	*I want a book*
liber mihi opus est	*a book is what I want*
opus mihi est libris	*I want books*
libri mihi opus sunt	*books are what I want*

142. The **Ablative** of **Price** is used with:

ĕmĕrĕ
rĕdĭmĕrĕ } *to buy*
mercārī
vendĕrĕ, *to sell* (**Pass.** vēnīrĕ)
līcērĕ, *to be for sale*

aestĭmārĕ, *to value*
lŏcārĕ } *to let*
collŏcārĕ
condūcĕrĕ, *to hire*
essĕ, stārĕ, constārĕ, *to cost*

patrĭam auro vendĭdit — *he sold his country for gold*
equus mihi talento stetit — *the horse cost me a talent.*

143. General **Value** or **Cost** is expressed by the following **Ablatives:**

magnō, *at a high price*
parvō, *at a low price*
nĭhĭlō, *for nothing*

plūrĭmō, *at a very high price*
mĭnĭmō, *at a very low price*

144. Verbs of *Filling* and *Depriving*, of *Plenty* and *Want* take the **Ablative.**

to abound	*to need*	*to fill*	*to deprive*
ăbundārĕ	ĕgērĕ	explērĕ	orbārĕ
rĕdundārĕ	indĭgērĕ	complērĕ	prīvārĕ
afflŭĕrĕ	cărērĕ	implērĕ	spŏlĭārĕ

Amerĭca abundat lacŭbus et flumĭnĭbus — *America abounds in lakes and rivers*
non egĕo medicīna — *I do not need medicine.*

145. Verbs signifying *to remove, abstain, set free*, take the **Ablative** with or without the Prepositions ex, dē, ăb; but with persons a Preposition (usually ăb) must be used.

arcērĕ, *to keep off*
abstĭnērĕ, *to refrain*
exclūdĕrĕ, *to shut out*

pellĕrĕ, expellĕrĕ, *to drive*
lībĕrārĕ, *to set free*
lĕvārĕ, *to relieve*

(See *Exercises 55, 56,* p. 60.)

Relations of Time and Place.

I. Time.

146. **Time** *when* is expressed by the **Ablative** of words denoting time, such as: tempŭs, aetās, vēr, aestās, &c., as: Hannibălis milĭtes vere convenērunt, *Hannibal's soldiers assembled in spring*.

147. **Time** *how long* is put in the **Accusative**, as:

Appĭus caecus multos annos fuit, *Appius was blind many years*.

The Preposition **pĕr** may be used to denote *from beginning to end*, as: est mecum per totum diem, *he is with me the livelong day*.

148. **Time** *how long before the present moment* is expressed by **ăbhinc** with the **Accusative**, as: abhinc sex menses, *six months ago*.

149. **Distance** of time *how long before* or *after* is expressed by the **Ablative** with antĕ or pŏst following:

paucis diēbus ante, *a few days before*,
paucis diēbus post, *a few days afterward*.

The **Accusative** can also be employed, but then the Preposition precedes, thus: ante, post paucos dies.

150. **Time** *within which* is expressed by the **Ablative** or by intrā with the **Accusative**, as:

Agamemnon vix decem annis (intra decem annos) unam cepit urbem *Agamemnon in ten years hardly took one city*.

151. **Time** *for how long* is expressed by **in** with the **Accusative**, as:

Phaëton currum paternum in diem rogăvit *Phaeton asked his father's chariot for a day*.

152. The **Question** *how old?* is answered in different ways:

By **nātŭs** *(born)* with the **Accusative**, as: puer decem annos natus est, *the boy is ten years old;*

By the **Genitive of Quality**, as: Hamilcar secum duxit filĭum Hannibălem annōrum novem, *Hamilcar took with him his son Hannibal 9 years of age;*

By **ăgĕrĕ**, *to pass*, with annŭs and an ordinal number, as: quartum annum ago et octogesĭmum, *I am 83 years old*.

Older and *younger* are expressed by **mājŏr** and **mĭnŏr** with following **Ablative**, as:

major quinque et triginta annis, *older than 35 years*.

(See *Exercises 57, 58*, p. 61.)

II. Space and Place.

153. The **Accusative of Extent in Space** accompanies Verbs, Adjectives and Adverbs in answer to the questions *how long, how wide, how high, how deep?* as: fossa pedes trecentos longa, *a ditch 300 feet long.* With Substantives the **Genitive of Quality** is used, as: colossus centum viginti pedum, *a coloss of 120 feet (in height).*

154. The place *in which* is in the **Ablative** with ĭn; the place *from which,* in the **Ablative** with ex, and the place *to which,* in the **Accusative** with ĭn or ăd; as: in urbe, *in town;* ex Italĭa, *from Italy;* in Americam, *to America;* ad urbem, *to town.*

155. The place *in which* is in the **Ablative without a Preposition** with nouns when qualified by tōtŭs or cunctŭs, and with lŏcō, lŏcīs when qualified by Adjectives, as: tota Graecia, *in all Greece;* multis locis, *in many places.* The way *by which* is put in the **Ablative,** as: via Appĭa profectus est, *he set out by the Appian way.*

156. In like manner the Prepositions are not used with the names of **Towns** and **small Islands.**

In answer to the question *whither?* names of towns and small islands are put in the **Accusative Case,** as: Romam venit, *he came to Rome.*

In answer to the question *whence?* the names of towns and small islands are put in the **Ablative Case,** as: Roma cessit, *he retired from Rome.*

In answer to the question *where?* the names of towns and small islands, if of the first or second Declension and in the Singular, are put in the **Genitive Case,** as: Romae mansit, *he remained at Rome.* But if the names are of the Plural Number or belong to the third Declension, they are put in the **Ablative Case,** as: Babylōne mortŭus est, *he died at Babylon.*

157. The following words are used like names of towns without a Preposition:

rŭs, *into the country*   dŏmŭm, *home*
rŭrĕ, *from the country* dŏmō, *from home*   hŭmō, *from the ground*
rŭrī, *in the country*   dŏmī, *at home*   hŭmī, *on the ground*
    domī militĭaeque, *at home and in the field*
    belli domīque, *in war and in peace.*

(See *Exercises 59, 60,* p..62.)

Ablative in Special Constructions.

158. The **Ablative of Cause** designates that *by which, by reason of which, because of which, in accordance with which* something is, or is done, as: Dei providentĭa mundus administrătur, *the world is governed by God's providence.* In the Passive construction, however, the **Person** or **Living Agent by whom** any thing is done is put in the **Ablative** with ā, ăb, as: a Deo mundus administrătur, *the world is governed by God.*

159. The **Ablative** is used to denote the **Means** or **Instrument** by which any thing is effected, as: Pyrrhus lapĭde interfectus est, *Pyrrhus was killed by a stone.* The person considered as means or instrument is expressed by pĕr with the Accusative, as: Caesar certĭor factus est **per** legătos, *Caesar was informed by (means of) ambassadors.*

160. That *in respect to which*, or *in accordance with which* any thing happens, or is done, is denoted by the **Ablative of Limitation**, as: aurum cetĕra metalla pondĕre supĕrat, *gold surpasses in weight the rest of the metals;* nostro more, *according to our custom.*

161. The **Ablative** with an Adjective is used to denote **Quality**, as: Cicĕro magna fuit eloquentĭa, *Cicero was (a man) of great eloquence.* The **Genitive** may be used in the same way, and must be used to define *measure, number, time, space*, as: fossa quindĕcim pedum, *a ditch of 15 feet.*

162. The **Ablative of Manner** answers the question **how?** It is used with the Preposition cŭm when it has no Adjective, with or without cŭm when it has an Adjective, as: Miltiădes summa aequitāte res constitŭit, *Miltiades settled the affairs with the greatest fairness;* cum voluptāte alĭquem audīre, *to hear some one with pleasure.* But words of manner: mŏdō, ratiōne, more, viā, *in (such) a manner*, &c. never take cŭm.

163. The **Ablative of Measure** is used to denote the *Degree of Difference*, especially with Comparatives, as: turris vigĭnti pedĭbus altĭor erat quam murus, *the tower was (by) twenty feet higher than the wall.* Mark the expressions: multō, *much;* paulō, *little;* altĕrō tantō, *twice as much;* quō..eō, *the..the.*

164. The **Ablative of Comparison** may be used with the *Comparative*, instead of quäm, *than*, with the Nominative or Accusative, as: filĭus melĭor est patre, *the son is better than his father.*

(See *Exercises 61, 62*, p. 62.)

Use of Tenses.

165. The use of the Tenses corresponds, upon the whole, pretty closely in Latin and in English. The principal points of difference are the following:

166. The **Perfect** has two different uses. As the **Perfect Definite** it denotes an action as now completed, and is rendered by the English Perfect with *have*, as: Graecas litĕras senex didĭci, *I have learned Greek in my old age*. As the **Historical Perfect** it denotes an action as completed in past time, when no reference is to be made to the time of other events, as: Caesar exercĭtum finĭbus Italĭae admōvit, Rubicōnem transīit, Romam et aerariŭm occupāvit, &c., *Caesar advanced with his army to the frontiers of Italy, passed the Rubicon, took possession of Rome and the treasury*.

167. While the general statement is given by the Historical Perfect, the particulars of the action *(situations, manners, customs)* are in the **Imperfect**, as: Verres in forum venit; ardēbant ocŭli, *Verres came into the forum; his eyes were blazing*.

168. The **Present** is regularly used with **dŭm**, *while*, though the time referred to is past, as: dum haec aguntur, Caesări nuntiātum est, *while this is going on, word was brought to Caesar*.

169. The **Historical Perfect** is regularly used with postquam, posteāquam, *after;* ubi, ut, simŭlac, ubi primum, ut primum, *as soon as*. The English translation is often the Pluperfect, as: postquam adspexi, illĭco cognōvi, *after I had looked at it, I recognized it immediately*.

170. The **Future Perfect** is used with much greater exactness in Latin than in English, as: ut sementem fecĕris, ita metes, *as you sow, so shall you reap*.

(See *Exercises 63, 64,* p. 63.)

Sequence of Tenses.

171. Tenses, in regard to their connection, are divided into two classes:

Principal, including the *Present*, both *Futures* and the *Perfect Definite;*

Historical, including the *Imperfect*, the *Historical Perfect* and the *Pluperfect*.

172. The Tense used in any *Subjunctive Clause* is governed by the Tense of the Verb upon which it depends. When depending upon a **Principal Tense**, the **Present Subjunctive** is used for *contemporary* action, and the **Perfect Subjunctive** for *antecedent* action.

Principal Clause.		Dependent Clause.
Present.	cognosco, *I am finding out*	quid facĭas, *what you are doing*
Future.	cognoscam, *I shall find out*	
Fut. Perf.	cognovĕro, *I shall have found out (shall know)*	quid fecĕris, *what you have done, what you have been doing, what you did*
Perf. Defin.	cognōvi, *I have found out (I know)*	

173. When the *Subjunctive Clause* depends upon an **Historical Tense**, the **Imperfect Subjunctive** is used for *contemporary* action, and the **Pluperfect Subjunctive** for *antecedent* action.

Principal Clause.		Dependent Clause.
Imperf.	cognoscēbam, *I was finding out*	quid facĕres, *what you were doing*
Pluperf.	cognovĕram, *I had found out (I knew)*	quid fecisses, *what you had done, had been doing*
Hist. Perf.	Caesar cognōvit, *Caesar found out*	quid facĕrent hostes, *what the enemy was doing*
		quid fecissent hostes, *what the enemy had done*

174. The **Future Tenses** are wanting in the *Subjunctive*. After a Future or Future Perfect, their place is supplied by the Present or Perfect Subjunctive; after the other Tenses by the Active Periphrastic Subjunctive, Present or Imperfect; as:

cognoscam, quid facĭas, *I shall find out what you are doing;*
cognovĕro, quid fecĕris, *I shall have found out what you have done;*
cognosco, quid factūrus sis, *I am finding out what you will do;*
cognovĕram, quid factūrus esses, *I had found out what you would do.*
(See *Exercises 65, 66*, p. 63.)

The Imperative.

175. The **Present Imperative** denotes that an action is to be performed at once, as: si quid in te peccāvi, ignosce, *if I have sinned against you, forgive me.*

The **Future Imperative** is used where there is a distinct relation to future time, as: regĭo imperĭo duo sunto, *there shall be two officers with royal power.*

176. The regular negative of the Imperative is **nē**, which is, however, in classical Latin only found with the Future Imperative. Instead of the *Positive Imperative*, the third person of the **Present Subjunctive** may be employed, as: amet, *let him love;* instead of the *Negative Imperative* the second person of the **Perfect Subjunctive** or the third person of the **Present Subjunctive** with **nē** may be employed, as: ne transiĕris Ibĕrum, *do not cross the Ebro;* ne amet, *let him not love.*

177. Instead of the simple Imperative several **Imperative Phrases** are common:

cūrā ŭt, *take care that*   } each with   căvē nē, *beware lest* } each with
făc ŭt, *cause that*   } the **Subj.** căvē, *beware*   } the **Subj.**
făc, *do*   }   nōlī, *be unwilling*, with the **Inf.**

The Infinitive.

178. The **Infinitive** is really a Verbal Noun which governs the case of its Verb and is modified by Adverbs and not by Adjectives, as: diligenter legĕre librum, *the careful reading of a book.*

179. The **Infinitive** may be used as the **Subject** of a Verb, as: numquam est utīle peccāre, *to do wrong is never useful,* or as the **Object**, as: vincĕre scis, Hannĭbal, victorĭa uti nescis, *how to win victory, Hannibal, you know; how to make use of victory you know not.*

(See *Exercises 67, 68*, p. 64.)

Gerund.

180. As the Infinitive is used as a Verbal Noun in the Nominative and Accusative cases, so the **Gerund** is used in the remaining cases, viz:

Nom.	scribĕre est utīle	*writing is useful*
Gen.	ars scribendi	*the art of writing*
Dat.	scribendo adfŭi	*I was present at the writing*
Acc.	scribĕre disco	*I learn to write*
	ad scribendum utīlis	*useful for writing*
Abl.	scribendo discīmus	*we learn by writing.*

The Gerund governs the same case as the Verb, as:

ars scribendi epistŭlam	*the art of writing a letter*
cupĭdus te audiendi	*desirous of hearing you*
injurĭas ferendo	*by bearing wrongs*
ad beāte vivendum	*for living happily*
parendo legĭbus	*by obeying the laws.*

Gerundive.

181. The **Gerundive** of Verbs governing the Accusative is frequently used instead of the Gerund in the following manner:
The **Accusative** is put in the same Case as the Gerund;
The **Gerund** is then changed into the Gerundive;
The **Gerundive** is made to agree with the Substantive in *Gender, Number* and *Case;* thus:

	Gerund.	Gerundive.
Gen.	scribendi epistŭlam	scribendae epistŭlae
Dat.	scribendo epistŭlam	scribendae epistŭlae
Acc.	ad scribendum epistŭlam	ad scribendam epistŭlam
Abl.	scribendo epistŭlam	scribenda epistŭla.

(See *Exercises 69, 70*, p. 64.)

Accusative with the Infinitive.

182. The **Accusative with the Infinitive** is used like the English Objective with the Infinitive in such sentences, as: hoc verum esse scimus, *we know this to be true.* In English we might also say: *We know that this is true,* but Latin permits only of the Infinitive Construction.

183. The **Accusative with the Infinitive** may be the **Subject** of the sentence. The Predicate is either a Noun or Adjective with est, or an Impersonal Verb, as: certum est libĕros a parentĭbus amări, *it is certain that children are loved by their parents.*

The most common phrases under this rule are:

certŭm est, *it is certain*
vĕrŭm est, *it is true*
nōtŭm est, *it is known*
vĕrī sĭmĭlĕ est, *it is probable*

constăt, *it is agreed, it is evident*
ŏportĕt, *there is need, ought*
trădĭtŭm est, *it is handed down, there is a tradition*

184. The **Accusative with the Infinitive** is used as the **Object** of Verbs of *perceiving* and *declaring*, such as:

nĕgărĕ, *to deny*
narrārĕ, *to relate*
sentīrĕ, *to feel, perceive*
dīcĕrĕ, *to say*
testārī, *to testify*
arbĭtrārī, *to be of opinion, believe*

intellĕgĕrĕ, *to understand*
pŭtārĕ, *to consider, think*
vĭdērĕ, *to see*
spērārĕ, *to hope*
scīrĕ, *to know*
nescīrĕ, *not to know*
dŏcērĕ, *to teach*

Examples are:
aves vidēmus construĕre nidos   *we see that birds build nests*
nemo negābit se esse mortālem   *no one will deny that he is mortal.*

185. Verbs followed by the **Accusative and Infinitive** are especially those of *wishing* and *desiring*, as:

vŏlō, *I wish*   cŭpĭō, *I desire*   sĭnō, *I permit*
nōlō, *I do not wish* jŭbĕō, *I bid*   pătĭŏr, *I suffer*
mālō, *I like better* vĕtō, *I forbid*

discipŭlum me habēri volo, non doctōrem, *I wish to be taken for a learner, not for a teacher.*

186. To translate such clauses as are introduced in English by the Conjunction *that*, and require in Latin the **Accusative with the Infinitive**
take no notice of *that;*
translate the **English Nominative** following *that* by the **Latin Accusative**;
translate the **English Verb** by the **Latin Infinitive**.

The **Future Infinitive** is often expressed by **fŏrĕ** or **fŭtūrŭm essĕ ŭt** — necessarily so when the Verb has no **Supine**, as:

credo fore ut pluat   *I believe it will rain*
credēbam fore ut pluĕret   *I believed it would rain.*

(See *Exercises 71, 72*, p. 65.)

Participles.

187. The **Participles** are more frequently used in Latin than in English and may have the value

of *a Relative*, as: divitĭae semper duratūrae, *riches which will last forever;*

of *while, when, after*, as: Plato scribens mortŭus est, *Plato died while writing;*

of *if*, as: mendāci homĭni ne verum quidem dicenti credĭmus, *we do not believe a liar, even if he speaks the truth;*

of *since, because,* as: cantus olorīnus recte fabulōsus habētur nunquam audītus, *the swan's song is justly regarded as fabulous, because it has never been heard;*

of *though, although*, as: ocŭlus se non videns alĭa cernit, *the eye, though not seeing itself, sees other things;*

of *to, in order to* (expressing a purpose), as: Scipio in Afrĭcam trajēcit Carthagĭnem deletūrus, *Scipio crossed over into Africa to destroy Carthage.*

188. The **Participle** with a **negative** (nōn, nĭhĭl) is often best rendered

by ***without*** and a *Participial Noun*, as: multi homĭnes vitupĕrant libros non intellectos, *many men find fault with books without understanding them.*

189. The **Passive Participle** is often used in Latin where the English idiom requires a Verbal Noun, as: Tarentum captŭm, *the taking of Tarent;* ab urbe condĭta, *from the building of the city;* ante Christum natum, *before the birth of Christ.*

(See *Exercises 73, 74*, p. 65.)

Periphrastic Conjugation.

190. The **Periphrastic Conjugation** is formed by combining the tenses of essĕ with the **Future Participle (Active)**, as: amatūrus sum, *I am about to love;* and with the **Gerundive (Passive)**, as: amandus sum, *I ought to be loved.*

191. The **Active Periphrastic Conjugation** denotes *intention* or *being on the point of doing something*, as: scriptūrus sum, *I purpose to write,* or *I am about to write.* The **Passive Periphrastic Conjugation** expresses *necessity* or *propriety*, as: parentes amandi sunt, *parents ought to be loved;* the person *by whom* is put in the **Dative**, as: parentes libĕris amandi sunt, *parents ought to be loved by their children.*

192. The neuter of the Gerundive with est, ĕrăt, etc., is used impersonally if what is said holds good of people in general, as: vivendum est, *we* or *you must live.*

But the person *by whom* may also be added in the **Dative**, thus:

mihi scribendum est, *I must* or *should write*
tibi scribendum est, *thou must* or *shouldst write*
ei scribendum est, *he must* or *should write*
nobis scribendum est, *we must* or *should write*
vobis scribendum est, *you must* or *should write*
eis scribendum est, *they must* or *should write.*

(See *Exercises 75, 76*, p. 66.)

Ablative Absolute.

193. A Noun or Pronoun with a Participle is used in the **Ablative Case** absolutely to express some accompanying circum-

The **Ablative Absolute** may be translated by the English *Nominative Absolute* which is a close equivalent; but, as a rule, the same change of form is required as in translating Participles in general. (See *187*.)

Examples are:

Numa Pompilio regnante	*Numa Pompilius reigning. When Numa Pompilius was reigning. In the reign of Numa Pompilius.*
Tito imperante	*In the reign of the emperor Titus.*
Caesăre interfecto	*Caesar being, having been murdered. When Caesar had been murdered. After the murder of Caesar.*

An **Adjective**, or another **Noun** may take the place of the Participle, as:

Xerxe rege	*Xerxes being king.*
natūra dūce	*Nature being the leader. Under the guidance of nature.*
nolentĭbus nobis	*While we are unwilling. Against our will. In spite of us.*
patre invīto	*While father is, was unwilling. Against father's will.*

194. The want of a Perfect **Active** Participle in Latin is frequently supplied by the Ablative Absolute with the **Passive** Participle, thus:

Caesar, urbe capta, redīit { *The city being taken, Caesar returned.* *Having taken the city, Caesar returned.*

(See *Exercises 77, 78*, p. 66.)

The Supine and its Equivalents.

195. The **Former Supine** (in **ŭm**) is used after Verbs of *motion* to express the *purpose* of the motion; it has an *Active meaning*, as:

venĭo te rogātum   *I come to ask you.*

196. The **Latter Supine** (in **ū**) has a *Passive meaning;* it is used only with a few Adjectives denoting *ease* or *difficulty, pleasure* or *displeasure, right* or *wrong;* with the nouns **fās**, *right*, **nĕfās**, *wrong;* sometimes with **ŏpŭs**, *need*, as:

quid est tam jucundum audītu?   *what is so agreeable in hearing?*

197. The **Former Supine**, as an expression of *purpose*, is not very common, its place being supplied in various ways. Thus the sentence:

The Carthaginians sent ambassadors to sue for peace,

may be rendered:

Supine.	Carthaginienses legātos misērunt **pacem petītum**.
Gerundive w.	⎰ C. legātos misērunt **ad pacem petendam**.
ǎd, causā	⎱ C. legātos misērunt **pacis petendae causā**.
Fut. Part.	C. legātos misērunt **pacem petitūros**.
ŭt w. Subj.	C. legātos misērunt, **ut pacem petěrent**.
quī w. Subj.	C. legātos misērunt, **qui pacem petěrent**.

198. The use of the **Latter Supine** is confined to a few Verbs, as: dictū, *to tell;* factū, *to do;* audītū, *to hear;* vīsū, *to see*. With făcĭlis, diffĭcĭlis, jūcundŭs, the construction of **ǎd** with the Gerund is more common, as: res est facĭlis ad cognoscendum (cognĭtu), *the thing is easy to know.*

(See *Exercises* **79, 80**, p. 67.)

The Subjunctive.

199. Dependent **Subjunctive** Clauses may be classified as follows:

Conjunctive Clauses introduced by *Conjunctions,*
Relative   "   "   " *Relatives,*
Indirect Questions   "   " *Interrogative words.*

Subjunctive after Conjunctions.

200. **ŭt,** *that,* governs the **Subjunctive**:

I. When it means *so that* (often rendered by *to, so as to*), to express a *result;* its negative is **ŭt nōn,** *so that not.* It is used after such words as tǎm, ĭtǎ, sīc, ădĕō, *so;* tālis, *such;* tantŭs, *so great,* and after Verbs denoting *it happens, it remains,* accĭdit. restat, and the like, as: Atticus ita vixit, ut Atheniensĭbus carissĭmus esset, *Atticus so lived that he was very dear to the Athenians.*

II. When it means *that, in order that* (often to be translated by *to, in order to*); its negative is **nē,** *that not, lest.* It expresses *purpose* and is regularly used with Verbs denoting *purpose* or *intent,* as: oro te ut dilĭgens sis, *I entreat you to be diligent.*

III. When it means *granted that*, to express a *concession;* its negative is **nē; as:** ut desint vires, tamen est laudanda voluntas, *granted that strength fails, still the will should be approved.*

IV. With Verbs of *fearing*, **nē** is translated *that*, and **ūt**, *that not;* timĕo, ne venĭat, *I am afraid that he will come* (it is my purpose that he shall not) — timĕo, ut venĭat, *I am afraid that he will not come* (it is my purpose that he shall).

201. The Ablative **quō** (= ūt ĕō, *that thereby*), *in order that, so that,* is used with **Comparatives**, as: ager arātur, quo meliōres fructus edĕre possit, *a field is plowed that it may yield better fruit.*

202. **quōmĭnŭs**, *that..not*, is used after expressions of *hindering* where also **nē** may be used, as: nihil obstat quomĭnus scribam, *nothing hinders me from writing.*

203. **quīn**, *but that, but that..not*, is used with *negative* expressions, as: nemo est quin hoc vidĕat, *there is no one but sees this*, and after negative expressions implying *doubt, omission*, and the like, as: non dubĭto quin domi sit, *I do not doubt that he is at home.*

204. The Conjunctions of Comparison:

tamquăm, quăsī, vĕlŭt sī, pĕrindĕ ăc sī, *as if*, take the Subjunctive, as: me adspicĭtis quasi monstrum sim, *you look at me as if I were a monster.*

205. The Subjunctive is used in *conditional wishes* with **dummŏdŏ, dŭm, mŏdŏ**, *if only, provided*, as: odĕrint dum metŭant, *let them hate if they only fear.* The negative is **nē**.

206. The Concessive Conjunctions

    lĭcĕt, ŭt, cŭm, *though, suppose, whereas*
    quamvīs, quantumvīs, *however much*

take the Subjunctive, while

    etsī, tămetsī, quamquăm, *although*

regularly take the Indicative.

EXAMPLES: Vitĭa mentis, quamvis exigŭa sint, in majus excēdunt, *defects of the mind, no matter how slight they be, go on increasing.* — Quamquam intellĕgunt, tamen numquam dicunt, *though they understand, they never speak.*

207. Causal **cŭm**, meaning *as, since*, takes the Subjunctive, as: quae cum ita sint, perge, *since these things are so, proceed.* — Temporal **cŭm**, meaning *when, at the time when*, takes the

Indicative of all the tenses, as: ager cum multos annos quiēvit, uberiōres fructus efferre solet, *when a field has rested many years, it usually produces a more abundant crop.*—Historical **cŭm**, meaning *when, as*, takes the **Imperfect** or **Pluperfect Subjunctive**, involving cause as well as time, as: cum Caesar Ancōnam occupasset, urbem reliquīmus, *when Caesar had occupied Ancona, we left the city.*

208. There are three classes of **Conditional Sentences**:

I. The condition is represented as a *fact:* **sī** with the **Indicative** in both clauses:

    si Deus **est**, aeternus **est**   *if there is a God, he is eternal.*

II. The condition is represented as *possible* or *likely to be realized:* **sī** with **Present** or **Perfect Subjunctive** in both clauses:

    si quis ita **agat**, imprūdens **sit**   *if anybody were to act thus, he would not be wise.*

III. The condition is represented as *contrary to fact:* **sī** with **Imperfect** or **Pluperfect Subjunctive** in both clauses:

    facĕrem, si **possem**   *I should do it if I could.*

    (See *Exercises 81—84*, p. 68.)

The Subjunctive after Relatives.

209. The Subjunctive is used in **Relative Sentences**:

To denote **purpose** or **motive; quī** = **ŭt ĕgŏ, ŭt tū, ŭt ĭs**, etc., as: missi sunt delecti cum Leonīda, qui Thermopўlas occupārent   *picked men were sent with Leonidas to take possession of Thermopylae.*

To denote the **cause** *on account of which*, or the **hindrance** *in spite of which;* **quī** = **cŭm ĕgŏ, cŭm tū, cŭm ĭs**, etc. (often with **ŭt, ŭtpŏtĕ,** *as;* **quĭppĕ,** *namely*), as:

o virum simplĭcem, qui nos nihil celet!   *O guileless man who hidest nothing from us!*

After general expressions of *existence* and *non-existence*, as:

est qui } *there is, there are*   habĕo quod, *I have to*
sunt qui }   *some who*   reperiuntur qui, *persons are*
nemo est qui, *there is none to*   *found who*
nihīl est quod, *there is nothing*

sunt qui censĕant una animum cum corpŏre interīre, *there are some who believe that the soul perishes together with the body.*

After **dignŭs, indignŭs, ĭdōnĕŭs, aptŭs,** as:
indignus es, cui fides habeātur, *you are unworthy of being believed.*

    (See *Exercises 85, 86,* p. 69.)

Subjunctive in Indirect Questions.

210. The **Subjunctive** is used in such questions as are dependent upon some word in the former part of the sentence (**Indirect Questions**).

The words: ubi fuisti? *where have you been?* are a **Direct Question**, with the Verb in the **Indicative**; in the sentence:

dic mihi ubi fuĕris, *tell me where you have been,*

the same words are an **Indirect Question**, and the dependent Verb is in the **Subjunctive** Mood.

qualis sit animus ipse animus   *the mind itself knows not what*
  nescit   *the mind is*
quis ego sim me rogĭtas?   *do you ask me who I am?*

Indirect Questions have the same particles as the direct, **num** and **ně**, corresponding to *whether* in English.

Indirect Disjunctive Questions.

quaero utrum verum an falsum sit
quaero verumne an falsum sit   } *I ask whether it is true or*
quaero verum an falsum sit   *false*
quaero verum falsumne sit

When the interrogative particle is omitted in the first member, **ně** may stand in the second, but only in **Indirect Questions**.

Or not in *Indirect Questions* is **necně**, as: dii utrum sint, necne sint, quaerĭtur, *the question is whether there are gods or not.*

(See *Exercises 87, 88*, p. 69.)

Part Second.
PARALLEL EXERCISES
ON THE FOREGOING LESSONS.

ETYMOLOGY (Continued).

Declension.—Gr. 1—22.

1. Vita parentum filiis et filiabus cara est. Bonus paterfamilias diligentiam¹ et parsimoniam amat. Tria pondo auri non sunt graviora quam tria pondo plumarum². Tyranni³ perpetuo⁴ insidias⁵ metuunt. · Noctu plerique homines domi sunt. Multi homines divitias amant, pauci virtutem.

¹*diligence* ²*feather* ³*tyrant* ⁴*constantly* ⁵*treachery*

2. Good health is more desirable¹ than great riches. Soldiers like the life of the camp. Diligent boys are the joy and delight of (their) parents and teachers. My father's letter was very pleasing to me. The cares of a good father of a family are great. Truth loves the light (and) falsehood² darkness.

¹optābĭlĭs, -ĕ ²mendācĭŭm, -ī

First Conjugation.
Gr. 23—25.

RULE. *Cause, Manner,* and *Instrument* are put in the **Ablative**.

3. Natura dedit agros, ars humana aedificavit urbes. Eques equum calcari et freno domuit. Aethiopem¹ lavare supervacuus² labor est. Attus Navius³ augur⁴ cotem novacula⁵ secuit. Julius Caesar⁶ totam Galliam⁷ domuit⁸. Athenienses a Lacedaemoniis⁹ contra Persas adjuti sunt. Postquam¹⁰ tonuit, aer purus¹¹ et saluber¹² esse solet¹³.

¹*an Ethiopian* ²*needless, in vain* ³*Attus Navius*, proper name ⁴*augur* ⁵*razor* ⁶*Julius Caesar*, proper name ⁷*Gaul* ⁸*subjugate* ⁹*Lacedaemonian* ¹⁰*after* ¹¹*pure* ¹²*salubrious* ¹³*is wont*

RULE. Time *how long* is in the **Accusative**.

4. We tame wild beasts by hunger and blows. Alexander the Great subjugated a great part of Asia. How many years[1] has the Roman empire stood? God has given (to) us a short life. Tamed lions are rare. If riches afford happiness, avarice is the first virtue. Lycurgus[2] had prohibited[3] the use of gold and silver by law.

[1]Accusative [2]Lycurgŭs, -ī [3]vĕtō, ārē

Second Conjugation.
Gr. 96—35.

5. Post[1] bellum decem annōrum Graeci urbem Trojam delevērunt. Senātus[2] servitūtem abolēvit. Multi parentes vitĭa liberōrum indulgentĭa[3] auxērunt. Discipŭli a magistris docentur. Puĕri manēre jussi sunt, sed non manēbunt. Pastor fugāvit[4] lupum, qui unam ovem momordĕrat. Si visus es a nullo, tamen Deus te vidit.

[1]*after* [2]*the senate* [3]*indulgence* [4]*to put to flight*

6. Pains are increased by impatience[1]. Poverty has taught men many useful arts. How long[2] will your brother stay in Virginia[3]? Six months[4]. Who destroyed the city (of) Carthage[5]? Scipio[6]. The father wept over[7] the death of (his) son. Some[8] people have never laughed. Sheep are shorn once or[9] twice every year.

[1]impătĭentĭă, -ae [2]quamdĭu [3]Virgĭnĭă, -ae [4]Acc. [5]Carthāgŏ, -ĭnĭs [6]Scĭpĭŏ, -ōnĭs [7]dē, with Ab'ative [8]quĭdăm [9]vĕl

Third Conjugation.
Verbs ending in ŭō, vō. — Gr. 36. 37.

7. Danubĭus[1] orientem, Rhenus[2] septentriōnem versus[3] fluit. Cuilĭbet homĭni quaedam beneficĭa a deo tribuuntur. Hodĭe[4], amīci, optĭmas induĭte vestes[5]: est natālis patris patrĭae. Nemo justus esse potest, qui mortem, qui dolōrem, qui egestātem[6] metŭit. Justus est is, qui suum cuīque tribŭit. Interdum per[7] tres continŭos[8] dies pluit.

[1]*Danube* [2]*Rhine* [3]*toward;* versus takes the Acc.; it is put after the word it governs; here orientem .. septentriōnem [4]*to-day* [5]*clothing* [6]*want* [7]*for* [8]*continuous*

8. Knives are sharpened with a whetstone. Brave soldiers do not fear death. This medicine¹ will lessen your pain. The beaver builds a wonderful² house. Some³ insects live one day⁴ only. King Arganthonīus⁵ lived 120 years⁶. The deeds⁷ of some men do not agree with⁷ (their) words⁸.

¹medĭcīnā, -ae ²mīrīfĭcŭs, -ă, -ŭm ³quīdăm ⁴Accus. ⁵Arganthŏnĭŭs, -ī ⁶factŭm, -ī ⁷cŭm, w. Abl. ⁸verbŭm, -ī

Verbs ending in Iō. — Gr. 38. 39.

9. Prudens est is, quem facĭunt aliēna¹ perĭcŭla cautum. Quid faciet is homo in tenĕbris, qui nihil² timet nisi³ testem⁴ et judĭcem? Elephantum ex⁴ mure facis, amīce. Quo plura homĭnes habent, eo plura cupĭunt. In magno magni capiuntur flumĭne⁵ pisces. Testudĭnes⁶ parĭunt⁷ ova⁸ avĭum ovis simĭlĭa.

¹of others ²nothing but ³witness ⁴of ⁵river ⁶tortoise ⁷to lay ⁸egg

10. Death snatches away young men as well as¹ old men. The drones are killed by (ăb) the bees. In the sea and in the rivers innumerable² fishes are caught every year. The more a miser has, the more he desires. Nobody will dig the earth with³ golden mattocks. We call him wise whom the dangers of others make cautious.

¹t.im..quam ²innŭmĕrābĭlĭs, -ĕ ³Abl.

Verbs in dō, tō. — Gr. 40—42.

11. Puĕri Romāni, sicut¹ nostri, pila² et trocho³ lusērunt. Solis cursus⁴ annŭus⁵ divīsus est in quattŭor partes: in ver et aestātem et autumnum et hiĕmem. Bonus dux bonum reddit comĭtem⁶. Caesar, ille clarissĭmus imperātor Romānus, etĭam librum grammatĭcum⁷ edĭdit. Quod quisque sperat⁸, facĭle⁹ credit.

¹like ²ball ³hoop ⁴course ⁵yearly ⁶follower ⁷grammar (book) ⁸to hope for ⁹easily

12. The year is divided into spring, summer, autumn (and) winter. Agesilaus¹, king of the Spartans, sometimes played with² his children. Romulus founded the city (of) Rome. The hunters have spread (their) nets. I have read your letter which our friend had delivered to me. The Greeks founded many cities in Italy and Sicily.

¹Agēsĭlāŭs, -ī ²cŭm, w. Abl.

Gr. 43. 44.

13. Carthaginienses¹ frustra² a Romānis pacem petivērunt. Boves cornĭbus, canes dentĭbus, aves rostris et ungŭlis³ se defendunt. Plebs Romāna magnam vim⁴ frumenti ex agro Tarquiniōrum⁵ in Tibĕrim⁶ fudit. Scipĭo⁷ Numantĭam⁸ operĭbus⁹ clausit. Cimbri¹⁰ et Teutŏni¹¹ complūres exercĭtus¹² Romānos fudĕrant. Aves super¹³ arbŏres sidĕre solent¹⁴.

¹*Carthaginian* ²*in vain* ³*claim* ⁴*quantity* ⁵*the Tarquinians* ⁶*Tiber* ⁷*Scipio* ⁸*Numantia* ⁹*military works* ¹⁰*Cimbrians* ¹¹*Teutons* ¹²*army* ¹³*on top of* ¹⁴*are accustomed*

14. The moon sends the light which she receives from¹ the sun (in)to² the earth. Horses defend themselves with (their) hoofs³, dogs and other animals with (their) teeth, bulls⁴ with (their) horns. Truth defends itself. Ten thousand (of) Athenians routed more than⁵ a hundred thousand (of) Persians. The riches of others kindle the envy of the miser.

¹², with the Abl. ²In, with the Acc. ³ungŭlā, -ae ⁴taurūs, -ī ⁵amplĭūs, *more than*

Verbs ending in bŏ, pŏ. — Gr. 45. 46.

15. Octavĭa¹, Augusti² soror, nupsit Antonĭo. Simŭlac³ epistŭlam⁴ scripsĕro, ambulābo⁵. Darēus⁶ in fuga⁷ aquam turbĭdam⁸ bibit; numquam jucundĭus⁹ bibĕrat, numquam enim¹⁰ sitĭens¹¹ bibĕrat. Cicĕro librum de¹² officĭis¹³ scripsit. Quid agis¹⁴, carissĭme? Scribo, ut¹⁵ vides. Quid scribis? Littĕras ad patrem scribo. Corpŏra animalĭum serpentĭum sunt mollĭa¹⁶.

¹*Octavia* ²*Augustus* ³*as soon as* ⁴*letter* ⁵*to take a walk* ⁶*Dareus* ⁷*flight* ⁸*muddy* ⁹*more deliciously* ¹⁰*for* ¹¹*when thirsty* ¹²*on* ¹³*duty* ¹⁴*to do* ¹⁵*as* ¹⁶*soft*

RULE. Time *when* is in the **Ablative**.

16. Horses crop the grass. Many men can neither¹ read nor¹ write. The boys have already² plucked the cherries³; in autumn⁴ we shall pluck the fruit⁵ of all the trees. Men drink water, wine (and) milk⁶. Some men have never drunk wine. The art of writing was known to the Phenicians. Cicero wrote many letters to his friend Atticus⁷.

¹nequĕ..nequĕ ²jăm ³cĕrăsŭm, -ī ⁴Abl. without prepos. ⁵pōmă, -ōrŭm, ⁶lăc, lactĭs ⁷Attĭcŭs, -ī

Verbs ending in cō, gō (gŭō), quō, hō, ctō. — Gr. 47—51.

17. Si nos non ipsi regēmus, regēmur ab aliis. Insŭla est terra aqua cincta. Apud Romānos fur¹ dicebātur homo trium litterārum. Pisces squamis² tecti sunt. Curae nos sollicĭtant³ anguntque. Adulescentes praeceptis senum ad virtūtem ducuntur. Nobĭlis⁴ equus umbrā⁵ virgae⁶ regētur.

¹thief ²scale ³to disturb ⁴noble ⁵shadow ⁶switch

18. God rules the destinies¹ of men. It is God who rules this whole world. Bias², one of³ the seven wise men⁴, said: I carry my all⁵ with me⁶. In winter the banks' of rivers are joined by ice⁸. Precepts lead, examples draw. It is difficult to rule the minds of men. The ox draws the cart⁹, not the cart the ox.

¹fātŭm, -ī ²Bĭās, -antis ³ex, w. Abl. ⁴săpĭens, -tis ⁵omnĭā mĕā ⁶mēcŭm ⁷rīpă, -ae ⁸gĕlŭ, -ūs (Abl.) ⁹currūs, -ūs

Gr. 52—54.

19. Quid egisti, amīce? Epistŭlam scripsi. Caeci¹ sunt ocŭli, cum² animŭs aliās res agit³. Athenienses Aristīdem⁴, civem omnĭum justissĭmum, in exsilĭum egērunt⁵. Tarquinĭus Superbus rex foedus⁶ cum Latīnis⁷ icit. Marcellus⁸ primus Hannibălem⁹ aciē¹⁰ vicit. Gades¹¹, ultĭma urbs Hispaniae, oceănum¹² tangit. Romāni milĭtes neque sacris neque profānis¹³ aedificĭis¹⁴ Carthagĭnis pepercērunt.

¹blind ²when ³to be intent on ⁴Aristĭdes ⁵to drive ⁶treaty ⁷Latin ⁸Marcellus ⁹Hannibal ¹⁰battle ¹¹Cadix ¹²ocean ¹³profane ¹⁴building

20. I was reading, you were writing, your brother was painting. We break and overcome all diseases by abstinence¹. The general Duilius² held³ the first naval⁴ triumph⁵. Dionysius⁶, the tyrant⁷ of Syracuse⁸, led⁹ (his) life in constant¹⁰ fear¹⁰. Danger will never be overcome without¹⁰ danger. In summer the streets¹² are sprinkled with water.

¹abstĭnentĭă, -ae (Abl.) ²Duillĭŭs, -ī ³ăgō, -ĕrĕ ⁴marĭtĭmŭs, -ă, -ŭm ⁵trĭumphŭs, -ī ⁶Dĭŏnȳsĭŭs, -ī ⁷tyraunŭs, -ī ⁸Syrăcūsae, -ārŭm ⁹perpĕtŭŭs, -ă, -ŭm ¹⁰mĕtŭs, -ūs ¹¹sĭnĕ, w. Abl. ¹²vĭă, -ae

Verbs ending in lō, mō, nō, rō. — Gr. 55—57.

21. Caesar pecunĭam publĭcam¹ ex aerarĭo² promserat. Caesar a militĭbus quoque pecunĭam mutŭam³ sumpserat³. Aristīdes Atheniensis inter omnes integritāte⁴ excellēbat. Jure⁵ ii contemnuntur, qui nec sibi nec aliis prosunt. Qui bonam famam⁶ contemnit, contemnit virtūtem. Morbis quoque natūra quasdam leges posŭit.

¹*public* ²*treasury* ³mutŭum sumĕre, *to borrow* ⁴*integrity* ⁵*justly* ⁶*reputation;* bona fama, *a good name*

22. Not all the fields, which are tilled, are fruitful. The Egyptians worshipped the dog and the cat¹ as² gods. The larger beasts are caught, the smaller (ones) despised by³ lions. A fire is nourished by its own ashes⁴. In spring the nightingale sings during⁵ the whole night⁶. We worship one God.

¹ellīs, - ²ūt ³ā, w. Abl. ⁴Abl. without prepos. ⁵pĕr, w. Acc. ⁶nox, noctīs

Gr. *58. 59.*

23. Numa, secundus Romanōrum rex, nullum bellum gessit¹. Argus² centum ocŭlos gerēbat (*had*). Res familiāris³ quaeri debet labōre et parsimonĭa. Filĭi non semper patrum vestigĭa⁴ premunt⁵. Vetĕres Germāni⁶ vinum ad se importāri⁷ non sivērunt. Britanni olim frumenta non serēbant, sed lacte et carne⁸ vivēbant.

¹*to carry on* ²*Argus* ³*property* ⁴*footstep* ⁵vestigĭa premĕre, *to walk in the footsteps* ⁶*German* ⁷*to import* ⁸Abl. to be translated by *on*

24. My grandfather had planted many trees with his own hand. (*Abl.*) When¹ father sends² money, we shall buy these very useful books. Socrates always sought after³ truth. God has not a body; for this reason⁴, though⁵ he is everywhere, he can nowhere⁶ be seen. Very many wars have been carried on by the Romans.

¹cŭm ²Translate: *shall have sent* ³quaerō, -ĕrĕ, *to seek after* ⁴idcircō ⁵etsī ⁶nusquăm

Verbs ending in sō, xō, scō. — Gr. *60—62.*

25. Homĭnes dum¹ docent, discunt. Quid heri egistis? Scripsĭmus et didicĭmus fabŭlam², quam magister dictavĕrat³. Semper cogĭta, primam esse virtūtem compescĕre lingŭam⁴. Aranĕae⁵ retĭa texunt tenuissĭma. Omnes, qui in Graecĭam iter fecērunt, Athēnas visērunt. Non scholae, sed vitae discĭmus.

¹*whilst* ²*fable* ³*to dictate* ⁴*tongue* ⁵*spider*

26. Without¹ air neither plants can grow nor animals live. Even² without a master vices are learned. Below³ the earth the bones of the dead repose. You will learn the Latin⁴ language in a short time⁵, boys, if you are⁶ diligent and attentive. In the most ancient⁷ times Egypt was visited by⁸ no stranger⁹.

¹sĭnĕ, w. Abl. ²ĕtĭăm ³sŭb, w. Abl. ⁴Lătīnŭs, -ă, -ŭm ⁵brĕvī tempŏrĕ ⁶Translate: *if you will be* ⁷antīquŭs, -ă, -ŭm ⁸ā, w.Abl. ⁹pĕrĕgrīnŭs, -ī

Fourth Conjugation.
Gr. 63. 64.

27. Lex erat apud Romānos: Nemo in urbe sepelītor. Innumĕrae¹ artes ab hominĭbus inventae sunt. Apes et formīcae victum² comportant³ memōres hiĕmis ventūrae. Olim capti⁴ reges et duces catēnis⁵ vincti sunt. Alexandri Magni jussu⁶ sepulcrum⁷ Cyri⁸ apertum est. Optĭma praecepta vitae ex⁹ sacris libris hauriuntur.

¹*innumerable* ²*food* ³*to collect* ⁴*captive* ⁵*chain* ⁶*by order* ⁷*grave* ⁸*Cyrus* ⁹*from*

28. Alexander the Great opened the grave of Cyrus. Of all the Romans Trajan¹ alone was buried within² the city. Spring opens the rivers and lakes to navigation³. The time of death will come, and quickly⁴ indeed⁵. Letters were invented by the Phenicians. The enemies were conquered and bound with chains.

¹Trājānŭs, -ī ²intrā, w. Acc. ³nāvīgātĭō, -ōnĭs ⁴cĕlĕrĭtĕr ⁵quĭdĕm

Deponent Verbs.
Gr. 65—68.

29. Hannĭbal optĭmum ratus est, bellum cum Romānis in ipsa Italĭa gerĕre. Impăres¹ nati sumus, pares² moriēmur, aequat³ omnes sepulcrum. Qui duos lepōres sequĭtur, neutrum capit. Quam multi indigni⁴ sunt luce⁵, et tamen⁶ dies orītur. Apud vetĕres Germānos pedĭtes proeliabantur inter equĭtes.

¹*unequal* ²*equal* ³*to level* ⁴*unworthy* ⁵The Abl. to be translated by *of* ⁶*nevertheless*

30. A good conscience will everywhere accompany an upright man and comfort him in adversity. A good man suffers

all misfortunes[1] for[2] his country. When[3] we die, only the body dies, not the soul. Spring follows winter. The greatest evils have arisen from[4] avarice. Most birds awake when[5] the sun rises.

[1]călămĭtās, -ātis [2]pro, w. Abl. [3]si [4]ex, w. Abl. [5]cŭm

Semi-Deponents and Derivative Verbs.
Gr. 69—77.

31. Frumenta autumno seruntur et aestāte sequentis anni maturescunt. Avus meus in publĭcis munerĭbus[1] senŭit. Magna[2] puerōrum multitūdo[3] per[3] prāta cursābat. Caesar virtūti milĭtum in omnĭbus rebus fīsus est. Hic puer mendacii causa[4] vapulāvit. In schola legĭmus historĭam viri, qui in monte obdormīvit et post viginti annos revixit.

[1]office [2]a very great number [3]through [4]in consequence of; causā is put after the word it governs, here mendacii, lying

32. A mouse does not trust to one hole[1]. This servant[2] has been flogged most undeservedly[3]. Some animals are accustomed to dwell both[4] in[5] the water and[4] on[5] the land. Nothing dries quicker[6] than a tear[7]. In consequence[8] of the cold[9], grain[10] ripens later[11] in Germany[12] than in Italy.

[1]antrŭm, -ī [2]servŭs, -ī [3]immerĭtissĭmō [4]et..et [5]in, w. Abl. [6]citĭus [7]lacrĭmā, -ae [8]propter, w. Acc. [9]frĭgŏrā, -ŭm [10]frūmentā, -ōrum [11]sērĭus [12]Germānĭā, -ae

Irregular Verbs.
ĕdĕrĕ, vellĕ, nollĕ, mallĕ, īrĕ. — Gr. 78—82.

33. In Aegypto brassĭca[1] propter[2] amaritudĭnem[3] non estur. Malŭmus paupĕres esse et probi, quam divītes et imprŏbi. Vulpes vult fraudem, lupus agnum[4], femĭna laudem[5]. Puĕris in scholam euntĭbus dare solēbant Romāni custōdes[6]. Nudus[7] in hanc terram veni, nudusque redībo. Noli oblivisci, quantum[8] parentĭbus debĕas. Noli me tangĕre.

[1]cabbage [2]on account of [3]bitterness [4]lamb [5]praise [6]custodian [7]naked [8]how much

34. Merchants[1] prefer to dwell near[2] the market[3]. A full belly[4] will not (nōlō) study[5] willingly[6]. If we wish to be happy, we must be contented with our lot¹. After death the body perishes, the soul will never perish. The seasons go and return, but never⁵ to me returns day. Death will pass by⁶ nobody.

¹mercātŏr, -ōrĭs ²ăpŭd, w. Acc. ³fŏrŭm, -ī ⁴ventĕr, -rĭs ⁵stŭdĕō, -ērĕ ⁶lĭbentĕr ⁷with our lot, Abl. ⁸numquăm ⁹praetĕrĕō, -īrĕ

quĕō, nĕquĕō, fĕrō, fīō. — Gr. 83—87.

35. Animalĭa magnam utilitātem¹ affĕrunt¹ hominĭbus. Aristippus² servo, qui pecunĭam ferēbat onerĕque premebātur, dixit: Abjĭce³, quod nimĭum⁴ est, et fer, quod ferre potes. Onus, quod bene fertur, leve fit. Principĭo⁵ rerum Deus dixit: 'Fiat lux', et lux facta est. Si dilĭgens esses, labōres tibi facīles fĭĕrent.

¹to do service ²Aristippus ³to throw away ⁴too much ⁵beginning, Abl. to denote time when

36. Not every field which is sown yields¹ fruits. Aristides bore poverty most patiently². Virtue and learning³ are riches which no thief can carry away. Fish cannot live without water. Every burden becomes lighter by patience⁴. In winter time (time of winter) the days become shorter, and the nights longer. Without light there cannot be (any) colors.

¹ferrĕ ²pătĭentissĭmē ³doctrīnā, -ae ⁴pătĭentĭā, -ae

Defective and Impersonal Verbs.
Gr. 88—93.

37. Uva, inquit vulpes, nondum¹ matūra² est, nolo acerbam³ sumĕre. Quis foret egēnus⁴, si divītes semper paupĕrum meminissent? Salvēte amīci, jamdūdum⁵ vos exspectāvi⁶. Tempus, inquis, praetĕrit; erras⁷, inquam, tempus manet; nos praeterīmus. Pluit et ningit, non poterīmus ambulāre. Non licēbat vinum femīnis Romānis bibĕre.

¹not yet ²ripe ³sour ⁴needy ⁵a long time ⁶to wait for ⁷to be mistaken

38. It thunders and lightens, we shall stay at home. To no one it is allowed to break¹ the laws of his country. Elephants hate the mouse most² among all animals. God is the author² of all things; therefore⁴, you will say, he is also the author of evils. You are mistaken, I say, for men have turned⁵ blessings⁶ into⁷ evils. It seldom⁸ thunders in winter, and it snows seldom in summer.

¹vŏlŏ, -ārĕ ²maxĭmē ³auctŏr, -ōrĭs ⁴ergō ⁵vertŏ, -ĕrĕ ⁶bŏnā. -ōrŭm ⁷in, w. Acc. ⁸rārō

CONSTRUCTIONS OF SYNTAX.
Agreement of the Predicate.   Questions.
Gr. 94—102.

39. Somnus est imāgo mortis. Maxĭmum anĭmal terrestre est elephantus. Leges sunt optĭmae patrōnac¹ civĭum. Roma omnĭum Italĭae populōrum victrix fuit. Tu et frater tuus epistŭlas ad me scripsistis. Pater et ego fratresque pro² patrĭa arma tulĭmus. Pater et mater mihi carissĭmi sunt. Vita rustĭca³ parsimonĭae, diligentĭae, justitĭae magistra est.

¹protector ²for ³country life

40. The lion is the king of quadrupeds and the eagle is the king¹ of birds. Pain, fear, labor, old age are troublesome to most men. The beginning and the end² are often very different. The walls and gates³ of the city were destroyed by⁴ the soldiers. Father and son died on the same day⁵.

¹Translate: queen ²fĭnĭs, - ³portă, -ae ⁴ā, w. Abl. ⁵Abl. without prepos.

Gr. 103—111.
41. Sol nobis minor appāret¹ quam est. Hispanĭa postrēma omnĭum provinciārum domĭta est. Socrātes,cujus sapientĭam admirāmur, ab Atheniensĭbus injuste² capĭtis³ damnātus⁴ est. Utrum major est sol quam terra, an minor? Audisne cantum avĭum? Ubi sunt, qui ante nos in mundo fuērunt? Romŭlus, qui Romam condĭdit, a pastōre regis educātus erat⁵.

¹to seem ²unjustly ³to death ⁴to condemn ⁵to bring up

42. There is a God who rules this whole world. No animal which has blood can be without a heart. The worst friends are those who always praise us. What is the sun? The fixed¹ star which is nearest to our earth. Is the sun or the moon the greater? Is not iron more useful than gold? Do we not owe the greatest thanks² to our parents?

¹fixŭs,-ă,-ŭm ²gratĭae,-ārŭm

Cases with Prepositions.
Gr. 112.

43. Caelum, non anĭmum mutant, qui trans mare migrant[1]. Pauci homĭnes supra nonaginta annos vivunt. Ante meridĭem[2] curāmus[3] negotĭa nostra, post meridĭem ambulāmus per prata et silvas. Homĭnes divĭtes prope urbem magnifĭcas villas habent. Plurĭma Romanōrum sepulcra propter viam Appĭam[4] erant. Penes Deum imperĭum totīus mundi est. Non utĭlis est somnus post cenam.

[1]*to migrate, remove* [2]*noon* [3]*to attend to* [4]*the Appian way*

44. Physicians have remedies against diseases; against death they have no remedy. Fish swim through the water. The women commonly attend to the homes[1] and domestic affairs[2], the men to the occupations without the house. A good judge will judge[3] according to the laws. There is a great variety of languages among men. The teacher praises these scholars on account of (their) diligence, he blames[4] those on account of (their) laziness.

[1]dŏmŭs, -ūs [2]res dŏmestĭca [3]jūdĭco, -āre [4]vĭtŭpĕro, -āre

Gr. 113. 114.

45. Magna cum voluptāte cantum avĭum audīmus. Facilĭor est a virtūte transĭtus[1] ad vitĭa, quam a vitĭis ad virtūtem. Caecus de colorĭbus judicāre non potest. A bove majōre discit arāre[2] minor. Sine virtūte nemo beātus est. Mors pro patrĭa decōra[3] est. Jucundum mihi est cum amīcis per campos[4] et silvas ambulāre. Non omnes fluvĭi, qui in hac terra sunt, in mare fluunt.

[1]*passage* [2]*to plow* [3]*glorious* [4]*field*

46. The Atlantic[1] ocean separates[2] America from Europe. The deeds of men do not always agree with (their) words. (Out) of all animals which live with us, dogs are the most faithful[3]. Nothing without great labor! A dog is small in comparison with an elephant, and large in comparison with a mouse. It is sweet and glorious to die for one's country. An upright life is the road into heaven.

[1]Atlantĭcŭs, -a, -um [2]divĭdo, -ĕre [3]fĭdēlĭs, -e

Cases with Adjectives.

Gr. *116—118.*

47. Vetĕres Romāni glorīae cupidissĭmi fuērunt. Ex¹ Themistŏclis tempŏre Athenienses peritissĭmi belli navālis² fuērunt. Gallĭa plena erat civĭum Romanōrum. Genĕri³ humāno cultūra⁴ agrōrum salutāris⁵ est. Amo veritātem, etiamsi⁶ mihi jucunda non est. Virtus vel⁷ in hoste laude digna est. Quam multi luce indigni sunt, et tamen sol orĭtur.

¹*from* ²*naval warfare* ³*race* ⁴*cultivation* ⁵*beneficial* ⁶*even if* ⁷*even*

48. Human life is full of dangers. Men are often more desirous of riches than of wisdom. Caesar was most skilful in military affairs¹. Nothing is so² like death as³ sleep. Old age is troublesome to most men. To the unhappy man² time is very long, to the happy man very short. Flies are not less worthy of admiration⁴ than elephants.

¹rēs mīlĭtārĭs ²tăm..quăm ³infēlīx, -Icĭs ⁴admīrātĭō, -ōnĭs

Cases with Verbs.

Genitive. — Gr. *119—128.*

49. Homĭnes facilĭus beneficĭa quam injurĭas oblivisci solent. Tiberĭus¹ judĭces legum et religiōnis² admonēbat. Lycurgus maxĭmos honōres non divĭtum sed senum esse volŭit. Nostrum est parentes amāre. Roscĭus³ parricidĭi⁴ accusātus quidem, sed hujus facinŏris⁵ omnĭum judĭcum sententĭis⁶ absolūtus est. Homĭnem inconstantem⁷ saepissĭme paenĭtet primi consilĭi⁸.

¹*Tiberius* ²*oath* ³*Roscius* ⁴*parricide* ⁵*crime* ⁶*omnĭum judĭcum sententĭis, by the unanimous decision of the judges* ⁷*inconstant* ⁸*design*

50. He is a fool¹ who is ashamed of his parents, but² virtuous³ parents are justly ashamed of their wicked sons. Miltiades⁴ was accused of treason⁵. Homer⁶ was highly valued by (ăb) Alexander the Great. The whole kingdom⁷ of the Persians came⁸ under Alexander's dominion. My conscience is of more account to me than the talk⁹ of all men.

¹stultŭs, -ī ²ăt ³prŏbŭs, -ă, -ŭm ⁴Miltĭădēs, -ĭs ⁵prōdĭtĭō, -ōnĭs ⁶Hŏmērŭs, -ī ⁷regnŭm, -ī ⁸Translate: *became Alexander's* ⁹sermō, -ōnĭs

Dative. — Gr. 129—132.

51. Facĭle omnes, cum valēmus[1], bona consilĭa[2] aegrōtis damus. Filĭa Caesăris Pompējo[3] nupsit. Reae Silvĭae[4], Numitōris[5] filĭae, duo erant filĭi, quorum altĕri erat nomen Romŭlus, altĕri Remus[6]. Perĭcles[7] agros suos rei publĭcae dono dedit. Omnes homĭnes libertāti student et condiciōnem[8] servōrum[9] odērunt. Spes vitae futūrae misĕris magno solatĭo[10] est.

[1]*to be well* [2]*advice* [3]*Pompey* [4]*Rea Silvia* [5]*Numitor* [6]*Remus* [7]*Pericles* [8]*condition* [9]*slave* [10]*consolation*

52. The soldiers spared neither women nor children. Old age is a disease which no physician can cure. The upright man envies nobody. Flowers have not always the same colors. Attălus[1], a king of Asia, gave his kingdom to the Romans as a present. My name is Henry[2]. I have many books. Virtues bring[3] honor and glory to men.

[1]Attălŭs, -I [2]Henrīcŭs, -I [3]Translate: *are for*

Accusative. — Gr. 133—139.

53. Romăni Cicerōnem patrem patrĭae appellavērunt. Providentĭa[1] divīna res futūras nos sapienter celāvit. Aquam a pumĭce[2] postŭlas. Persae tria[3] praecipŭe[4] libĕros suos docēbant, equitāre[5], jaculāri[6], vera[7] dicĕre. Paupertas homĭnem ad multas virtūtes aptiōrem facit. Romŭlus urbem, quam condidĕrat, ex[8] nomĭne suo Romam vocāvit. Ingenŭum verĭtas decet.

[1]*providence* [2]*pumice-stone* [3]*three things* [4]*principally* [5]*to ride* [6]*to throw the javelin* [7]*truth* [8]*from* [9]*gentleman*

54. Alexander founded in Egypt a city which from his own name he called Alexandria[1]. Anthony called his flight victory, because he had come off[2] alive[3]. Good boys conceal nothing from their parents. Modesty becomes as well[4] boys as[4] girls. Verres[5] demanded[6] from parents a price[7] for[8] the burial[9] of (their) children.

[1]Alěxandrĭă, -ae [2]exĕō, -īrĕ [3]vīvŭs, -ă, -ŭm [4]tăm..quăm [5]Verrēs, -Is [6]poscō, -ĕrĕ [7]pretĭŭm, -I [8]prō, w. Abl. [9]sĕpultūră, -ae

Ablative. — Gr. 140—145.

55. Nulla res carĭus constat, quam quae precĭbus[1] emĭtur. In magnis et frequentĭbus[2] urbĭbus domus plurĭmo locantur.

Arīon⁰ nomĭnis sui fama⁴ omnes terras implevĕrat. Hiems arbŏres follis spoliāvit⁵. Corpŏri animōque nonnumquam⁶ recreatiōne⁷ opus est. Qui bona fruĭtur valetudĭne, non indĭget medicīna. Boni assiduīque⁸ domĭni villa semper abundat lacte, casĕo⁹, melle.

¹*prayers* ²*crowded* ³*Arion* ⁴*glory* ⁵*to strip* ⁶*sometimes* ⁷*recreation* ⁸*industrious* ⁹*cheese*

56. Death releases¹ men from all cares. America abounds in gold. The sun fills the whole world with its light. There is need not of many books, but of good (ones). The old painters² used but³ few colors. Most people will enjoy greater happiness in heaven than they have enjoyed upon⁴ this earth. We cannot buy virtue and wisdom with gold.

¹lībĕrō, -āre ²pictŏr, -ōrIs ³tantŭm (to be placed after the word to which it belongs; here, *few*) ⁴In, w. Abl.

Relations of Time and Place.

Time. Gr. 146—152.

57. Romŭlus duodevicesĭmum annum aetātis agens urbem exigŭam in monte Palatīno¹ condĭdit. Quot annos abhinc ars typographĭca² inventa est? Nonnullae³ aves per totum annum cantant, aliae nonnīsi⁴ quibusdam⁵ anni temporĭbus. Persae apud⁶ Salamīna⁷, et Carthaginienses ad Himĕram, eōdem die victi sunt. Arganthonĭus ad imperĭum quadraginta annos natus accessit⁸, octoginta annos regnāvit⁹, et centum et viginti vixit.

¹*Palatine* ²*the art of printing* ³*some* ⁴*only* ⁵*certain* ⁶*near* ⁷*Salamis* ⁸ad imperĭum accedĕre, *to come to the throne* ⁹*to reign*

58. My friend's father died about¹ twenty years ago. In autumn storks² migrate³ to⁴ other lands and return in spring. The city (of) Veii⁵ was besieged⁶ during ten summers and winters. Corinth⁷ was destroyed by Mummius⁸, and Carthage by Scipio on the same day. Rome was founded in the 754th year before Christ⁹. The planet Saturn¹⁰ completes¹¹ its course in nearly¹ 30 years.

¹fĕrē ²cĭcōnĭă, -ae ³mĭgrō, -āre ⁴In, w. Acc. ⁵Veji, -ōrŭm ⁶obsĭdĕō, -ēre ⁷Cŏrinthŭs, -ī ⁸Mummĭŭs, -ī ⁹ante Chrĭstŭm nātŭm ¹⁰stellă Sāturnī ¹¹conficĭō, -ĕre

Space and Place. Gr. *153—157*.

59. Archĭas¹ poëta Antiochīa² Romam venit. Hodĭe non cenābo domi. Quis te invitāvit³ ad cenam? Avuncŭlus⁴ meus. Ubi ille nunc habĭtat? In domo conductitĭa⁵ in Platēa Lata⁶. Xerxes⁷ eādem via, qua sex mensĭbus iter in Graecĭam fecĕrat, triginta diēbus in Asĭam redīit. Justum⁸ Nili incrementum⁹ est cubitōrum¹⁰ sexdĕcim. Hodĭe domi manēbo.

¹*Archias* ²*Antioch* ³*to invite* ⁴*uncle* ⁵*rented* ⁶*Broadway* ⁷*Xerxes* ⁸*regular* ⁹*increase* ¹⁰*cubit*

60. The trunk¹ of the elephant is seven or eight feet long. The sun does not always rise or set² in the same place. My uncle has determined³ to pass⁴ (his) life in the country. The largest libraries⁵ were in former times at Alexandria and Pergamum⁶. The weary⁷ sleep well even on the ground. The most famous oracle⁸ of all Greece was at Delphi⁹. Marius¹⁰ died at his home an old man.

¹prŏboscĭs, -ĭdĭs ²occĭdō, -ĕrĕ ³constĭtŭō, -ĕrĕ ⁴ăgō, -ĕrĕ ⁵bibliŏthēcă, -ae ⁶Pergămŭm, -ī ⁷fessŭs, -ă, -ŭm ⁸ōrācŭlŭm, -ī ⁹Delphī, -ōrŭm ¹⁰Marĭŭs, -ī

Ablative in Special Constructions.
Gr. *158—164*.

61. Duārum civitātum civis esse nostro jure civīli¹ nemo potest. Voluptāte capiuntur homĭnes, ut² hamo³ pisces. Quo debilĭor⁴ est hostis, eo major est ignominĭa⁵, si ab eo vincĭmur. Multos comētas⁶ non vidēmus, quod⁷ obscurantur⁸ radĭis solis. Croesus⁹ specĭe¹⁰ quidem beātus fuit, re vera¹¹ autem¹² admŏdum¹³ miser. Nullus patrĭa locus tibi carĭor esse debet.

¹*civil* ²*as* ³*hook* ⁴*weak* ⁵*disgrace* ⁶*comet* ⁷*because* ⁸*to obscure* ⁹*Croesus* ¹⁰*appearance* ¹¹res vera, *reality* ¹²*yet* ¹³*very*

62. Friendships are known by affection¹ and love². Alexandria was founded by Alexander the Macedonian. No one is dearer to me than my parents. The peacock is handsomer³ than other birds, not more useful. Birds are covered with feathers, quadrupeds with hairs⁴, fish with scales. The wise man bears an injury with an even² mind⁶. My country is much dearer to me than life.

¹cārĭtās, -ātis ²āmŏr, -ōris ³pulchĕr, -rā, -rŭm ⁴plūs, -ī ⁵aequŭs, -ă, -ŭm ⁶Abl. without prepos.

Use of Tenses.
Gr. *165—170.*

63. Agesilāus, rex Lacedaemoniōrum, cum libĕris, quos magnopĕre¹ diligēbat, interdum ludēbat. Dum ea² Romāni parant³, jam Saguntum⁴ summa vi oppugnabātur⁵. Hannĭbal postquam domo profŭgit⁶, Magōnem⁷ fratrĕm ad se evocāvit⁸. Donec eris felix, multos numerābis amīcos; tempŏra si fuĕrint nubīla, solus eris. Caesar Pontĭco⁹ triumpho trium verbōrum praetŭlit¹⁰ titŭlum¹¹: veni, vidi, vici.

¹*greatly* ²*these things* ³*to prepare* ⁴*Saguntum* ⁵*to besiege* ⁶*to flee* ⁷*Mago* ⁸*to summon* ⁹*Pontic;* Abl. to denote time *when* ¹⁰*to carry before* ¹¹*inscription*

64. The cowardly¹ soldier fled, as soon as he saw the enemy. After Hannibal had taken Saguntum, he raised² three armies; of³ these he sent one into Africa; the second he left with his brother Hasdrubal⁴ in Spain; the third he brought⁵ with himself into Italy. While Pompey was deliberating⁶, Caesar with the utmost⁷ speed⁸ approached⁹ Rome.

¹ignāvŭs, -ă, -ŭm ²compărō, -ārĕ ³ex ⁴Hasdrŭbăl, -ĭs ⁵dūcō, -ĕrĕ ⁶consultō, -ārĕ ⁷maxĭmŭs, -ă, -ŭm ⁸cĕlĕrĭtās, -ātis ⁹apprŏpinquō, -ārĕ.

Sequence of Tenses.
Gr. *171—174.*

65. Non intellĕgunt homĭnes, quantum vectīgal¹ parsimonĭa sit. An² dives sit omnes quaerunt³, nemo an bonus. Tune⁴ tam pauca in schola didicisti, ut hoc nescĭas? Tanta est stellārum multitūdo, ut numerāri non possint. Vita brevis est, etiamsi⁵ supra⁶ centum annos duret⁷. Dic mihi quis mane⁸ quattŭor, meridĭe duos, vespĕre⁹ tres pedes habĕat.

¹*income* ²*if* ³*to ask* ⁴-ne, interrog. particle, not to be translated ⁵*even if* ⁶*over* ⁷*to last* ⁸*in the morning* ⁹*at night*

The words which are to be expressed by the Subjunctive are underlined.

66. Your father does not know where you <u>have been</u>. In former times it was a question¹ whether² the earth <u>was</u> round³.

We have two ears and one mouth that we may hear much⁴ and speak little⁵. Our ancestors often fought⁶ that they might free⁷ their country. There is no state that has not wicked⁸ citizens.

¹quaestĭŏ, -ōnĭs ²nūm ³rŏtundŭs, -ă, -ŭm ⁴multă, -ōrŭm ⁵paucă, -ōrŭm ⁶dīmĭcŏ, -ārĕ ⁷lībĕrŏ, -ārĕ ⁸prăvŭs, -ă, -ŭm

Imperative and Infinitive.
Gr. 175—179.

67. Imitāre formīcam, quae etĭam noctu operātur. Noli oblivisci, mi fili, quantum parentĭbus debĕas. Proxĭmus¹ este bonis¹, si non potes optĭmus esse. Et² monĕre et² monēri proprĭum³ est verae amicitĭae. Adsuesce⁴ et dicĕre verum⁵ et audīre. Plurĭmi cupidĭtātes suas regĕre nesciunt, et tamen⁶ alĭos regĕre volunt. Nocĕre facĭle est, prodesse diffĭcĭle.

¹next best ²both....and ³mark ⁴to accustom one's self ⁵truth ⁶nevertheless

68. Pray¹ and work²! Philip, king of the Macedonians, used to say: Fight with silver weapons³ and you will conquer every thing. To receive a benefit is to sell (one's) liberty. It is beautiful to speak the truth; it is more beautiful to hear (it) willingly. To lose a friend is the greatest of losses⁴. To dwell in the city is irksome⁵ to him who has been accustomed⁶ to live in the country.

¹ōrŏ, -ārĕ ²lăbōrŏ, -ārĕ ³tēlŭm, -ī ⁴damnŭm, -ī ⁵mōlestŭs, -ă, -ŭm ⁶consuescŏ, -ĕrĕ

Gerund and Gerundive.
Gr. 180—181.

69. Parsimonĭa est scientĭa vitandi¹ sumptus² supervacŭos. Summa voluptas ex discendo capĭtur. Boves onerĭbus gestandis³ non sunt idonĕi⁴. In magnēte⁵ mira vis inest attrahendi⁶ ferrum. Multi in equis parandis⁷ adhĭbent⁸ curam, in amīcis eligendis neglegentes⁹ sunt. De eligendo genĕre¹⁰ vitae deliberatĭo¹¹ est omnĭum diffĭcillĭma.

¹to avoid ²expense ³to carry ⁴proper ⁵magnet ⁶to attract ⁷to get ⁸to use ⁹careless ¹⁰a line ¹¹deliberation

70. The art of writing was invented by the Phenicians. No age is too late¹ for² learning. The short time of life is long enough³ to² live well and happily. The only⁴ art of improving⁵ the memory is practice⁶. Night time⁷ is more suited to sleeping than to studying. In reading we must imitate the bees. Brave soldiers are ready⁸ to² meet⁹ all dangers.

¹too late, sērŭs, -ă, -ŭm ²ăd ³sătīs ⁴ūnŭs, -ă, -ŭm ⁵augĕō, -ērĕ ⁶exercĭtātĭō, -ōnĭs ⁷tempŭs nocturnŭm ⁸părātŭs, -ă, -ŭm ⁹sŭbĕō, -īrĕ

Accusative with the Infinitive.
Gr. 182—186.

71. Historĭa narrat Romam a Romŭlo condĭtam esse. Sentīmus calēre¹ ignem, nivem esse albam, dulce mel. Verum est nemĭnem in hac terra semper felīcem esse. Facĭle intellĕgi potest anĭmum et audīre et vidēre, non eas partes, quae quasi fenestrae² sunt anĭmi. Vere dici potest magistrātum esse legem loquentem, legem autem mutum³ magistrātum. Scio me mortālem esse.

¹to be hot ²window ³mute, dumb

72. It is agreed among all writers¹ that Romulus was the first king of the Romans. We know that the sun is larger than the moon. Anaxagoras² denied that snow is white. All believe that the knowledge of future things is not very³ useful to us. It is known that the Romans were often conquered by Hannibal. We see that the moon is sometimes eclipsed⁴ by the shadow of the earth.

¹scriptŏr, -ōrĭs ²Anaxăgŏrās, -ae ³părŭm, not very ⁴obscūrō, -ārĕ

Participles.
Gr. 187—189.

73. Alexander morĭens anŭlum¹ dedit Perdiccae². Solent puĕri interdum ludentes imitāri ea quae³ maxĭme scrĭa⁴ sunt. Dives paupĕrem saepe juvāre potest se ipsum non spolĭans⁵. Stellae nobis parvae videntur, immenso⁶ intervallo⁷ a nobis sejunctae⁸. Aranti⁹ Cincinnāto¹⁰ nuntiātum¹¹ est cum dictatōrem¹² esse factum. Hephaestĭon¹³ omnĭum amicōrum carissĭmus erat Alexandro cum ipso parĭter¹⁴ educātus.

¹a ring ²Perdiccas ³those things which ⁴serious ⁵to rob ⁶immense ⁷space ⁸to separate ⁹to plow ¹⁰Cincinnatus ¹¹to bring word ¹²dictator ¹³Hephaestion ¹⁴together

The words which illustrate the lesson are underlined.

74. The master punishes the scholars who learn carelessly[1]. Plato[2] died, while writing, in the 81st year of (his) life. In daytime[3] we do not see the stars, because they are obscured by the light of the sun. Numa was made king in the forty first year after the founding of the city. Lions when satiated[4] and not provoked[5] are perfectly[6] harmless[7].

[1]neglĕgentĕr [2]Plătō, -ōnĭs [3]interdĭū [4]sătĭō, -ārĕ [5]lăcessō, -ĕrĕ [6]plānē [7]innoxĭŭs, -ă, -ŭm

Periphrastic Conjugation.
Gr. 190—192.

75. Alexander Magnus imperĭo totĭus orbis terrārum potitūrus erat. Moriendum certe est, at quo die moriendum sit incertum est. Discipŭlis Pythagŏrae[1] per quinque annos tacendum erat. Diligentes discipŭli magistro laudandi sunt. Non scholae sed vitae discendum est. Ocŭlis magis habenda[2] est fides quam aurĭbus. Etĭam post malam segĕtem serendum est.

[1]*Pythagoras* [2]fidem habēre, *to trust*

76. A thief ought to be punished. Must we not[1] all die? My father is on the point of setting out for[2] California[3]. Bees when[4] they are about to fly out[5] hum[6] very loudly[7]. A good book ought to be read a second time[8]. Virtue must be cultivated that we may be able to live well and happily. Every scholar must learn that he may sometime be useful[9] to society[10].

[1]nonnĕ [2]in w. Acc. [3]Călĭfornĭă, -ae [4]cŭm [5]ēvŏlō, -ārĕ [6]consŏnō, -ārĕ [7]vĕhĕmentĕr, *very loudly* [8]ĭtĕrŭm, *a second time* [9]prōsum, prōdessĕ [10]sŏcĭĕtās, -ātĭs

Ablative Absolute.
Gr. 193. 194.

77. Vespasiāno[1] regnante Hierosolўma[2] vastāta[3] sunt. Pythagŏras Tarquinĭo Superbo regnante in Italĭam venit. Lacrĭmae[4] cadunt nolentĭbus nobis. Cessante[5] causa cessat effectus[6]. Appropinquante hiĕme hirundĭnes in terras calidiōres[7] migrant.

Latrante⁸ uno statim⁹ et¹⁰ alter latrat canis. Etiam sanāto vulnĕre cicātrix¹¹ manet. Vetĕres Germāni pellĭbus utebantur¹² magna corpŏris parte nuda.

¹Vespasian ²Jerusalem ³to demolish ⁴tear ⁵to cease ⁶effect ⁷warm ⁸to bark ⁹at once ¹⁰also ¹¹scar ¹²pellĭbus uti, to wear skins

78. When the cause of disease has been found out, the physicians think that the cure¹ has² been found. After Troy was taken by the Greeks, Aeneas³ came (in) to Italy. When the sea is calm³, it is easy to steer⁴ a ship. A wise man having lost⁵ all his goods remains rich, and that saying⁶ of Bias is known: "I carry my all with me". When spring returns, the swallows return.

¹cūrātĭō, -ōnĭs ²Aenēās, -ae ³tranquillŭs, -ă, -ŭm ⁴gŭbernō, -āre ⁵āmittō, -ĕre ⁶dictŭm, -ī

The Supine.

Gr. 195—198.

79. Muliĕres spectātum¹ veniunt, veniunt spectentur ut ipsae. Hannĭbal — incredibĭle² dictu — bidŭo³ et duābus noctĭbus Hadrumētum⁴ pervēnit⁵, quod distat⁶ a Zama⁷ circĭter milĭa passŭum⁸ trecenta. Virtus diffĭcĭlis inventu est; rectōrem⁹ ducemque desidĕrat¹⁰; vitĭa etiam sine magistro discuntur. Scio multos ad me non gratulātum¹¹, sed edendi et bibendi causā¹² venisse.

¹to look (at) ²incredible ³two days ⁴Hadrumetum ⁵to reach ⁶to be (distant) from ⁷Zama ⁸pace; mille passŭum, a mile ⁹master ¹⁰to require ¹¹to congratulate ¹²for the sake of

80. Hannibal was recalled¹ to defend his native country. This book is very difficult to understand. Pears² are sweet to (the) taste. Merchants³ go to market⁴ either⁵ to buy or⁶ to sell various wares⁶. What is more beautiful to see than a tree in blossom⁷? The ambassadors of the Gauls⁸ came to Rome to ask aid. The shorter a narrative⁹ is, the clearer¹⁰ it is and the easier to understand.

¹rĕvŏcō, -āre ²pĭrŭm, -ī ³mercātŏr, -ōrĭs ⁴mercātŭs, -ūs ⁵aut.. ⁶merx, -cĭs ⁷flōrens, -tĭs ⁸Gallŭs, -ī ⁹narrātĭō, -ōnĭs ¹⁰dīlūcĭdŭs, -ă, -ŭm

Subjunctive after Conjunctions.

Gr. *199—204.*

81. Persārum reges voluptātis causa ita dividēbant annum, ut hiĕmem Babylōnĕ¹, in Medĭa² aestātem agĕrent³. Avārus timet, ne bona sibi eripiantur⁴. Stultum est in luctu⁵ sibi capillum⁶ evellĕre⁷, quasi calvitĭo⁸ maeror⁹ levētur¹⁰. Socrătes ita in judicĭo capitĭs¹¹ pro se dixit, ut non reus¹², sed domĭnus esse viderētur judĭcum. Demosthĕni non offēcit¹³ vitĭum¹⁴ linguăae¹⁵, quomĭnus summus evadĕret¹⁶ orātor.

¹*Babylon* ²*Media* ³*to spend* ⁴*to take away* ⁵*grief* ⁶*hair* ⁷*to pluck out* ⁸*baldness* ⁹*grief* ¹⁰*to lessen* ¹¹*trial for life,* judicĭum capĭtis ¹²*defendant* ¹³*to hinder* ¹⁴*defect* ¹⁵*speech* ¹⁶*to become*

82. It happens, I do not know how, that we see the faults of others more sharply than our own. The physician feared that you would not recover¹ from² this disease. There is no doubt³ that God rules the world. The rain⁴ hinders⁵ (us) from walking. The fear at Rome was great that the Gauls would again come to Rome. Parents send their children (in) to school in order to learn something.

¹convălescō, -ĕrĕ ²ex ³dŭbĭum nōn est ⁴plŭvĭae, -ārŭm ⁵impĕdĭō, -īrĕ

Gr. *205—208.*

83. Medĭci quamquam intellĕgunt saepe, tamen numquam aegris¹ dicunt, illo morbo eos esse moritūros. Labōra, dum potes, ut, cum imbecillus² eris, quiescas. Apelles³, pictor clarissĭmus, Alexandrum Magnum pinxĕrat equitantem. Rex imagĭnem minus laudāvit quam merebātur. Cum autem equus Alexandri picto equo sic adhinnīret⁴ quasi verus esset equus, Apelles, o rex inquit, equus tuus artis pingendi peritĭor⁵ quam tu esse vidētur.

¹*a patient* ²*feeble* ³*Apelles* ⁴*to neigh to* ⁵*a better judge*

84. Physicians, if they could cure¹ all diseases, would be very happy. You will be sad if you are alone. Since the soul of man is immortal, it can in no manner² perish. Socrates although he was the most innocent of all men, nevertheless was accused and condemned. So live with men as if God saw you; so speak with God, as if men heard you. If the masters of the house are not at home, danger more easily threatens⁸ (to) the houses.

¹mĕdĕŏr, -ĕrī w. Dat. ²nullō mŏdō ³immĭnĕō, -ĕrĕ w. Dat.

Subjunctive after Relatives.
Gr. 209.

85. Administratĭo¹ mundi nihil in se habet, quod reprehendi² possit. Famae ac fĭdĕi³ damna majōra sunt quam quae aestimāri possint. Inventae sunt leges, quae cum omnĭbus una atque eādem voce⁴ loquerentur. Bonum librum itĕrum atque itĕrum legas; sed multi libri non satis digni sunt, qui itĕrum legantur. Verba inventa sunt, non quae celārent, sed quae indicārent⁵ veritātem.

¹government ²to find fault with ³credit ⁴language ⁵to reveal

86. There is no speed which can be compared with the speed of the mind. There is no grief¹ which the length² of time may not assuage³. The old man plants trees to benefit⁴ the next⁵ generation⁶. Nothing is so useful that it cannot become hurtful⁷ by abuse⁸. There have been many found who were ready to give up⁹ not only (their) money, but even life for their country.

¹dŏlŏr, -ōrĭs ²longinquĭtās, -ātĭs ³mollĭō, -īrĕ ⁴Translate: which may benefit (prōdessĕ w. Dat.) ⁵altĕr, -ă, -ŭm ⁶saecŭlŭm, -ī ⁷noxĭŭs, -ă, -ŭm ⁸ăbūsŭs, -ūs ⁹prŏfundō, -ĕrĕ

Subjunctive in Indirect Questions.
Gr. 210. 211.

87. Quis fuit eloquentĭor¹ quam Demosthenes? Utrum anĭmus immortālis est an simul cum corpŏre interībit? Quis hunc librum legit? Dic, quis hunc librum legĕrit. Judĭces reos interrogāre solent, quibus causis ad scelĕra² impulsi sint³. Non intellĕgunt homĭnes, quam magnum vectīgal parsimonĭa sit. Vix⁴ dici potest, quot quantisque pericŭlis vita humāna circumdăta sit.

¹eloquent ²crime ³to drive ⁴hardly

88. It is uncertain how long the life of each of us will be. Is there one world or several[1]? The question is[2] whether there is one world or several. Were you in school yesterday? Tell me were you in school yesterday. I was. Will the physician ask a patient whether he wants to be healed? Whether or not wisdom makes men happy is a question. Think how long winter is. The boy asks his father whether wolves are similar to dogs.

[1] plūrēs, -a [2] quaerĭtur

VOCABULARY
TO THE FOREGOING EXERCISES.
LATIN AND ENGLISH.

NOTE. Changeable parts of words are printed in **bold-faced** type, so as to indicate the manner of forming the Genitive and the Gender endings, and to show the principal parts of Verbs.

The - simply added to a noun indicates that the Genitive is like the Nominative.

(m.), (f.), (n.), (pl.) mean: masculine, feminine, neuter, plural, respectively.

A.

ā, ăb (with ablat.), *by, from*

ăbhinc, *ago*

abjĭcĭō, -ĕrĕ, abjēcī, abjectŭm, *to throw away*

ăbŏlĕō, -ērĕ, ăbŏlēvī, ăbŏlĭtŭm, *to abolish*

absolvō, -ĕrĕ, absolvī, absŏlūtŭm. *to acquit*

abstĭnentĭă, -ae (f.), *abstinence*

abstĭnĕō, -ērĕ, abstĭnŭī, abstentŭm, *to refrain*

ăbundō, -ārĕ, -āvī, -ātŭm, *to abound*

ăbūsŭs, -ūs (m.), *abuse*

ăbūtŏr, -ī, ăbū-ŭs sŭm, *to abuse*

accēdō, -ĕrĕ, accessī, accessŭm, *to approach;* ăd impĕrĭŭm accēdĕrĕ. *to come to the throne*

accendō, -ĕrĕ, accendī, accensŭm. *to kindle*

acceptŭs, -ă, -ŭm, *acceptable*

accĭpĭō, -ĕrĕ, accēpī, acceptŭm. *to receive*

accūsō, -ārĕ, -āvī. -ātŭm, *to accuse*

ăcerbŭs, -ă, -ŭm, *sour*

ăcĭēs, -ēī (f.), *a battle*

acquīrō, -ĕrĕ, acquīsīvī, acquīsītŭm, *to acquire*

ācrĭŭs, *more sharply*

ăcŭō, -ĕrĕ, ăcŭī, ăcūtŭm, *to sharpen, whet*

ăd (with accus.), *to*

ădhĭbĕō, -ērĕ, -ŭī, -ĭtŭm, *to use;* cūrăm ădhĭbērĕ, *to use care*

adhinnĭō, -īrĕ, -īvī, -ītŭm, *to neigh to*

ădĭpiscŏr, -ī, ădeptŭs sŭm, *to obtain, acquire*

adjŭvō, -ārĕ, adjūvī, adjūtŭm, *to help, assist*

administrātĭō, -ōnĭs (f.), *government*

admīrātĭō, -ōnĭs (f.), *admiration*

admīrŏr, -ārī, -ātŭs sŭm, *to admire*

admŏdŭm, *in a high degree, very*

admŏnĕō. -ērĕ, -ŭī, -ĭtŭm. *to remind*

Ădŏlescens, -tĭs (m.), see Ădŭlescens

adspĭcĭō, -ĕrĕ, adspexī, adspectŭm, *to see*

adsuescō, -ĕrĕ, adsuēvī, adsuētum, *to accustom one's self*

Ădŭlescens, -tĭs (m.), *a youth, a young man*

adversŭm, adversŭs (w. acc.), *against, toward*

adversŭs, -ă, -ŭm, *adverse;* rēs adversae. *adversity*

aedĭfĭcĭŭm, -ī (n.), *a building*

aedĭfĭcō, -ārĕ. -āvī, -ātŭm, *to build*

aegĕr, -ră, -rŭm, *sick, ill; a patient*

aegrōtŭs, -ă, -ŭm. *sick*

Aegyptĭŭs, -ī (m.), *an Egyptian*

Aegyptŭs, -ī (f.), *Egypt*

Aenēās, -ae (m.), *Aeneas, ancestor of the Romans*

— 72 —

acquō, -āre, -āvī, -ātum, to be equal, to level
aequus, -a, -um, even
āēr, āěrīs (m.), the air
aerārīum, -ī (n.), a treasury
aestās, -ātis (f.), the summer
aestimō, -āre, -āvī, -ātum (cx), to estimate, to value (by); magnī aestimāre, to value highly
aetās, -ātis (f.), an age
Aethiops, -ŏpis (m.), an Ethiopian
afferō,-re, attulī, allātum, to bring; utilitātem afferre, to do service
Āfrica, -ae (f.), Africa
agens, -tis, passing; duodevicesimum aetātis annum agens, in the 18th year of one's age
ăgěr, -rī (m.), a field
Āgēsīlaus, -ī (m.), Agesilaus, one of the Spartan kings
agnus, -ī (m.), a lamb
ăgō, -ěre, ēgī, actum, to drive; do, hold; vītam agěre, to pass one's life; hiěměm, aestātěm agěre, to spend the winter, summer; aliās rēs agěre, to be intent on other matters; in exsilium agěre, to drive into exile
albus, -a, -um, white
Ālexander, -rī (m.), Alexander
Ālexandrīa, -ae (f.), Alexandria
ălīēnus, -a, -um, of others
ălīquandō, some time
ălīquis, -a, -ŏd, -ĭd, some one, some thing
ălīus, -a, -ud, other, another
allĭcĭō, -ěre, allexī, allectum, to entice
ălō, -ěre, ălŭī, ălĭtum or altum, to nourish
Alpēs, -ium (pl. f.), the Alps
altěr, -a, -um, second, the other, next; altěrō tantō, twice as much
āmārĭtūdō, -ĭnis (f.), bitterness
ambŭlō, -āre, -āvī, -ātum, to take a walk, to walk
Ămĕrĭca, -ae, (f.), America
ămĭcĭō, -īre, (no perf.), ămictum, to clothe
ămĭcĭtĭa, -ae, (f.), friendship
ămĭcus, -ī (m.), a friend

ămĭcus, -a, -um, friendly
ămittō, -ěre, āmīsī, āmissum, to lose
ămō, -āre, -āvī, -ātum, to love, like
ămŏr, -ōris (m.), love
amplectŏr, -ī, amplexus sum, to embrace
amplĭus, more, more than
ăn, or, if
Anaxăgŏrās, -ae (m.), Anaxagoras, a Greek philosopher
angō, -ěre, anxī, (no sup.), to torment, vex
ănĭmăl, -ālis (n.), an animal; animal terrestre, a land animal
ănĭmus, -ī (m.), the mind, soul
annōn, or not
annus, -ī (m.), a year
annuus, -a, -um, yearly
antě (w. acc.), before
Antĭŏchīa, -ae (f.), Antioch
antīquus, -a, -um, old, ancient
Antōnĭus, -ī (m.), Anthony, a Roman family name
antrum, -ī (n.), a cave
ānŭlus, -ī (m.), a finger-ring
Ăpellēs, -is (m.), Apelles, a distinguished Greek painter
ăpěrĭō, -īre, ăpěrŭī, ăpertum, to open
ăpis, - (f.), a bee
appārěō, -ēre, -ŭī, -ĭtum, to appear
appellō, -āre, -āvī, -ātum, to call
Appĭus, -a, -um, Appian
apprŏpinquō, -āre, -āvī, -ātum, to approach
aptus, -a, -um ad, apt, suited, suitable
ăpŭd (w. acc.), among, near
ăqua, -ae (f.), water
ăquĭla, -ae (f.), an eagle
ărānĕa, -ae (f.), a spider
arbĭtrŏr, -ārī, -ātus sum, to believe, think, be of opinion
arbŏr, -is (f.), a tree
arcĕō, -ēre, -ŭī, (no sup.), to keep off, restrain

arcessō, -ĕrĕ, arcessīvī, arcessītŭm, to summon
Archĭās, -ae (m.), Archias, a Greek
poet
ardĕō, -ĕrĕ, arsī, arsŭm, to burn
ārescō, -ĕrĕ, ārŭī, (no sup.), to (become) dry
Arganthōnĭŭs, -ī (m.), king Arganthonius
argentĕŭs, -ă, -ŭm, silver (adj.)
argentŭm, -ī (n.), silver, money
argŭō, -ĕrĕ, argŭī, argūtŭm, to
argue, accuse
Argŭs, -ī (m.), Argus, a fabulous being, said to have had a hundred eyes
Arīŏn, -ŏnīs (m.), Arion
Arīstĭdēs, -īs (m.), Aristides, re-
nowned for his integrity
Arīstippŭs, -ī, (m.), Aristippus
armă, -ōrŭm (pl. n.), arms
ărō, -ārĕ, -āvī, -ātŭm, to plow
ars, -tīs (f.), an art
Asĭă, -ae (f.), Asia
assentĭŏr, -īrī, assensŭs sŭm, to
assent
assĭdŭŭs, -ă, -ŭm, industrious
ăt, but
Ăthēnae, -ārŭm (pl. f.), Athens
Ăthēnĭęnsīs, - (m.), an Athenian
Atlantĭcŭs, -ă, -ŭm, Atlantic
Attălŭs, -ī (m.), Attalus, king of Per-
gamos
attentŭs, -ă, -ŭm, attentive
Attĭcŭs, -ī (m.), Atticus, the intimate
friend of Cicero
attrăhō, -ĕrĕ, attraxī, attractŭm,
to attract
Attŭs Nāvĭŭs, -ī -ī (m.), Attus Navius
auctŏr, -ōrīs (m.), an author
audĕō, -ĕrĕ, ausŭs sŭm, to dare
audĭō, -īrĕ, -īvī. -ītŭm, to hear
aufĕrō, -rĕ, abstŭlī, ablātŭm, to
carry away
augĕō, -ĕrĕ, anxī, auctŭm, to increase; mĕmŏrĭăm augērĕ, to improve
the memory
augŭr, -īs (m.), an augur
Augustŭs, -ī (m.), Augustus, the first
emperor of Rome

aurĕŭs, -ă, -ŭm, of gold, golden
aurīs, - (f.), the ear
aurŭm, -ī (n.), gold
aut, or; aut..aut, either..or
autĕm (follows the first word in the sentence or clause), but, yet
autumnŭs, -ī (m.), autumn
auxĭlĭŭm, -ī (n.), help, assistance,
aid
ăvārĭtĭă, -ae (f.), avarice
ăvārŭs, -ă, -ŭm, greedy; ăvā. ŭs,
-ī (m.), a miser
ăvīs, - (f.), a bird
ăvuncŭlŭs, -ī (m.), an uncle
ăvŭs, -ī (m.), a grandfather

B.

Băbўlōn, -īs (f.), Babylon
bĕātŭs, -ă, -ŭm, happy, blessed
bellŭm, -ī (n.), war; bellum nāvāle,
naval warfare
bĕnĕ, well
bĕnĕfĭcĭŭm, -ī (n.), a benefit
bestĭă, -ae (f.), a beast
Bĭās, -antīs (m.), Bias, one of the
7 wise men
bĭblĭŏthēcă, -ae (f.), a library
bĭbō, -ĕrĕ, bĭbī, bĭbĭtŭm, to drink
bĭdŭŭm, -ī (n.), the space of 2 days
bĭs, twice
bŏnŭm, -ī (n.), a good, possession,
blessing
bŏnŭs, -ă, -ŭm, good
bōs, bŏvīs (m.), an ox
brassĭcă, -ae (f.), cabbage
brĕvīs, -ĕ, short
Brĭtannŭs, -ī (m.), a Briton

C.

cădō, -ĕrĕ, cĕcĭdī, cāsŭm, to fall
caecŭs, -ă, -ŭm, blind
caedō, -ĕrĕ, cĕcĭdī, caesŭm, to
fell
caelŭm, -ī (n.), heaven, the sky, the
open sky; pl. caelī, -ōrŭm (m.),
Written also: coelum
Caesăr, -īs (m.), Caesar
călămĭtās, -ātīs (f.), misfortune
calcăr, -ārīs (n.), a spur
călĕō, -ĕrĕ, -ŭī, (no sup.), to be hot

— 74 —

călescō, -ĕrĕ, călŭī, (no sup.), to become hot
călĭdŭs, -ă, -ŭm, hot, warm
Călĭfornĭă, -ae (f.), California
calvĭtĭŭm, -ī (n.), baldness
campŭs, -ī (m.), a field
cănĭs, - (m.), a dog
cănō, -ĕrĕ, cĕcĭnī, cantŭm, to sing
cantō, -ārĕ, -āvī, -ātŭm, to sing
cantŭs, -ūs (m.), song
căpessō, -ĕrĕ, căpessīvī, căpessītŭm, to lay hold of
căpillŭs, -ī (m.), a hair
căpĭō, -ĕrĕ, cēpī, captŭm, to take, catch
căpŭt, -ĭtĭs (n.), the head; capĭtis damnāre, to condemn to death
captŭs, -ă, -ŭm, captive
cărĕō, -ērĕ, -ŭī, -ĭtŭm, to need
cārĭtās, -ātĭs (f.), affection
cărō, carnĭs (f.), meat, flesh
carpō, -ĕrĕ, carpsī, carptŭm, to pluck, crop
Carthāgĭnĭensĭs, -ĕ, Carthaginian
Carthāgō, -ĭnĭs (f.), Carthage
cārŭs, -ă, -ŭm, dear; cārissĭmĕ, my dearest
cāsĕŭs, -ī (m.), a cheese
castŏr, -ŏrĭs (m.), a beaver
castrŭm, -ī (n.), a fort; castră, -ōrŭm (pl. n.), a military camp
cătēnă, -ae (f.), a chain
causă, -ae (f.), a cause; causā (abl.), in consequence, for the sake of
cautŭs, -ă, -ŭm, cautious
căvĕō, -ĕrĕ, cāvī, cautŭm, to be on one's guard, beware of
cēdō, -ĕrĕ, cessī, cessŭm, to yield
cĕlĕrĭtās, -ātĭs (f.), speed
cĕlĕrĭtĕr. quickly
cēlō, -ārĕ, -āvī, -ātŭm, to conceal from
cēnă, -ae (f.), dinner, meal. Written also: coenă
cēnō, -ārĕ, -āvī, -ātŭm, to dine; cēnātŭs, -ă, -ŭm, having dined. Written also: coenō
censĕō, -ērĕ, censŭī, censŭm, to value, think

centŭm, a hundred; centŭm mīllĭă, a hundred thousand
cĕrăsŭm, -ī (n.), a cherry
cernō, -ĕrĕ, crēvī, crētŭm, to see, discern
certē, to be sure, certainly
certŭs, -ă, -ŭm, certain
cessō, -ārĕ, -āvī, -ātŭm, to cease
Christŭs, -ī (m.), Christ
cĭcātrīx, -īcĭs (f.), a scar
Cĭcĕrō, -ōnĭs (m.), Cicero
cĭcōnĭă, -ae (f.), a stork
cĭĕō, -ērĕ, cĭvī, cĭtŭm, to arouse
Cimbrī, -ōrŭm (pl. m.), the Cimbrians
Cincinnātŭs, -ī (m.), Cincinnatus
cingō, -ĕrĕ, cinxī, cinctŭm, to gird, surround
cĭnĭs, -ĕrĭs (m.), ashes
circā (w. acc.), around, near, about
circĭtĕr (w. acc.), about, near
circŭm (w. acc.), around, about
circumdō,-ārĕ, circumdĕdī, circumdătŭm, to surround
circumstō, -ārĕ, -stĕtī, (no sup.), to stand around
cĭs (w. acc.), on this side of
cĭtĭŭs, sooner, more quickly
citrā (w. acc.), on this side of .
cĭvĭs, - (m.), a citizen
cĭvĭtās, -ātĭs (f.), a state
clāmĭtō, -ārĕ, -āvī, -ātŭm, to cry out aloud
clangō,-ĕrĕ,(no perf. & sup.), to clang
clārŭs, -ă, -ŭm, famous
claudō, -ĕrĕ, clausī, clausŭm, to shut, close
cŏarguō, -ĕrĕ, -ī, (no sup.), to convict
coepī, -issĕ, coeptŭm, to have begun
cōgĭtō, -ārĕ, -āvī, -ātŭm, to think
cognoscō, -ĕrĕ, cognōvī, cognĭtŭm, to know
collĭgō, -ĕrĕ, collēgī, collectŭm, to collect
collŏcō, -ārĕ, -āvī, -ātŭm, to let
cŏlō, -ĕrĕ, cŏlŭī, cultŭm, to cultivate, worship; agrŭm colĕrĕ, to till the field

cŏlŏr, -ŏrĭs (m.), *color*
cŏmĕs, -ĭtĭs (m.), *a follower*
cŏmētēs-ae (m.), *a comet*
cŏmĭtŏr, -ārī, -ātŭs sŭm, *to accompany*
commŏnĕfăcĭŏ,-ĕrĕ,-fēcī,-factŭm, *to remind*
commŏnĕŏ, -ēre, -ŭī, -ĭtŭm, *to remind*
commūnĭs, -ĕ, *common*
cōmŏ, -ĕrĕ, compsī, comptŭm, *to adorn*
compărŏ, -āre, -āvī, -ātŭm, *to get, to compare;* exercĭtŭm compărărĕ, *to raise an army*
compescŏ,-ĕrĕ,compescŭī,(no sup.), *to restrain*
complĕŏ, -ēre, complēvī, complētŭm, *to fill up*
complūrēs, -ă or -ĭă (pl.), *several, very many*
comportŏ, -āre, -āvī, -ātŭm, *to collect*
compŏs, -ŏtĭs, *capable*
condemnŏ, -āre, -āvī, -ātŭm. *to condemn, find guilty*
condĭcĭŏ, -ōnĭs (f.), *a condition*
condŏ, -ĕrĕ, condĭdī, condĭtŭm, *to build, found*
condūcŏ, -ĕrĕ, conduxī, conductŭm, *to hire*
conductĭtĭŭs, -ă, -ŭm, *rented*
confĭcĭŏ, -ĕrĕ, confēcī, confectŭm, *to complete*
confĭtĕŏr, -ērī, confessŭs sŭm, *to confess*
congrŭŏ, -ĕrĕ, congrŭī, (no sup.), *to agree*
cŏnīvĕŏ, -ēre, cōnīvī & cōnixī, (no sup.), *to shut the eyes*
conscĭentĭă, -ae (f.), *conscience*
consĭlĭŭm, -ī (n.), *counsel, design*
consōlŏr, -ārī, -ātŭs sŭm, *to comfort*
consŏnŏ, -āre, -āvī, -ātŭm, *to hum*
constăt, *it is evident, it is agreed*
constĭtŭŏ, -ĕrĕ, constĭtŭī, constĭtūtŭm, *to determine*
constŏ,-āre,constĭtī,(no sup.),*to cost*

consuescŏ, -ĕrĕ, consuēvī, consuētŭm, *to accustom, to be accustomed*
consŭlŏ,-ĕrĕ,consŭlŭī,consultŭm, *to counsel*
consultŏ, -āre, -āvī, -ātŭm, *to deliberate*
contemnŏ, -ĕrĕ, contempsī, contemptŭm, *to despise*
contentŭs, -ă, -ŭm, *contented*
contĭnŭŭs, -ă, -ŭm, *continuous*
contrā (w. acc.), *against*
convălescŏ, -ĕrĕ, convălŭī, (convălĭtŭm), *to recover*
convincŏ,-ĕrĕ,convĭcī,convictŭm, *to convict*
cōpĭă, -ae (f.), *abundance;* cōpĭae, -ārŭm (pl. f.), *troops, forces*
cōquŏ,-ĕrĕ,coxī,coctŭm,*to cook, bake*
cŏr, cordĭs (n.), *the heart*
cōrăm (w. abl.), *in presence of*
Cŏrinthŭs, -ī (f.), *the city of Corinth*
cornū, -ūs (n.), *a horn*
corpŭs, -ŏrĭs (n.), *a body*
cōs, cōtĭs (f.), *a grindstone, whetstone*
crēdŏ. -ĕrĕ, crēdĭdī, crēdĭtŭm. *to believe*
crĕŏ, -āre, -āvī, -ātŭm, *to create, make*
crĕpŏ. -āre, crĕpŭī, crĕpĭtŭm, *to creak, clank*
crescŏ, -ĕrĕ, crēvī, crētŭm, *to grow, increase*
Croesŭs, -ī (m.), *Croesus, celebrated for his riches*
cŭbĭtŭm, -ī (n.), *a cubit*
cŭbŏ,-āre, cŭbŭī, cŭbĭtŭm, *to lie down*
cūdŏ, -ĕrĕ, cūdī, cūsŭm, *to forge*
cultĕr, -rī (m.), *a knife*
cultūră, -ae (f.), *the culture*
cŭm (w. abl.), *with*
cŭm (conjunct.), *when, at the time when, as, though, suppose, whereas, since*
cŭpĭdĭtās, -ātĭs (f.), *passion, desire*
cŭpĭdŭs, -ă, -ŭm, *eager, desirous*
cŭpĭŏ, -ĕrĕ, cŭpīvī, cŭpĭtŭm, *to wish, desire*
cūră, -ae (f.), *care*
cūrātĭŏ, -ōnĭs (f.), *a cure*

cūrō, -ārĕ, -āvī, -ātŭm, to attend to
currō, -ĕrĕ, cŭcurrī, cursŭm, to run
currŭs, -ūs (m.), a cart
cursō, -ārĕ, -āvī, -ātŭm, to run about
cursŭs, -ūs (m.), a course
custōs, -ōdīs (m.), a custodian
Cȳrŭs, -ī (m.), Cyrus

D.

damnō, -ārĕ, -āvī, -ātŭm, to condemn, find guilty; căpĭtīs damnāre, to condemn to death
damnŭm, -ī (n.), loss
Dānŭbĭŭs, -ī (m.), the Danube
Dārēŭs, -ī (m.), Dareus, a Persian king
dē (w. abl.), of, from, on, concerning
dēbĕō, -ĕrĕ, -ŭī, -ĭtŭm, to owe; I ought, must, should; dēbērī, to be due
dēbĭlĭs, -ĕ, weak
dĕcĕm, ten
dĕcĕt, it becomes; -ĕrĕ, dĕcŭĭt
dĕcōrŭs, -ă, -ŭm, glorious
dēdĕcĕt, it is unbecoming; -ĕrĕ, dēdĕcŭĭt
dēfendō, -ĕrĕ, dēfendī, dēfensŭm, to defend
dēfĭcĭō, -ĕrĕ, dēfēcī, dēfectŭm, to be wanting
dēfungŏr, -ī, dēfunctŭs sŭm, to discharge
dēlĕō, -ĕrĕ, dēlēvī, dēlētŭm, to destroy
dēlībĕrātĭō, -ōnĭs (f.), deliberation
dēlĭcĭae, -ārŭm (pl. f.), delight
Delphī, -ōrŭm (pl. m.), Delphi
deltă, - (n. indecl.), delta
dēmō, -ĕrĕ, dempsī, demptŭm, to take away
dens, -tĭs (m.), a tooth
Dēmosthĕnēs, -ĭs (m.), Demosthenes
depsō, -ĕrĕ, depsŭī, depstŭm, to knead
dēsĕrō, -ĕrĕ, dēsĕrŭī, dēsertŭm, to forsake
dēsīdĕrō, -ārĕ, -āvī, -ātŭm, to require

dēsignō, -ārĕ, -āvī, -ātŭm, to appoint
dĕŭs, -ī (m.), a god; Dĕŭs, God
dīcō, -ĕrĕ, dixī, dictŭm, to say, tell, call
dictātŏr, -ōrĭs (m.), a dictator
dictō, -ārĕ, -āvī, -ātŭm, to dictate
dictŭm, -ī (n.), a saying
dĭēs, -ēī (m. & f. in the sing., m. in the plur.), a day
diffĭcĭlĭs, -ĕ, difficult
diffĭtĕŏr, -ērī, (no perf.), to disavow
dignŏr, -ārī, -ātŭs sŭm, to deem worthy
dignŭs, -ă, -ŭm, worthy; laudĕ dignŭs, praiseworthy
dīlĭgens, -tĭs, diligent
dīlĭgentĭă, -ae (f.), diligence
dīlĭgō, -ĕrĕ, dīlexī, dīlectŭm, to love
dīlūcĭdŭs, -ă, -ŭm, clear
dīmĭcō, -ārĕ, -āvī, -ātŭm, to fight
Dĭōnȳsĭŭs, -ī (m.), Dionysius, tyrant of Syracuse
discĭpŭlŭs, -ī (m.), a pupil, scholar
discō, -ĕrĕ, dĭdĭcī, (no sup.), to learn
dispār, -ārĭs, unlike
dissĭmĭlĭs, -ĕ, unlike
distō, -ārĕ, (no perf. & sup.), to be distant
dīvĕs, -ĭtĭs, rich
dīvĭdō, -ĕrĕ, dīvīsī, dīvīsŭm, to divide, separate
dīvīnŭs, -ă, -ŭm, divine
dīvĭtĭae, -ārŭm (pl. f.), riches
dō, -ārĕ, dĕdī, dătŭm, to give
dŏcĕō, -ĕrĕ, dŏcŭī, doctŭm, to teach
doctrīnă, -ae (f.), learning
dŏlŏr, -ōrĭs (m.), pain, grief
dŏmestĭcŭs, -ă, -ŭm, domestic
dŏmĭnŭs, -ī (m.), a master, a lord
dŏmō, -ārĕ, dŏmŭī, dŏmĭtŭm, to tame, to subjugate
dŏmŭs, -ūs (f.), a house; dŏmī, at home; dŏmŭm, home; dŏmō, from home
dōnĕc, as long as, while

dōnŭm, -ī (n.), *a gift, present;* dōnō dărĕ, *to give as a present*
dormĭō, -īrĕ, -īvī, -ītŭm, *to sleep*
dŭbĭŭm, -ī (n.), *a doubt*
dūcō, -ĕrĕ, duxī, ductŭm, *to lead, bring, to count*
Dūillŭs, -ī (m.), *Duilius*
dulcĭs, -ĕ, *sweet (to the taste)*
dŭm, *while; if only, provided*
dummŏdŏ, *if only, provided*
dŭŏ, -ae, -ŏ, *two*
dŭŏdēvīcēsĭmŭs, -ă, -ŭm, *the eighteenth*
dūrō, -ārĕ, -āvī, -ātŭm, *to last*
dux, dŭcĭs (m.), *a leader*

E.

ē (w. abl. and only before consonants), *from, of, out of*
ĕdō, -ĕrĕ, ēdī, ēsŭm, *to eat*
ēdō, -ĕrĕ, ēdĭdī, ēdĭtŭm, *to give out, publish*
ēdūcō, -ārĕ, -āvī, -ātŭm, *to bring up, educate*
effectŭs, -ūs (m.), *an effect*
effĭcĭō, -ĕrĕ, effēcī, effectŭm, *to make*
ĕgēnŭs, -ă, -ŭm, *needy*
ĕgĕō, -ērĕ, -ŭī, (no sup.), *to (be in) need*
ĕgestās, -ātĭs (f.), *want*
ĕgō, *I;* ĕgŏmĕt, *I*
ĕlēmentŭm, -ī (n.), *an element*
ĕlĕphantŭs, -ī (m.), *an elephant*
ĕlĕphās, -antĭs (m.), *an elephant*
ēlĭgō, -ĕrĕ, ēlēgī, ēlectŭm, *to choose, elect*
ēlŏquens, -tĭs, *eloquent*
ĕmō, -ĕrĕ, ēmī, emptŭm, *to buy, purchase*
ēnĕcō, -ārĕ. -āvī, -ātŭm; -ŭī, enectŭm, *to slay*
ĕnĭm, *for*
ĕō, īrĕ, īvī, ĭtŭm, *to go*
ĕpistŏlă, -ae } (f.), *a letter*
ĕpistŭlă, -ae }
ĕquĕs, -ĭtĭs (m), *a rider, horseman*
ĕquĭtō, -ārĕ, -āvī, -ātŭm, *to ride*
ĕquŭs, -ī (m.), *a horse*

ergā (w. acc.), *toward, unto*
ērĭpĭō, -ĕrĕ, ērĭpŭī, ēreptŭm, *to take away* [taken
errō,-ārĕ,-āvī,-ātŭm, *to be mis-*
ēsŭrĭō, -īrĕ, -īvī, (no sup.), *to be hungry*
ĕt, *and;* ĕt..ĕt, *both..and*
ĕtĭăm, *even*
ĕtĭamsī, *even if, although*
etsī, *although, though*
Eurōpă, -ae (f.), *Europe*
ēvādō, -ĕrĕ, ēvāsī, ēvāsŭm, *to become, turn out*
ēvellō, -ĕrĕ, ēvellī, ēvulsŭm, *to pluck out*
ēvŏcō, -ārĕ, -āvī, -ātŭm, *to summon*
ēvŏlō,-ārĕ,-āvī,-ātŭm, *to fly out*
ex (w. abl.), *from, of*
exardescō, -ĕrĕ, exarsī, exarsŭm, *to take fire* [excel
excellō, -ĕrĕ, (no perf. & sup.), *to*
exclūdō, -ĕrĕ, exclūsī, exclūsŭm, *to shut out*
exemplŭm, -ī (n.), *an example*
exĕō, -īrĕ, -ĭī, -ĭtŭm, *to depart, come off*
exercĭtătĭō, -ōnĭs (f.), *practice*
exercĭtŭs, -ūs (m.), *an army*
exĭgŭŭs, -ă, -ŭm, *small*
existĭmō, -ārĕ, -āvī, -ātŭm, *to regard, believe*
expellō, -ĕrĕ, expŭlī, expulsŭm, *to drive away*
expergiscŏr, -ī, experrectŭs sŭm, *to awake*
expĕrĭŏr. -īrī, expertŭs sŭm, *to try, exercise*
expers, -tĭs, *free, without share*
explĕō,-ĕrĕ,explēvī,explētŭm, *to fill*
explĭcō, -ārĕ;-āvī,-ŭī;-ātŭm, -ĭtŭm, *to unfold*
exsĭlĭŭm, -ī (n.), *exile*
exspectō, -ārĕ, -āvī, -ātŭm, *to wait for*
exstinguō, -ĕrĕ, exstinxī, exstinctŭm, *to put out*
extrā (w. acc.), *without*
exŭō,-ĕrĕ, exŭī, exūtŭm, *to put off*

F.

făbŭlă, -ae (f.), *a fable*
făcessō, -ĕrĕ, făcessīvī, făcessī-tŭm, *to accomplish*
făcĭlĕ, *easily, readily*
făcĭlĭs, -ĕ, *easy*
făcĭlĭŭs, *more easily*
făcĭnŭs, -ŏrĭs (n.), *a crime*
făcĭō, -ĕrĕ, fēcī, factŭm, *to make, do*
factŭm, -ī (n.), *a deed*
fallō, -ĕrĕ, fĕfellī, falsŭm, *to cheat*
fāmă, -ae (f.), *reputation, glory;* bona fama, *a good name*
fămēs, -ĭs (f.), *hunger*
fămĭlĭārĭs, -ĕ, *belonging to the family;* rēs fămĭlĭārĭs, *property*
farcĭō, -īrĕ, farsī, fartŭm, *to stuff*
fās (indecl. n.), *right*
fătĕŏr, -ērī, fassŭs sŭm, *to confess*
fātŭm, -ī (n.), *destiny*
făvĕō, -ĕrĕ, fāvī, fautŭm, *to favor*
fēlĭcĭtās, -ātĭs (f.), *happiness*
fēlĭcĭtĕr, *happily*
fēlĭs, - (f.), *a cat*
fēlīx, -īcĭs, *happy, fortunate*
fēmĭnă, -ae (f.), *a female, woman*
fĕnestră, -ae (f.), *a window*
fĕrē, *almost, nearly*
fērĭae, -ārŭm (pl. f.), *holidays*
fĕrō, ferrĕ, tŭlī, lātŭm, *to bear, carry;* fructus ferre, *to yield fruits*
ferrŭm, -ī (n.), *iron*
fĕrŭs, -ă, -ŭm, *wild*
fervĕō, -ĕrĕ, fervī & ferbŭī. (no sup.), *to glow*
fessŭs, -ă, -ŭm, *weary (of)*
fĭdēlĭs, -ĕ, *faithful*
fĭdēs, -ĕī (f.), *faith;* fĭdĕm hăbērĕ, *to trust*
fīdō, -ĕrĕ, fīsŭs sŭm, *to trust*
fīgō, -ĕrĕ, fixī, fixŭm, *to fix*
fīlĭă, -ae (f.), *a daughter*
fīlĭŭs, -ī (m.), *a son*
findō, -ĕrĕ, fĭdī, fissŭm, *to split, cleave*
fingō, -ĕrĕ, finxī, fictŭm, *to fashion*
fīnĭs, - (m.), *an end*
fīō, fĭĕrī, factŭs sŭm, *to become, happen, be made*
fixŭs, -ă, -ŭm, *fixed*

flăgĭtō, -ārĕ, -āvī, -ātŭm, *to ask*
flectō, -ĕrĕ, flexī, flexŭm, *to bend*
flĕō, -ĕrĕ, flēvī, flētŭm, *to weep*
flōrens, -tĭs, *flourishing;* in blossom
flōs, -ōrĭs (m.), *a flower*
flūmĕn, -ĭnĭs (n.), *a river*
flŭō, -ĕrĕ, fluxī, fluxŭm, *to flow*
flŭvĭŭs, -ī (m.), *a river*
fŏdĭō, -ĕrĕ, fōdī, fossŭm, *to dig*
foedŭs, -ĕrĭs (n.), *a treaty*
fŏlĭŭm, -ī (n.), *a leaf*
fŏrĕm, *I should be*
formīcă, -ae (f.), *an ant*
fortĭs, -ĕ, *brave*
fŏrŭm, -ī (n.), *the forum, market*
fŏvĕō, -ĕrĕ, fōvī, fōtŭm, *to cherish*
frangō, -ĕrĕ, frēgī, fractŭm, *to break*
frātĕr, -rĭs (m.), *a brother*
fraus, -dĭs (f.), *a fraud*
frĕmō, -ĕrĕ, frĕmŭī, (no sup.), *to growl*
frēnă, -ōrŭm (pl. n.) } *a bridle, a bit*
frēnī, -ōrŭm (pl. m.) }
frēnŭm, -ī (n.), *a bridle*
frĕquens, -tĭs, *crowded*
frētŭs, -ă, -ŭm, *trusting, relying*
frĭcō, -ārĕ, -ŭī, -ātŭm, frictŭm, *to rub*
frĭgĕō, -ĕrĕ, frixī, (no sup.), *to be cold*
frĭgŭs, -ŏrĭs (n.), *cold*
frūgĭfĕr, -ă, -ŭm, *fruit-bearing, fruitful*
frūmentŭm, -ī (n.), *corn;* frūmentă, -ōrŭm (pl. n.), *grain*
frŭŏr, -ī, frŭĭtŭs & fructŭs sŭm, *to enjoy*
frustrā, *in vain*
fūcŭs, -ī (m.), *a drone*
fŭgă, -ae (f.), *a flight*
fŭgĭō, -ĕrĕ, fūgī, fŭgĭtŭm, *to flee or fly*
fŭgō, -ārĕ, -āvī, -ātŭm, *to put to flight*
fulcĭō, -īrĕ, fulsī, fultŭm, *to support*
fulgĕō, -ĕrĕ, fulsī, (no sup.), *to shine*
fulmĭnō, -ārĕ, -āvī, -ātŭm, *to lighten*

fundō, -ĕrĕ, fūdī, fūsŭm, to pour; to rout
fungŏr, -ī, functŭs sŭm, to discharge
fūr, -īs (m.), a thief
fūrō, -ĕrĕ, (no perf. & sup.), to rage
fŭtūrŭs, -ă, -ŭm, about to be, future

G.

Gādēs, -īŭm (pl. f.), Cadiz
Gallīă, -ae (f.), Gaul
Gallŭs, -ī (m.), a Gaul
gaudĕō, -ērĕ, gavīsŭs sŭm, to rejoice
gaudĭŭm, -ī (n.), joy
gĕlū, -ūs (n.), (icy) cold, ice
gĕnŭs, -ĕrīs (n.), a kind; race; gĕnŭs vītae, a line of life
Germānīă, -ae (f.), Germany
Germānŭs, -ī (m.), a German [on
gĕrō, -ĕrĕ, gessī, gestŭm, to carry
gestō, -ārĕ, -āvī, -ātŭm, to carry
gignō, -ĕrĕ, gĕnŭī, gĕnĭtŭm, to beget, bring forth
glōrīă, -ae (f.), glory, honor
glūbō, -ĕrĕ, glupsī, gluptŭm, to peel
grădĭŏr, -ī, gressŭs sŭm, to step
Graecĭă, -ae (f.), Greece
Graecŭs, -ă, -ŭm, Greek
grāmĕn. -ĭnĭs (n.), grass
grammatĭcŭs,-ă, -ŭm. grammatical; liber grammatĭcŭs, a grammar
grātĭae, -ārŭm (pl. f.) thanks
grātŭlŏr, -ārī, -ātŭs sŭm, to congratulate
grātŭs, -ă, -ŭm, pleasing
grăvīs, -ĕ, burdensome
gŭbernō, -ārĕ, -āvī, -ātŭm, to steer
gustō, -ārĕ, -āvī, -ātŭm, to taste

H.

hăbĕō, -ērĕ, -ŭī, -ĭtŭm, to have, consider; fidem habēre, to trust
hăbĭtō, -ārĕ, -āvī, -ātŭm, to dwell, live
Hădrūmētŭm, -ī (n.), Hadrumetum
haerĕō, -ērĕ, haesī, haesŭm, to hang

hāmŭs, -ī (m.), a hook
Hannĭbăl, -īs (m.), Hannibal, a Carthaginian general
Hasdrŭbăl, -īs (m.), Hasdrubal
haurĭō, -īrĕ, hausī, haustŭm, to draw
Henrĭcŭs, -ī (m.), Henry
Hĕphaestĭōn, -ŏnĭs (m.), Hephaestion
hĕrī, yesterday
hīc, haec, hōc, this (of mine)
hĭems, hĭĕmĭs (f.), winter
Hĭĕrŏsŏlўmă, -ōrŭm (pl. n.), Jerusalem
Hīmĕră, -ae (f.), Himera
hīrundō, -ĭnĭs (f.), a swallow
Hīspānĭă, -ae (f.), Spain
histōrĭă, -ae (f.), history, a story
hŏdĭē, to-day
Hŏmērŭs, -ī (m.), Homer
hŏmō, -ĭnĭs (m.), man; hŏmĭnēs (pl. m.), people; men
hŏnŏr, -ōrĭs (m.), an honor, office
hostĭs, - (m.), an enemy
hūmānŭs, -ă, -ŭm, human
hŭmŭs. -ī (f.), soil; hŭmō, from the ground; hŭmī, on the ground

I.

īcō, -ĕrĕ, īcī, ictŭm, to strike; foedus icĕre, to make a treaty
idcircō, for this reason, therefore
īdĕm, ĕădĕm, ĭdĕm, the same
īdōnĕŭs, -ă, -ŭm, fit, proper
ignārŭs, -ă, -ŭm, ignorant
ignāvŭs, -ă, -ŭm, cowardly
ignĭs, - (m.), fire
ignōmĭnĭă, -ae (f.), disgrace
illĕ, illă, illŭd, that (yonder)
īmāgō, -ĭnĭs (f.), an image
imbĕcillŭs, -ă, -ŭm, feeble, weak
imbŭō, -ĕrĕ, imbŭī, imbūtŭm, to dip, dye
ĭmĭtŏr, -ārī, -ātŭs sŭm, to imitate
immĕmŏr, -ĭs, forgetful, unmindful
immensŭs, -ă, -ŭm, immense, immeasurable
immĕrĭtissĭmō, most undeservedly
immĭnĕō, -ērĕ, (no perf. & sup.), to threaten

immortālīs, -ĕ, *immortal*
impār, -ārīs, *unequal*
impătĭentĭā, -ae (f.), *impatience*
impĕdīmentŭm, -ī (n.), *a hindrance;* impĕdīmentă, -ōrŭm (pl. n.), *baggage*
impĕdĭō, -īrĕ, -īvī, -ītŭm, *to hinder*
impellō, -ĕrĕ, impŭlī, impulsŭm, *to drive*
impĕrātŏr, -ōrīs (m.), *a general*
impĕrĭŭm, -ī (n.), *empire;* ăd impĕrĭŭm accēdĕrĕ, *to come to the throne*
implĕō,-ērĕ,implēvī,implētŭm, *to fill, fill up*
importō, -ārĕ, -āvī, -ātŭm, *to import*
impŏs, -ŏtīs, *not in possession of*
impŏtens, -tīs, *unable*
imprŏbŭs, -ă, -ŭm, *bad, wicked*
ĭn (w. acc.), *into;* (w. abl.), *in, on, upon*
incertŭs, -ă, -ŭm, *uncertain*
incessō, -ĕrĕ, incessīvī, incessītŭm, *to fall upon*
inconstans, -tīs, *inconstant*
ĭncrēdĭbĭlĭs, -ĕ, *incredible*
incrēmentŭm, -ī (n). *increase*
incūsō, -ārĕ, -āvī, -ātŭm. *to accuse* [*reveal*
indīcō, -ārĕ, -āvī, -ātŭm, *to*
indĭgĕō,-ērĕ,-ŭī, (no sup.), *to need*
indignŭs, -ă, -ŭm, *unworthy*
indulgentĭă, -ae (f.), *indulgence*
indulgĕō,-ērĕ, indulsī, indultŭm, *to indulge*
induō, -ĕrĕ, indŭī, indūtŭm, *to put on*
infrā, *below, under*
infēlīx,-īcīs, *unhappy*
ingĕnŭŭs, -ī (m.), *a gentleman*
ingrātŭs, -ă, -ŭm, *unpleasant*
inĭmīcŭs, -ă, -ŭm, *unfriendly*
ĭnĭtĭŭm, -ī (n.), *a beginning*
injūcundŭs, -ă, -ŭm, *disagreeable*
injūrĭă, -ae (f.), *an injury*
innŏcens, -tīs, *innocent*
innoxĭŭs, -ă, -ŭm, *harmless*
innŭmĕrābĭlĭs, -ĕ } *innumerable*
innŭmĕrŭs, -ă, -ŭm }
inquăm, *I say, quoth I*

insciŭs, -ă, -ŭm, *ignorant*
insectŭm, -ī (n.), *an insect*
insĭdĭae, -ārŭm (pl. f.), *treachery*
insĭmŭlō, -ārĕ, -āvī, -ātŭm, *to accuse, charge*
instăr (n. indecl.), *like, kind*
insŭlă, -ae (f.), *an island*
insŭm, ĭnessĕ, infŭī, *to be in*
intĕgrĭtās, -ātīs (f.), *integrity*
intellĕgō, -ĕrĕ, intellexī, intellectŭm, *to understand*
intĕr (w. acc.), *among, between*
interdĭū, *in day-time*
interdŭm, *sometimes*
intĕrĕō, -īrĕ, intĕrĭī, intĕrĭtŭm, *to perish*
interfĭcĭō, -ĕrĕ, interfēcī, interfectŭm, *to kill*
interrŏgō,-ārĕ,-āvī,-ātŭm,*to ask*
intersŭm, intĕressĕ, interfŭī, *to be present at;* intĕrest, *it concerns, is of importance*
intervallŭm, -ī (n.), *a space*
intrā (w. acc.), *within*
invĕnĭō, -īrĕ, invēnī, inventŭm, *to find (out), invent, to devise*
invĭdĕō, -ērĕ, invĭdī, invĭsŭm, *to envy*
invĭdĭă, -ae (f.), *envy*
invītō,-ārĕ,-āvī,-ātŭm,*to invite*
ipsĕ, -ă, -ŭm, *himself, herself, itself*
īrascŏr, -ī, -īātŭs sŭm. *to grow angry*
ĭs, ĕă, ĭd, *that; he, she, it;* ĕă, -ōrŭm (pl. n.), *those things*
ĭtă, *thus, so*
Ĭtălĭă, -ae (f.), *Italy*
ĭtĕr, ĭtĭnĕrĭs (n.), *a journey*
ĭtĕrŭm, *a second time, again*

J.

jăcĭō, -ĕrĕ, jēcī, jactŭm, *to throw, cast*
jăcŭlŏr, -ārī. -ātŭs sŭm, *to throw the javelin*
jăm, *already*
jamdūdŭm, *a long time*
jŏcŭs, -ī (m.), *a jest, joke;* pl. jŏcī, -ōrŭm (m.) & jŏcă, -ōrŭm (n.), *jokes*

— 81 —

jŭbĕō, -ērĕ, jussī, jussŭm, to order
jŭcundē, *pleasantly, deliciously*
jŭcundŭs, -ă, -ŭm, *agreeable*
jŭdex, -Icis (m.), *a judge*
jŭdĭcĭŭm, -ī (n.), *a court;* jŭdĭcĭŭm căpĭtĭs, *a trial for life*
jŭdĭcō, -ārĕ, -āvī, -ātŭm, *to judge*
Jūlĭŭs, -ī (m.), *Julius* [*ioin*
jungō, -ĕrĕ, junxī, junctŭm, *to*
jŭrō, -ārĕ, -āvī, -ātŭm, *to swear;* jūrātŭs, -ă, -ŭm, *having sworn*
jūs, jūrĭs (n.), *right, law;* jūs cīvĭlĕ, *civil law;* jūrĕ, *justly*
jussū, *by order*
justĭtĭă, -ae (f.), *justice*
justŭs, -ă, -ŭm, *just, regular*
jŭvĕnĭs (without n.), *young*
jŭvō, -ārĕ, jūvī, jūtŭm, *to assist, help*
juxtă (w. acc.), *near to, beside*

L.

lăbōr, -ōrĭs (m.), *labor*
lābōr, -ī, lapsŭs sŭm, *to glide ·*
lăbōrō, -ārĕ, -āvī, -ātŭm, *to work*
lăc, lactĭs (n.), *milk*
Lăcĕdaemŏnĭŭs, -ī (m.), *a Lacedaemonian*
lăcessō, -ĕrĕ, lăcessīvī, lăcessītŭm, *to excite, provoke*
lăcrĭmă, -ae } (f.), *a tear*
lăcrymă, -ae
lăcŭs, -ūs (m.), *a lake*
lambō, -ĕrĕ, lambī, (lambĭtŭm), *to lick*
Lătĭnŭs, -ă, -ŭm, *Latin*
lătrō, -ārĕ, -āvī, -ātŭm, *to bark*
lātŭs, -ă, -ŭm, *broad, wide*
laudō, -ārĕ, -āvī, -ātŭm, *to praise*
laus, -dĭs (f.), *praise*
lăvō, -ārĕ, lăvī, lăvātŭm, (lautŭm, lōtŭm), *to wash*
lēgātŭs, -ī (m.), *an ambassador*
lĕgō, -ĕrĕ, lēgī, lectŭm, *to read*
lĕō, -ōnĭs (m.), *a lion*
lĕpŭs, -ōrĭs (m.), *a hare*
lĕvĭs, -ĕ, *light*

lĕvō, -ārĕ, -āvī, -ātŭm, *to lessen, relieve*
lex, lēgĭs (f.), *a law*
lībentĕr, *willingly*
lībĕr, -rī (m.), *a book;* lībĕr grammătĭcŭs, *a grammar*
lībĕrī, -ōrŭm (pl. m.), *children*
lībĕrō, -ārĕ, -āvī, -ātŭm, *to (set) free, release*
lībertās, -ātĭs (f.), *liberty, freedom*
lĭcĕō, -ērĕ, -ŭī, -ĭtŭm, *to be for sale*
lĭcĕōr, -ērī, -ĭtŭs sŭm, *to bid*
lĭcĕt, *though, suppose, whereas*
lĭcĕt, -ērĕ, -ŭĭt, *it is allowed*
lĭgō, -ōnĭs (m.), *a mattock*
linguă, -ae (f.), *the tongue, a language;* vitium linguae, *a defect of speech*
linquō, -ĕrĕ, līquī, (no sup.), *to leave*
littĕră, -ae (f.), *a letter (of the alphabet);* littĕrae, -ārŭm (pl. f.), *an epistle*
lŏcō, -ārĕ, -āvī, -ātŭm, *to let*
lŏcŭs, -ī (m.), *a place;* pl. lŏcī, -ōrŭm (m.), *passages in books;* lŏcă, -ōrŭm (n.), *places*
longinquĭtās, -ātĭs (f.), *length*
longŭs, -ă, -ŭm, *long*
lŏquōr, -ī, lŏcūtŭs sŭm, *to speak*
lūcĕō, -ērĕ, luxī, (no sup.), *to shine*
luctŭs, -ūs (m.), *grief*
lūdō, -ĕrĕ, lūsī, lūsŭm, *to play*
lūgĕō, -ērĕ, luxī, (no sup.), *to mourn*
lūmĕn, -ĭnĭs (n.), *light*
lūnă, -ae (f.), *the moon*
lŭō, -ĕrĕ, lŭī, lŭĭtŭm, *to pay, atone for*
lŭō, -ĕrĕ, lŭī, lūtŭm, *to wash*
lŭpŭs, -ī (m.), *a wolf*
luscĭnĭă, -ae (f.), *a nightingale*
lux, lūcĭs (f.), *light*
luxŭrĭă, -ae } (f.), *luxury*
luxŭrĭēs, -ēī
Lўcurgŭs, -ī (m.), *Lycurgus, the lawgiver of the Spartans*

M.

Măcĕdō, -ōnĭs (m.), *a Macedonian*
maerōr, -ōrĭs (m.), *sorrow*
măgĭs, *more*

magister, -rī (m.),) a teacher, master
magistra, -ae (f.);)
magistrātus, -ūs (m.), a magistrate
magnēs, -ētis (m.), a magnet
magnī, highly
magnifīcus, -a, -um, splendid
magnōpĕrĕ, greatly
magnus, -a, -um, great, large, big
Māgŏ, -ōnĭs (m.), Mago
mājŏr, -ūs, greater; mājōr nātū,
  older; mājōrēs, -um (pl. m.), the
  ancestors
mălĕdīcŏ, -ĕrĕ, -dīxī, -dictum,
  to curse
mālō, mallĕ, māluī, (no sup.), to be
  more willing, prefer, have rather
malum, -ī (n.), an evil
malus, -a, -um, bad
mandŏ, -ĕrĕ, mandī, mansum, to
  chew [ing
māne (n. indecl.), morning; in the morn-
mănĕō, -ĕrĕ, mansī, mansum,
  to stay, remain
manus, -ūs (f.), the hand
Marcellus, -ī (m.), Marcellus
măre, -ĭs (n.), the sea, ocean
marītimus, -a, -um, sea-, naval
Marius, -ī (m.), Marius, seven times
  consul
māter, -rĭs (f.), mother
mătĕrĭes, -ēī (f.), matter
mātūrus, -a, -um, ripe
mātūrescō, -ĕrĕ, mātūruī, (no sup.),
  to ripen
maxĭmē, most
maxĭmus, -a, -um, greatest
mĕdĕŏr,-ērī, (no perf.), to cure, heal
Mēdĭā, -ae (f.), Media
mĕdĭcīnā, -ae (f.), medicine
mĕdĭcus, -ī (m.), a physician
mel, mellĭs (n.), honey
mĕmĭnī, mĕminissĕ, to remember
mĕmŏr, -ĭs, mindful
mĕmŏrĭā, -ae (f.), memory
mendācĭum, -ī (n.), a falsehood, lying
mensĭs, - (m.), a month
mercātŏr, -ōrĭs (m.), a merchant
mercātus, -ūs (m.), a market
mercŏr, -ārī, -ātus sum, to buy
mĕrĕŏr, -ērī, -ītus sum, to deserve

mergō, -ĕrĕ, mersī, mersum, to
  dip in, plunge
mĕrĭdĭes, -ēī (m., midday, noon
merx, -cĭs (f.), ware
mētĭŏr,-īrī, mensūs sum,to measure
mĕtō, -ĕrĕ, messuī, messum, to
  reap
mĕtuō,-ĕrĕ, mĕtuī, (no sup.), to fear
mĕtus, -ūs (m.), fear
meus, -a, -um, my
mĭcō,-ārĕ, mĭcuī, (no sup.), to shine
migrō, -ārĕ, -āvī, -ātum, to migrate, remove
mīles, -ĭtĭs (m.), a soldier
mille, a thousand; mīllĭa, thousands
Miltĭădēs, -ĭs (m.), Miltiades
mĭnŏr, -ūs, less, smaller
mĭnuō, -ĕrĕ, mĭnuī, mĭnūtum, to
  lessen
mĭnus (adv.), less
mīrīfĭcus, -a, -um)
mīrus, -a, -um   ) wonderful
miscĕō, -ĕrĕ, miscuī, mixtum &
  mistum, to mix, mingle
mĭsĕr, -a, -um, wretched
mĭsĕrĕŏr, -ērī, mĭsĕrĭtus & miser-
  tus sum, to have pity
mĭsĕrĕt, it excites pity; mĭsĕrērĕ, mi-
  serĭtum & mĭsertum est
mittŏ, -ĕrĕ, mīsī, missum, to send
mŏdestĭă, -ae (f.), modesty
mŏdŏ, now, only, if only; mŏdŏ nĕ, provided only not
mŏdus, -ī (m.), manner; nullo modo,
  in no manner
mŏlestus, -a, -um, troublesome, irksome
molliō, -īrĕ, -īvī, -ītum, to assuage
mollĭs, -ĕ, soft, gentle
mŏlō, -ĕrĕ, mŏluī, mŏlĭtum, to
  grind
mŏnĕō, -ĕrĕ, -uī, -ĭtum, to advise, warn
mons, -tĭs (m.), a mountain, mount
morbus, -ī (m.), a disease
mordĕō,-ĕrĕ,mŏmordī,morsum,
  to bite
mŏrĭŏr, -ī, mortuus sum, to die
mors, -tĭs (f.), death

mortālis, -ĕ, *mortal*
mortŭus, -ă, -ŭm, *dead*
mŏvĕō, -ērĕ, mōvī, mōtŭm, *to move*
mulcĕō, -ērĕ, mulsī, mulsŭm, *to soothe*
mulgĕō, -ērĕ, mulsī, mulsŭm, *to milk*
mŭlĭĕr, -ĭs, (f.), *a woman*
multĭtūdŏ, -ĭnĭs (f.), *a multitude;* magnā multĭtūdŏ, *a very great number*
multŏ, *much, far*
multŭs, -ă, -ŭm, *much, many;* multa, *much*
Mummĭŭs, -ī (m.), *Mummius*
mundŭs, -ī (m.), *the world*
mūnŭs, -ĕrĭs (n.), *an office*
mūrŭs, -ī (m.), *a wall*
mūs, mūrĭs (m.), *a mouse*
muscă, -ae (f.), *a fly* [change
mūtŏ, -ārĕ, -āvī, -ātŭm, *to*
mūtŭs, -ă, -ŭm, *mute, dumb*
mūtŭŭs, -ă, -ŭm, *borrowed;* mūtŭŭm sūmĕrĕ, *to borrow*

N.

năm, *for*
nanciscŏr, -ī, nactŭs & nanctŭs sŭm, *to get*
narrātĭō, -ōnĭs (f.), *a narrative*
narrō, -ārĕ, -āvī, -ātŭm, *to relate*
nascŏr, -ī, nātŭs sŭm, *to be born*
nātālĭs, - (m.), *a birthday*
nătō, -ārĕ, -āvī, -ātŭm, *to swim*
nātū, *by birth;* mājŏr nātū, *older;* mĭnŏr nātū, *younger;* mājōrĕs nātū, *one's elders*
nātūră, -ae (f.), *nature*
nātŭs, -ă, -ŭm, *born;* antĕ, post Christŭm nātŭm, *before, after Christ*
nāvālĭs, -ĕ, *naval*
nāvĭgātĭō, -ōnĭs (f.), *navigation*
nāvĭs, -(f.), *a ship*
nē, *not, that not, lest; granted that not;* -nē (interrog. part.), *whether, if*
nĕc, *and not, nor;* nĕc..nĕc, *neither..nor*
nĕcessārĭŭs, -ă, -ŭm, *necessary*
nĕcessĕ est, *it must needs*
necnĕ, *or not*

nectō, -ĕrĕ, nexī & nexŭī, nexŭm, *to tie*
nĕfās (n. indecl.), *wrong, forbidden*
neglĕgens, -tĭs, *careless*
neglĕgō, -ĕrĕ, neglexī, neglectŭm *to neglect.* Written also: neglĭgĕrĕ
nĕgō, -ārĕ, -āvī, -ātŭm, *to deny*
nĕgōtĭŭm, -ī (n.), *affair, business, occupation*
nēmō, -ĭnĭs (m.), *nobody, no one*
nĕō, -ērĕ, nēvī, nētŭm, *to spin*
nĕquĕ, *and not;* nĕquĕ..nĕquĕ, *neither..nor*
nescĭō, -īrĕ, -īvī, -ītŭm, *not to know*
nescĭŭs, -ă, -ŭm, *ignorant*
neutĕr, -ră, -rŭm, *neither of the two*
nĭhĭl, *nothing;* nĭhĭl nĭsĭ, *nothing but*
Nīlŭs, -ī (m.), *the river Nile*
nĭmĭŭs, -ă, -ŭm, *too much, too great*
ningō, -ĕrĕ, ninxī, (no sup.), *to snow*
nĭsĭ, *but*
nītŏr, -ī, nīsŭs & nixŭs sŭm, *to stay one's self on*
nix, nĭvĭs (f.), *snow*
nōbĭlĭs, -ĕ, *noble*
nŏcĕō, -ērĕ, -ŭī, -ĭtŭm, *to do harm, hurt*
noctū, *at night*
nocturnŭs, -ă, -ŭm, *nightly;* tempŭs nocturnŭm, *night-time*
nōlō, nollĕ, nōlŭī, (no sup.), *to be unwilling, not to wish*
nōmĕn, -ĭnĭs (n.), *a name*
nōmĭnō, -ārĕ, -āvī, -ātŭm, *to call, name*
nōn, *not, no*
nōnāgintā, *ninety*
nondŭm, *not yet*
nonnĕ (interrog. part.), *not, if not*
nonnĭsĭ, *only*
nonnullī, -ae, -ă, *some*
nonnumquăm, *sometimes*
nosco, -ĕrĕ, nōvī, nōtŭm, *to learn to know*
nostĕr, -ră, -rŭm, *our*
nōtŭs, -ă, -ŭm, *known*
nŏvācŭlă, -ae (f.), *a razor*
nox, noctĭs (f.), *the night*
noxĭŭs, -ă, -ŭm, *noxious, hurtful*

nūbĭlŭs, -ă, -ŭm, *cloudy*
nūbō, -ĕrĕ, nupsī, nuptŭm, *to marry (of the woman)*
nūdŭs, -ă, -ŭm, *naked*
nullŭs, -ă, -ŭm, *no, none, not any, not one*
nŭm (interrog. part.), *whether, if*
Nŭmă, -ae (m.), *Numa, second king of Rome*
Nŭmantĭă, -ae (f.), *the city of Numantia*
nŭmĕrō, -ărĕ, -ăvī, -ātŭm, *to count*
nŭmĕrŭs, -ī (m.), *a number*
Nŭmĭtŏr, -ōrĭs (m.), *Numitor, king of Alba*
numquăm or nunquăm, *never*
nunc, *now*
nundīnae, -ārŭm (pl. f.), *market-day*
nunquăm, *never*
nuntĭō, -ărĕ, -ăvī, -ātŭm, *to bring word*
nuptĭae, -ārŭm (pl. f.), *a wedding*
nusquăm, *nowhere*

O.

o, O! *oh*
ŏb (w. acc.), *on account of*
obdormiscō, -ĕrĕ, obdormīvī, obdormītŭm, *to go to sleep*
oblīviscŏr, -ī, oblītŭs sŭm, *to forget*
ŏboedĭō, -īrĕ, -īvī, -ītŭm, *to obey*
obscūrō, -ărĕ, -ăvī, -ātŭm, *to obscure, eclipse*
obsĭdĕō, -ĕrĕ, obsēdī, obsessŭm, *to besiege*
obtrectō, -ărĕ, -ăvī, -ātŭm, *to decry*
occĭdō, -ĕrĕ, occĭdī, occāsŭm, *to set*
occŭlō, -ĕrĕ, occŭlŭī, occultŭm, *to conceal*
ŏcĕănŭs, -ī (m.), *the ocean*
Octāvĭă, -ae (f.), *Octavia*
octō, *eight*
octōgĭntă, *eighty*
ŏcŭlŭs, -ī (m.), *the eye*
ōdī, ōdissĕ, *to hate*
ŏdĭōsŭs, -ă, -ŭm, *hateful*

offĭcĭō, -ĕrĕ, offēcī, offectŭm, *to hinder*
offĭcĭŭm, -ī (n.), *a duty*
ōlĭm, *in former times, formerly*
omnĭs, -ĕ, *all, every*; omnĭă, -ĭŭm (pl. n.), *all things, every thing*; omnĭă sŭă, *all one's property*
ŏnŭs, -ĕrĭs (n.), *a burden, load*
ŏpĕrŏr, -ārī, -ātŭs sŭm, *to work, be busy*
ŏportĕt, *it is needful, ought*
oppĕrĭŏr, -īrī, oppertŭs sŭm, *to await*
oppugnō, -ărĕ, -ăvī, -ātŭm, *to besiege*
optăbĭlĭs, -ĕ, *desirable*
optĭmŭs, -ă, -ŭm, *best*
ŏpŭs, -ĕrĭs (n.), *a work*; ŏpĕră (pl. n.), *military works*; ŏpŭs est, *there is need*
ōrăcŭlŭm, -ī (n.), *an oracle*
ōrātŏr, -ōrĭs (m.), *an orator*
orbĭs, - (m.), *a circle*; orbĭs terrārŭm, *the world*
orbō, -ărĕ, -ăvī, -ātŭm, *to deprive*
ordĭŏr, -īrī, orsŭs sŭm, *to begin*
ōrĭens, -tĭs (m.), *the east*
ōrĭŏr, -īrī, ortŭs sŭm, *to rise, arise*
ornō, -ărĕ, -ăvī, -ātŭm, *to adorn*
ōrō, -ărĕ, -ăvī, -ātŭm, *to pray*
ōs, ōrĭs (n.), *the mouth*
ŏs, ossĭs (n.), *a bone*
ŏvĭs, - (f.), *a sheep*
ŏvŭm, -ī (n.), *an egg*

P.

păciscŏr, -ī, pactŭs sŭm, *to strike a bargain*
paenĭtĕt, *it causes sorrow*; paenĭtŭĭt, paenĭtĕrĕ. Written also: poenĭtĕt
Pălătīnŭs, -ă, -ŭm, *Palatine*
pandō, -ĕrĕ, pandī, passŭm, *to spread*
pangō, -ĕrĕ, panxī, panctŭm, *to strike, drive*
pangō, -ĕrĕ, pĕpĭgī, pactŭm, *to bargain*
păr, părĭs, *equal; a match for*
părātŭs, -ă, -ŭm, *ready*

parcō, -ĕrĕ, pĕpercī, parsŭm, to spare
pārens, -tīs (m. & f.), a parent
pārĕō, -ērĕ, -ŭī, -ītŭm, to obey
părĭō, -ĕrĕ, pĕpĕrī, partŭm, to bring forth; ova parĕre, to lay eggs
pārĭtĕr, together
părō, -ārĕ, -āvī, -ātŭm, to prepare for, get
parrĭcĭdĭŭm, -ī (n.), parricide
pars, -tĭs (f.), a part
parsĭmōnĭā, -ae (f.), frugality
partĭceps, -ĭpĭs, sharing, partaker of
pārŭm, not very
parvŭs, -ă, -ŭm, little, small
pascō, -ĕrĕ, pāvī, pastŭm, to graze, feed
pascŏr, -ī, pastŭs sŭm, to feed
passŭs, -ūs (m.), a pace; mīllĕ passŭŭm, a mile
pastŏr, -ōrĭs (m.), a shepherd
pătĕfăcĭō, -ĕrĕ, pătĕfēcī, pătĕfactŭm, to open
pătĕr, -rĭs (m.), a father
pătĕrfămĭlĭās, pătrĭsfămĭlĭās (m.), the father of a family
patĭentĕr, patiently
patĭentĭā, -ae (f.), patience
pătĭŏr, -ī, passŭs sŭm, to suffer
pătrĭā, -ae (f.), one's country, one's native land, home
pătrōnŭs, -ī (m.), a protector
paucī, -ae, -ă, few, a few; paucă, -ōrŭm (pl. n.), little
paulō, little
paupĕr, -ĭs, poor
paupertās, -ātĭs (f.), poverty
păvĕō, -ērĕ, pāvī, (no sup.), to quake for fear
păvō, -ōnĭs (m.), a pea-cock
pāx, -cĭs (f.), peace
pectō, -ĕrĕ, pexī, pexŭm, to comb
pĕcūnĭā, -ae (f.), money
pĕdĕs, -ĭtĭs (m.), a foot-soldier
pellĭs, - (f.), a skin
pellō, -ĕrĕ, pĕpŭlī, pulsŭm, to drive away
pendō, -ĕrĕ, pĕpendī, pensŭm, to hang [weigh
pendŏ, -ĕrĕ, pĕpendī, pensŭm, to
pĕnĕs (w. acc.), in the power of, in the hands of
pĕr (w. acc.), through, for, by, during
Perdiccās, -ae (m.), Perdiccas
perdō, -ĕrĕ, perdĭdī, perdĭtŭm, to lose, ruin
pĕrĕgrīnŭs, -ī (m.), a stranger
perfrŭŏr, -ī, perfructŭs sŭm, to enjoy fully
perfungŏr, -ī, perfunctŭs sŭm, to fulfil
Pergămŭm, -ī (n.), Pergamum
Pĕrĭclēs, -ĭs (m.), Pericles
pĕrĭcŭlŭm, -ī (n.), danger
pĕrītŭs, -ă, -ŭm, skilful; pĕrītĭŏr, a better judge
perpĕtŭō, constantly
perpĕtŭŭs, -ă, -ŭm, constant
Persă, -ae (m.), a Persian
pervĕnĭō, -īrĕ, pervēnī, perventŭm, to reach
pēs, pĕdĭs (m.), a foot
pessĭmŭs, -ă, -ŭm, worst
pĕtō, -ĕrĕ, pĕtīvī, pĕtītŭm, to seek, ask; pācĕm pĕtĕre, to sue for peace
Phĭlippŭs, -ī (m.), Philip, king of Macedonia
Phoenīx, -īcĭs (m.), a Phenician
pictŏr, -ōrĭs (m.), a painter
pĭgĕt, it grieves, it disgusts; pĭgērĕ, pĭgŭĭt or pĭgĭtŭm est
pigrĭtĭā, -ae (f.), laziness
pĭlā, -ae (f.), a ball (for playing)
pĭlŭs, -ī (m.), a hair
pingō, -ĕrĕ, pinxī, pictŭm, to paint
pinsō, -ĕrĕ, pinsŭī & pinsī, pinsĭtŭm, to pound, grind
pĭrŭm, -ī (n.), a pear
piscĭs, - (m.), a fish
plānē, perfectly
plangō, -ĕrĕ, planxī, planctŭm, to beat, lament
plantă, -ae (f.), a plant
plătĕă, (f.), a street
Plātō, -ōnĭs (m.), Plato, a famous Greek philosopher
plaudō, -ĕrĕ, plausī, plausŭm, to applaud
plēbēs, -ĕī) (f.), the common people, plēbs, -ĭs) populace

plectŏ, -ĕrĕ, (no perf. & sup.) to beat
plēnŭs, -ă, -ŭm, full
plērīquĕ, plēraequĕ, plērăquĕ, very many, most
plērumquĕ, commonly
plūmă, -ae (f.), a feather
plŭŏ, -ĕrĕ, plŭī, (no sup.), to rain
plūrīmŭs, -ă, -ŭm, most; plūrīmō (prĕtĭŏ), at a very high price
plūs, plūrĭs, more; plūrēs, -ă or -ĭă (pl.), many, several, (opposed to ūnŭs); plūrĭs, dearer
plŭvĭă, -ae (f.), rain
pŏĕtă, -ae (m.), a poet
pōmă, -ōrŭm (pl. n.), fruit
Pompējŭs, -ī (m.), Pompey
pondō (n. indecl.), in weight, pounds
pōnĕ (w. acc.), behind [place
pōnŏ, -ĕrĕ, pŏsŭī, pŏsĭtŭm. to
Pontĭcŭs, -ă, -ŭm, Pontic
pŏpŭlŭs, -ī (m.), a people, nation
portă, -ae (f.), a gate
portŏ, -ārĕ,-āvī, -ātŭm, to carry
poscŏ, -ĕrĕ, pŏposcī, (no sup.), to demand, to ask
possŭm, possĕ, pŏtŭī, to be able, can
post (w. acc.), behind, after
postquăm, after
postrēmŭs, -ă, -ŭm, last
postŭlŏ, -ārĕ, -āvī, -ātŭm, to require
pŏtĭŏr, -īrī, -ītŭs sŭm, to make one's self master of
pōtŏ, -ārĕ, pōtāvī, pōtŭm, to drink; pōtŭs, -ă, -ŭm, that has drunk
prae (w. abl.), before, for, in comparison with
praebĕŏ, -ērĕ, -ŭī, -ĭtŭm, to afford, give; sē praebērĕ, to show one's self
praeceptŭm, -ī (n.), a precept
praecĭpŭĕ, principally, especially
praefĕrŏ,-rĕ,praetŭlī,praelātŭm, to carry before
praestŏ,-ārĕ, praestĭtī, (no sup.), to afford; sē praestārĕ, to show one's self
praetĕr (w. acc.), past
praetĕrĕŏ, -īrĕ, praetĕrĭī, praetĕrĭtŭm, to pass by

prandĕŏ, -ērĕ, prandī, pransŭm, to breakfast; pransŭs, -ă, -ŭm, having breakfasted
prātŭm, -ī (n.), a meadow
prāvŭs, -ă, -ŭm, wicked
prĕcēs, -ŭm (pl. f.), prayers
prĕhendŏ, -ĕrĕ, prĕhendī, prĕhensŭm, to seize
prĕmŏ, -ĕrĕ, pressī, pressŭm, to press; vestĭgĭă prĕmĕrĕ, to walk in the footsteps
prĕtĭŭm, -ī (n.), a price
prīmŭs, -ă, -ŭm, the first
princĭpĭŭm, -ī (n.), beginning
prīvŏ, -ārĕ, -āvī, -ātŭm, to deprive
prō (w. abl.), for
prŏboscĭs, -ĭdĭs (f.), the trunk of an elephant
prŏbŭs, -ă, -ŭm, upright, virtuous
prōdĭtĭŏ, -ōnĭs (f.), treason
proelĭŏr, -ārī, -ātŭs sŭm, to fight
prŏfānŭs, -ă, -ŭm, profane
prŏfīciscŏr, -ī, prŏfectŭs sŭm,, to set out
prŏfŭgĭŏ, -ĕrĕ, prŏfŭgī, (no sup.), to flee
prŏfundŏ, -ĕrĕ, prŏfūdī, prŏfūsŭm, to give up
prŏindĕ ăc sī or quăsī, as if
prōmŏ, -ĕrĕ, prompsī, promptŭm, to take out
prŏpĕ (w. acc.), near
proprĭŭs, -ă, -ŭm, own, characteristic; proprĭŭm est, it is the mark
proptĕr (w. acc.), on account of, in consequence of; close by
prōsŭm, prōdessĕ, prōfŭī, to be useful, to do good, to benefit
prōvĭdentĭă, -ae (f.), providence
prōvincĭă, -ae (f.), province
proxĭmŭs, -ă, -ŭm, nearest, next; proxĭmŭs bŏnĭs, next best
prūdens, -tĭs, prudent
pūblĭcŭs, -ă, -ŭm, public
pŭdĕt, it shames; pŭdērĕ, pŭdŭĭt or pŭdĭtŭm est
pŭellă, -ae (f.), a girl
pŭĕr, -ī (m.), a boy [fight
pugnŏ, -ārĕ, -āvī, -ātŭm, to

pulchĕr, -ră, -rŭm, *beautiful, handsome*
pūmex, -ĭcĭs (m.), *a pumice-stone*
pungō, -ĕrĕ, pŭpŭgī, punctŭm, *to pierce, sting*
pūnĭō, -īrē -īvī, -ītŭm, *to punish*
pūrŭs, -ă, -ŭm, *pure*
pŭtō, -ārĕ, -āvī, -ātŭm, *to think, believe, consider*
Pȳthăgŏrās, -ae (m.), *Pythagoras, a celebrated philosopher*

Q.

quădrăgēsĭmŭs, -ă, -ŭm, *the fortieth*
quădrăgintă, *forty*
quădrŭpēs, -ĕdĭs (m.), *a four-footed animal, quadruped*
quaerō, -ĕrĕ, quaesīvī, quaesītŭm, *to ask, to seek (after, for), desire;* quaerĭtŭr, *the question is*
quaestĭō, -ōnĭs (f.), *a question*
quăm, *how, than*
quăm dĭū, *how long?*
quamquăm, *although*
quamvīs, *although, however (much)*
quantŭm, *how much? as much as*
quantumvīs, *however much*
quantŭs, -ă, -ŭm, *how great?*
quartŭs, -ă, -ŭm, *the fourth*
quăsī, *as, as if*
quătĭō, -ĕrĕ, (no perf. & sup.), *to shake*
quattŭŏr, *four*
-quĕ (to be appended to the word), *and*
quĕrŏr, -ī, questŭs sŭm, *to complain*
quī, quae, quŏd, *who, which, that;* quī, *he who*
quĭă, *because*
quīdăm, quaedăm, quiddăm, quoddăm, *some one, a certain one, a kind of*
quīdĕm, *indeed*
quĭescō, -ĕrĕ, quĭēvī, quĭētŭm, *to rest, repose*
quīlĭbĕt, quaelĭbĕt, quidlĭbĕt, quodlĭbĕt, *any one, every one, any thing you please*
quīn, *that not, but that, but that not*
quīnquāgēsĭmŭs, -ă, -ŭm, *the fiftieth*

quinquĕ, *five*
quĭs, quĭd, *who, what?*
quisquĕ, quaequĕ, quidquĕ, quodquĕ, *each one, every one, any one*
quō (w. compar.), *the;* quō..ĕō, *the..the*
quō, *that, in order that, so that*
quŏd, *because, that*
quōmĭnŭs, *that not*
quŏquĕ, *also, too*
quŏt, *how many?*
quŏtannĭs, *every year*

R.

rădĭŭs, -ī (m.), *a ray*
rādō, -ĕrĕ, rāsī, rāsŭm, *to scrape*
răpĭō, -ĕrĕ, răpŭī, raptŭm, *to snatch away*
rārō, *seldom*
rārŭs, -ă, -ŭm, *rare*
Rĕă Silvĭă (-ae, -ae) f., *Rea Silvia*
rĕcordŏr, -ārī, -ātŭs sŭm, *to remember*
rĕcrĕātĭō, -ōnĭs (f.), *recreation*
rectŏr, -ōrĭs (m.), *a master, ruler*
reddō, -ĕrĕ, reddĭdī, reddĭtŭm, *to restore, to make*
rĕdĕō, -īrĕ, rĕdĭī, rĕdĭtŭm, *to return*
rĕdĭmō, -ĕrĕ, rĕdēmī, rĕdemptŭm, *to buy, redeem*
rĕdundō, -ārĕ, -āvī, -ātŭm, *to abound*
rĕfert, *it concerns, matters*
rēgīnă, -ae (f.), *a queen*
regnō, -ārĕ, -āvī, -ātŭm, *to reign*
regnŭm, -ī (n.), *a kingdom*
rĕgō, -ĕrĕ, rexī, rectŭm, *to rule, govern*
rĕlĭgĭō, -ōnĭs (f.), *an oath*
rĕlinquō, -ĕrĕ, rĕlīquī, rĕlictŭm, *to quit, leave (behind)*
rĕmĕdĭŭm, -ī (n.), *a remedy* [ber
rĕmĭniscŏr, -ī, (no perf.), *to remem-*
Rĕmŭs, -ī (m.), *Remus, the brother of Romulus*
rĕŏr, -ērī, rătŭs sŭm, *to think*
rĕpĕrĭō, -īrĕ, reppĕrī, rĕpertŭm, *to find*
rēpō, -ĕrĕ, repsī, reptŭm, *to creep, crawl*

rĕprĕhendō, -ĕrĕ, rĕprĕhendī, rĕprĕhensŭm, *to find fault with*
rĕquĭescō, -ĕrĕ, rĕquĭēvī, rĕquĭētŭm, *to rest, repose*
rēs, rĕī (f.), *a thing, matter;* rēs pūblĭcă, *the commonwealth, state, republic;* res vera, *reality;* res famĭlĭāris, *property;* res mĭlĭtāris, *military affairs*
rētĕ, -ĭs (n.), *a net*
rĕŭs, -ī (m.), *the defendant;* rĕŭm făcĕrĕ, *to summon*
rĕvertŏr, -ī, rĕvertī (active), *to turn back*
rĕvīvisco, -ĕrĕ, rĕvixī, rĕvictŭm, *to come to life again*
rĕvŏcō, -ārĕ, -āvī, -ātŭm, *to recall*
rex, rēgĭs (m.), *a king*
Rhēnŭs, -ī (m.), *the Rhine*
rīdĕō, -ĕrĕ, rīsī, rīsŭm, *to laugh*
rīpă, -ae (f.), *the bank (of a stream)*
rōdō, -ĕrĕ, rōsī, rōsŭm, *o gnaw, slander*
rŏgō, -ārĕ, -āvī, -ātŭm, *to ask, beg*
Rōmă, -ae (f.), *Rome*
Rōmānŭs, -ă, -ŭm, *Roman*
Rōmŭlŭs, -ī (m.), *Romulus*
Roscĭŭs, -ī (m.), *Roscius*
rostrŭm, -ī (n.), *a beak;* pl. rostră, -ōrŭm (pl. n.), *a speaker's platform*
rŏtundŭs, -ă, -ŭm, *round*
rumpō, -ĕrĕ, rūpī, ruptŭm, *to break*
rŭō, -ĕrĕ, rŭī, rŭtŭm, *to rush (forth)*
rūs, rūrĭs (n.), *the country, a farm, a field;* rūrī, *in the country;* rūrĕ, *from the country;* rūs, *into the country*
rustĭcŭs, -ă, -ŭm, *country-*

S.

săcĕr, -ră, -rŭm, *sacred, holy*
saecŭlŭm, -ī (n.), *a generation*
saepĕ, *often, frequently;* saepĭŭs, *oftener;* saepissĭmē, *oftenest*
saepĭō, -īrĕ, saepsī, saeptŭm, *to fence in, inclose* [*tum*
Săguntŭm, -ī (n.), *the city of Sagun-*
sāl, sălĭs (m.), *salt;* pl. sălēs, -ĭŭm, *witty sayings*
Sălămĭs, -ĭnĭs (f.), *the island of Salamis* (acc. Sălămīnă)
sălĭō, -īrĕ, salŭī, saltŭm, *to leap*
sălūbĕr, -rĭs, -rĕ, *salubrious*
sălūtārĭs, -ĕ, *beneficial*
salvĕ, *hail*
sancĭō, -īrĕ, sanxī, sanctŭm & sancītŭm, *to sanction*
sanguĭs, -ĭnĭs (m.), *blood*
sānō, -ārĕ, -āvī, -ātŭm, *to heal*
săpĭens, -tĭs, *wise;* (m.), *a wise man*
săpĭentĕr, *wisely*
săpĭentĭă, -ae (f.), *wisdom*
săpĭō, -ĕrĕ, săpīvī & săpŭī, (no sup.), *to be wise*
sarcĭō, -īrĕ, sarsī, sartŭm, *to mend*
sătĭō, -ārĕ, -āvī, -ātŭm, *to satiate*
sătĭs, *enough*
Sāturnŭs, -ī (m.), *Saturn;* Sāturnī stellă, *the planet Saturn*
scăbō, -ĕrĕ, -ī, (no sup.), *to scratch*
scalpō, -ĕrĕ, scalpsī, scalptŭm, *to carve*
scandō, -ĕrĕ, scandī, scansŭm, *to climb*
scĕlŭs, -ĕrĭs (n.), *a crime*
schŏlă, -ae (f.), *a school*
scĭentĭă, -ae (f.), *a science, knowledge*
scindō, -ĕrĕ, scĭdī, scissŭm, *to cut*
scĭō, -īrĕ, -īvī, -ītŭm, *to know*
Scĭpĭō, -ōnĭs (m.), *Scipio, a Roman noble name* [*write*
scrībō, -ĕrĕ, scripsī, scriptŭm, *to*
scriptŏr, -ōrĭs (m.), *a writer*
sculpō, -ĕrĕ, sculpsī, sculptŭm, *to chisel*
sĕcō, -ārĕ, sĕcŭī, sectŭm, *to cut*
sĕcundŭm (w. acc.), *according to*
sĕcundŭs, -ă, -ŭm, *the second*
sĕd, *but*
sēdĕcĭm, *sixteen*
sĕdĕō, -ĕrĕ, sēdī, sessŭm, *to sit*
sĕgĕs, -ĕtĭs (f.), *a crop*
sĕgnĭtĭă, -ae } (f.), *slothfulness*
sĕgnĭtĭēs, -ēī }
sējungō, -ĕrĕ, sējunxī, sējunctŭm, *to separate*

sĕmĕl, *once*
sempĕr, *always, ever*
sĕnātŭs, -ūs (m.), *the senate*
sĕnectūs, -ūtĭs (f.), *old age*
sĕnescō, -ĕrĕ, sĕnŭī, (no sup.), *to grow old*
sĕnex, -ĭs (m.), *an old man*
sententĭă,-ae (f.), *a sentence; opinion, sentiment;* omnĭum jūdĭcŭm sententĭā, *the unanimous decision of the judges*
sentĭō, -īrĕ, sensī, sensŭm, *to perceive, feel*
sĕpĕlĭō, -īrĕ, sĕpĕlīvī, sĕpultŭm, *to bury*
septĕm, *seven*
septentrĭō, -ōnĭs (m.), *the north*
septingentēsĭmŭs, -ă, -ŭm, *the seven hundredth*
sĕpulchrŭm, -ī }
sĕpulcrŭm, -ī } (n.), *a grave*
sĕpultūră, -ae (f.), *a burial*
sĕquŏr, -ī, sĕcūtŭs sŭm, *to follow*
sērĭŭs, *later*
sērĭŭs, -ă, -ŭm, *serious*
sermō, -ōnĭs (m.), *a talk*
sĕrō, -ĕrĕ, sĕrŭī, sertŭm, *to join*
sĕrō, -ĕrĕ, sēvī, sătŭm, *to sow, plant*
serpō, -ĕrĕ, serpsī, serptŭm, *to creep (of animals)*
sērŭs, -ă, -ŭm, *too late*
servĭtŭs,-ūtĭs (f.), *slavery, servitude*
servŭs, -ī (m.), *a slave, servant*
sex, *siz;* sexdĕcim, *sixteen*
sī, *if, when*
sīc, *in this manner, so*
Sĭcĭlĭă, -ae (f.), *Sicily*
sīcŭt, *like*
sīdō, -ĕrĕ, sēdī, (no sup.), *to sit down*
silvă, -ae, (f.), *a wood, forest*
sĭmĭlĭs, -ĕ, *like, similar*
sĭmŭl, *together, at the same time*
sĭmŭlăc, sĭmŭlatquĕ, *as soon as*
sĭnĕ (w. abl.), *without*
sĭnō, -ĕrĕ. sīvī. sĭtŭm, *to let, suffer, permit*
sĭstō, -ĕrĕ, stĭtī, stătŭm, *to stop*
sĭtĭens, -tĭs, *thirsty*
sŏcĭĕtās, -ātĭs (f.), *society*
Sōcrătēs, -ĭs (m.), *Socrates*

sōl, -ĭs (m.), *the sun*
sōlātĭŭm, -ī (n.), *a consolation*
sŏlĕō,-ēre, sŏlĭtŭs sŭm, *to be wont, accustomed, to use*
sollĭcĭtō, -ārĕ, -āvī, -ātŭm, *to disturb*
sōlŭs, -ă, -ŭm, *alone*
solvō, -ĕrĕ, solvī, sŏlūtŭm. *to (dis)solve, free*
somnŭs, -ī (m.), *sleep*
sŏnō, -ārĕ, sŏnŭī. sŏnĭtŭm, *to sound*
sŏrŏr, -ōrĭs (f.), *a sister*
sors, -tĭs (f.), *a lot*
spargō, -ĕrĕ, sparsī, sparsŭm, *to cast, sprinkle*
Spartānŭs, -ī (m.), *a Spartan*
spĕcĭēs, -ēī (f.), *appearance*
spectō, -ārĕ, -āvī, -ātŭm, *to view, to look to, at*
spernō, -ĕrĕ, sprēvī, sprētŭm, *to despise*
spērō, -ārĕ, -āvī, -ātŭm, *to hope for*
spēs, spĕī (f.), *hope* [strip
spŏlĭō, -ārĕ,-āvī, -ātŭm, *to rob,*
spondĕō, -ērĕ, spŏpondī, sponsŭm, *to pledge*
spŭō, -ĕrĕ, spŭī, spūtŭm, *to spit*
squāmă, -ae (f.), *the scale (of a fish)*
stătĭm, *at once*
stătŭō, -ĕrĕ, stătŭī, stătūtŭm, *to set, place*
stellă, -ae (f.), *a star;* Sāturnī stellă, *the planet Saturn*
sternō, -ĕrĕ, strāvī, strātŭm, *to strew*
sternŭō, -ĕrĕ, sternŭī, (no sup.), *to sneeze*
stō,-ārĕ, stĕtī, stătŭm, *to stand, to cost*
strĕpō, -ĕrĕ, strĕpŭī, strĕpĭtŭm, *to make a noise*
stringō, -ĕrĕ, strinxī, strictŭm, *to bind*
strŭō, -ĕrĕ, struxī, structŭm, *to build*
stŭdĕō, -ērĕ, -ŭī, (no sup.), *to devote one's self, to study*
stŭdĭōsŭs, -ă, -ŭm, *devoted to*

stultŭs, -ă, -ŭm, *foolish;* stultŭs, -ī (m.), *a fool*
suādĕō, -ēre, suāsī, suāsŭm, *to advise*
sŭb (w. acc.), *under, toward;* (w. abl.), *under, below*
sŭbĕō, -īre, sŭbĭī, sŭbĭtŭm, *to meet*
subtĕr (w. acc.), *under, beneath*
suescō, -ĕre, suēvī, suētŭm, *to become used*
sūgō, -ĕre, suxī, suctŭm, *to suck*
sŭī, sĭbĭ, sĕ, *himself, herself, itself*
sŭm, essĕ, fŭī, *to be;* plūrĭs essĕ, *to be of more account*
summŭs, -ă, -ŭm, *utmost*
sūmō, -ĕre, sumpsī, sumptŭm, *to take;* mūtŭŭm sūmĕrĕ, *to borrow*
sumptŭs, -ūs (m.), *expense*
sŭō, -ĕre, sŭī, sūtŭm, *to sew*
sŭpĕr (w. acc.), *over, above, on top of;* sŭpĕr (w. abl.), *concerning*
supĕrbŭs, -ă, -ŭm, *proud*
sŭpervăcŭŭs, -ă, -ŭm, *needless*
sŭprā (w. acc.), *above, more than, over*
sŭŭs, -ă, -ŭm, *his, her, its, their (own);* omnĭă sŭă, *all one's property*
Syrācūsae, -ārŭm (pl. f.), *Syracuse*

T.

tăcĕō, -ēre, -ŭī, -ĭtŭm, *to be silent, still*
taedĕt, *it wearies, tires;* pertaesŭm est, taedēre
tăm, *so;* tăm..quăm, *as well..as*
tămĕn, *however, nevertheless*
tămetsī, *although*
tamquăm, *as, as if*
tangō, -ĕre, tĕtĭgī, tactŭm, *to touch*
tantŭm, *only, but* (to be placed after the word to which it belongs)
tantŭs, -ă, -ŭm, *so great*
Tarquĭnĭŭs, -ī (m.), *Tarquin, king of the Romans;* Tarquĭnĭī, -ōrŭm, (pl. m.), *the Tarquinians*
taurŭs, -ī (m.), *a bull*
tĕgō, -ĕre, texī, tectŭm, *to cover*
tēlŭm, -ī (n.), *a weapon*
tempŭs, -ŏrĭs (n.), *time;* tempŭs annī, *a season;* tempŭs nocturnŭm, *night-time;* brevi tempŏre, *in a short time*
tendō, -ĕre, tĕtendī, tensŭm, *to spread*
tĕnĕbrae, -ārŭm (pl. f.), *darkness*
tĕnĕō, -ēre, tĕnŭī, tentŭm, *to hold*
tĕnŭĭs, -ĕ, *thin*
tĕnŭs (w. abl.), *as far as, up to*
tergĕō & tergō, -ēre & ĕre, tersī, tersŭm, *to wipe*
tĕrō, -ĕre, trīvī, trītŭm, *to rub, wear out*
terră, -ae (f.), *the earth, land*
terrestrĭs, -ĕ, *land-*
tertĭŭs, -ă, -ŭm, *the third*
testĭs, - (m. & f.), *a witness*
testŏr, -ārī, -ātŭs sŭm, *to testify*
testūdō, -ĭnĭs (f.), *a tortoise*
Teutŏnī, -ōrŭm (m. pl.), *the Teutons*
texō, -ĕre, texŭī, textŭm, *to weave*
Thĕmistoclēs, -ĭs (m.), *Themistocles*
Tĭbĕrĭs, - (m.), *the Tiber*
Tĭbĕrĭŭs, -ī (m.), *Tiberius, a Roman name*
tĭmĕō, -ēre, -ŭī, (no sup.), *to fear*
tingō, -ĕre, tinxī, tinctŭm, *to stain*
tollō, -ĕre, sustŭlī, sublātŭm, *to take up, to take away*
tondĕō, -ēre, tŏtondī, tonsŭm, *to shear*
tŏnō, -āre, tŏnŭī, tŏnĭtŭm, *to thunder*
torquĕō, -ēre, torsī, tortŭm, *to torture*
torrĕō, -ēre, torrŭī, tostŭm, *to roast*
tōtŭs, -ă. -ŭm, *whole, all*
trādō, -ĕre, trādĭdī, trādĭtŭm, *to deliver;* trādĭtŭm est, *it is handed down, there is a tradition*
trăhō, -ĕre, traxī, tractŭm, *to draw*
Trājānŭs, -ī (m.), *Trajan, a Roman emperor*
tranquillŭs, -ă, -ŭm, *calm, tranquil*
trans (w. acc.), *across*
transĕō, -īre, transĭī, transĭtŭm, *to cross*
transĭtŭs, -ūs (m), *a passage*

trēcentī, -ā, -ae, *three hundred*
trĕmō, -ĕrĕ, trĕmŭī, (no sup.), *to tremble*
trēs, trĭă, *three;* trĭă, *three things*
trĭbŭō, -ĕrĕ, trĭbŭī, trĭbūtŭm, *to give, confer on*
trīgintā, *thirty*
tristĭs, -ĕ, *sad*
trĭumphŭs, -ī (m.), *a triumph*
trŏchŭs, -ī (m.), *a hoop*
Trōjă, -ae (f.), *the city of Troy*
trūdō,-ĕrĕ, trūsī, trūsŭm, *to thrust*
tū, *thou, you*
tundō, -ĕrĕ, tŭtŭdī, tŭsŭm, *to thump*
turbĭdŭs, -ă, -ŭm, *muddy*
turgĕō,-ēre, tursī, (no sup.), *to swell*
turpĭs, -ĕ, *disgraceful*
tŭŭs, -ă, -ŭm, *thy, your*
typŏgrăphĭcŭs, -ă, -ŭm, *of printing;* ars typŏgrăphĭcă, *the art of printing*
tўrannŭs, -ī (m.), *a tyrant*

U.

ŭbī, *where;* ŭbī, ŭbī prīmŭm, *as soon as*
ŭbĭquĕ, *everywhere*
ulciscŏr, -ī, ultŭs sŭm, *to avenge*
ultĭmŭs, -ă, -ŭm, *last, furthest*
ultrā (w. accus.), *beyond*
umbră, -ae (f.), *a shade, shadow*
ungŭlă, -ae (f.), *a claw, hoof*
ūnŭs, -ă, -ŭm, *one; only*
urbs, -ĭs (f.), *a city*
urgĕō, -ērĕ, ursī, (no sup.), *to urge*
ūrō, -ĕrĕ, ussī, ustŭm, *to burn*
ūsŭs, -ūs (m.), *use*
ŭt, *as;* ŭt (w. subj.), *in order that, so that; suppose, granted that;* ŭt nōn, *so that not;* ŭt prīmŭm, *as soon as*
ūtĭlĭs, -ĕ, *useful*
ūtĭlĭtās, -ātĭs (f.), *service*
ūtŏr, -ī, ūsŭs sŭm, *to use;* pellĭbŭs ūtī, *to wear skins*
ūtrŭm, *whether;* ŭtrŭm..ăn, *whether..or*
ūvă, -ae (f.), *a grape*

V.

vādō, -ĕrĕ, (no perf. & sup.), *to go*
vălĕō, -ērĕ, -ŭī, -ĭtŭm, *to be well*
vălētūdō, -ĭnĭs (f.), *health*

vāpŭlō, -ārĕ, -āvī, -ātŭm, *to be flogged*
vărĭĕtās, -ātĭs (f.), *variety*
vărĭŭs, -ă, -ŭm, *various, different*
vastō, -ārĕ, -āvī, -ātŭm, *to demolish*
vectīgal, -ālĭs (n.), *income*
vĕhĕmentĕr, *very loudly*
vĕhō, -ĕrĕ, vexī, vectŭm, *to carry*
Vĕiī, -ōrŭm (pl. m.), *Veii*
vĕl, *or, even*
vellō, -ĕrĕ, vellī (vulsī), vulsŭm, *to pluck, pull*
vĕlŭt sī, *as if*
vēnātŏr, -ōrĭs (m.), *a hunter*
vendō, vendĭdī, vendĭtŭm, -ĕrĕ, *to sell*
vēnĕō, -īrĕ, vēnīī, vēnĭtŭm, *to be sold* (vēnŭm-ĕō, *I go for sale*)
vĕnĭō, -īrĕ, vēnī, ventŭm, *to come*
ventĕr, -rĭs (m.), *the belly*
ventūrŭs, -ă, -ŭm, *coming*
vēr, vērĭs (n.), *spring*
verbĕr, -ĭs (n.), *a blow*
verbŭm, -ī (n.), *a word*
vērĕ, *truly*
vergō, -ĕrĕ, (no perf. & sup.), *to verge*
vērī sĭmĭlĭs, -ĕ, *probable*
vērĭtās, -ātĭs (f.), *truth*
Verrēs, -ĭs (m.), *Verres*
verrō, -ĕrĕ, verrī, versŭm, *to sweep*
versŭs (w. acc. and following its case), *toward, -ward;* ŏrĭentem versŭs, *toward the east*
vertō, -ĕrĕ, vertī, versŭm, *to turn, to interpret;* in fugam vertĕre, *to put to flight*
vērŭm, -ī (n.), *the truth*
vērŭs, -ă, -ŭm, *true, real;* res vera, *reality*
vescŏr, -ī, (no perf.), *to feed, live upon*
Vespăsĭānŭs, -ī (m.), *Vespasian*
vespĕrī, *in the evening, at night*
vestĕr, -ră, -rŭm, *your*
vestēs, -ĭŭm (pl. f.), *clothing*
vestīgĭŭm, -ī (n.), *a footstep*
vĕtō, -ārĕ, vĕtŭī, vĕtĭtŭm, *to forbid; prohibit*
vĕtŭs, -ĕrĭs, *ancient, old*

vĭă, -ae (f.), *a road; street*
victŏr, -ŏrĭs (m.), } *a conqueror*
victrīx, -īcĭs (f.),
victōrĭă, -ae (f.), *a victory*
victŭs, -ūs (m.), *food*
vĭdĕō, -ēre, vīdī, vīsŭm, *to see*
vĭdĕŏr, -ērī, vīsŭs sŭm, *to seem, appear*
vīgintī, *twenty*
villă, -ae (f.), *a country-house*
vincĭō, -īre, vīnxī, vīnctŭm, *to bind*
vincō, -ĕre, vīcī, victŭm, *to conquer, overcome*
vīnŭm, -ī (n.), *wine*
vĭŏlō, -āre, -āvī, -ātŭm, *to break (a law)*
vĭr, -ī (m.), *a man*
virgă, -ae (f), *a switch, a rod*
Virgĭnĭă, -ae (f.), *Virginia*
virtŭs, -ūtĭs (f.), *virtue*
vīs (without genit.) (f.), *force, power, violence;* vīrēs,-ĭŭm (pl. f.), *forces, strength;* magna vis, *a great quantity*
vīsō, -ĕre, vīsī, (no sup.), *to visit*
vītă, -ae (f.), *life*
vĭtĭŭm, -ī (n.), *a vice, fault, defect*

vītō, -āre, -āvī, -ātŭm, *to avoid*
vĭtŭpĕrō, -āre, -āvī, -ātŭm, *to blame*
vīvō, -ĕre, vīxī, victŭm, *to live*
vīvŭs, -ă, -ŭm, *alive*
vix, *hardly*
vŏcō, -āre, -āvī, -ātŭm, *to call, name*
vŏlō, vellĕ, vŏlŭī, (no sup.), *to be willing, wish, want*
vŏluptās, -ātĭs (f.), *pleasure*
volvō, -ĕre, volvī, volūtŭm, *to roll, turn*
vŏmō, -ĕre, vŏmŭī, vŏmĭtŭm, *to vomit*
vŏvĕō, -ēre, vŏvī, vōtŭm, *to vow*
vox, vōcĭs (f.), *language*
vulnŭs, -ĕrĭs (n.), *a wound*
vulpēs, -ĭs (f.), *a fox*

X.

Xerxēs, -ĭs (m.), *Xerxes, king of Persia*

Z.

Zămă, -ae (f.), *Zama*
Zeuxĭs, - (m.), *Zeuxis, a famous Grecian painter*

2. ENGLISH AND LATIN.

NOTE. For the principal parts of verbs and the inflection of nouns and pronouns, see the Latin and English Vocabulary.

A.

to be able, posse, quire; *not to be able*, nequire
to abolish, abolere
to abound, abundare, affluere; redundare
about, circiter, circa, fere
above (prep.), super, supra
abstinence, abstinentia
abundance, copia
abuse, abusus
to abuse, abuti
acceptable, acceptus
to accompany, comitari
to accomplish, facessere
according to, secundum
on account of, ob, propter; *to be of more account*, pluris esse
to accuse, accusare, arguere, incusare, insimulare
to accustom one's self, assuescere; *to be accustomed*, solere, assuescere, consuescere
to acquire, acquirere
to acquit, absolvere
across, trans
admiration, admiratio
to adorn, ornare, comere
adversity, res adversae
to advise, monere, suadere
Aeneas, Aeneas
an affair, res
affection, caritas
to afford, praebere, praestare
Africa, Africa
after, post; postquam
again, iterum
against, adversus, adversum, contra
an age, aetas
Agesilaus, Agesilaus

ago, abhinc
to agree, congruere
agreeable, jucundus
it is agreed, constat
aid, auxilium
the air, aër
Alexander, Alexander
Alexandria, Alexandria
alive, vivus
all, totus, omnis; *all one's property*, omnia sua; *all things*, omnia
it is allowed, licet
almost, fere
alone, solus
already, jam
also, etiam, quoque
although, etiamsi, etsi, tametsi, quamquam, quamvis
always, semper
an ambassador, legatus
America, America
among, inter, apud
Anaxagoras, Anaxagoras
the ancestors, majores
ancient, vetus, antiquus
and, et, ac, -que (appended); *and not*, nec, neque
an animal, animal
to anoint, unguere
another, alius
an ant, formica
Anthony, Antonius
Antioch, Antiochia
any one, any one you please, quivis, quilibet; *any thing you please*, quidlibet, quodlibet, quidvis, quodvis
Apelles, Apelles
to appear, videri
appearance, species
to applaud, plaudere
to apply, applicare
to appoint, designare
to approach, appropinquare
apt, aptus

Archias, Archias
Arganthonius, Arganthonius
Argus, Argus
Arion, Arion
to arise, oriri
Aristides, Aristides
an army, exercitus
around, circum
to arouse, ciere
an art, ars; *the art of printing*, ars typographica
as, ut; *as if*, quasi, velut si, tamquam, proinde ac si; *as far as*, tenus; *as long as*, dum, donec; *as soon as*, ubi, ubi primum, ut primum, simulac, simulatque; *as well as*, tam...quam
to be ashamed, pudere
ashes, cinis
Asia, Asia
to ask, rogare, interrogare, quaerere, poscere, flagitare, petere
to fall asleep, obdormiscere
to assent, assentiri
to assist, juvare, adjuvare
assistance, auxilium
to assuage, mollire
an Athenian, Atheniensis
Athens, Athenae
Atlantic, Atlanticus
to atone for, luere
Attalus, Attalus
attentive, attentus
Atticus, Atticus
to attract, attrahere
Attus Navius, Attus Navius
an augur, augur
Augustus, Augustus
an author, auctor
autumn, autumnus
avarice, avaritia
to avenge, ulcisci
to avoid, vitare
to await, opperiri
to awake, expergisci
away from, a, ab, abs

B.

Babylon, Babylon
bad, improbus
baggage, impedimenta
to bake, coquere
baldness, calvitium
a ball (for playing), pila
the bank (of a stream), ripa
to strike a bargain, pacisci
to bark, latrare
a battle, the (line of) battle, acies
to be, esse; *to be in*, inesse
a beak, rostrum
to bear, ferre
a beast, bestia
to beat, plangere, plectere
beautiful, pulcher
a beaver, castor
because, quod, quia
to become, fieri, evadere
it becomes, decet
a bee, apis
before, ante, prae
to beg, rogare
to beget, gignere
to begin, ordiri; *to have begun*, coepisse
a beginning, initium
behind (prep.), pone, post
to believe, credere, existimare, putare
the belly, venter
below, sub, infra
to bend, flectere
beneath, subter
beneficial, salutaris
a benefit, beneficium
to benefit, prodesse
beside, juxta
to besiege, obsidere, oppugnare
best (adj.), optimus
beyond, ultra
Bias, Bias
to bid, licere
big, magnus
to bind, stringere, vincire
a bird, avis
after the birth of Christ, post Christum natum
by birth, natu
a birthday, (dies) natalis
a bit, frena, freni; frustum
to bite, mordere
bitterness, amaritudo
to blame, vituperare
blessed, beatus

a blessing, bonum
blind, caecus
blood, sanguis
a blossom, flos; *in blossom*, florens
a blow, verber
a body, corpus
a bone, os
a book, liber
born, natus; *to be born*, nasci
to borrow, mutuum sumere
both..and, et..et
a boy, puer
brave, fortis
to break, frangere, rumpere; *to break the laws*, leges violāre
to breakfast, prandere; *having breakfasted*, pransus
a bridle, frenum, frena (pl.)
to bring, ducere; *to bring forth*, parere; gignere; *to bring up*, educare; *to bring word*, nuntiare
a Briton, Britannus
broad, latus
a brother, frater
to build, aedificare, struere, condere
a building, aedificium
a bull, taurus
a burden, onus
a burial, sepultura
to burn, ardere, urere
to bury, sepelire
to be busy, operari
but, sed, autem; tantum; *but..that, but that not*, quin
to buy, emere, redimere, mercari
by, a, ab

C.

cabbage, brassica
Cadiz, Gades
Caesar, Caesar
California, California
to call, appellare, vocare, nominare, dicere
calm, tranquillus
a camp, castra (pl.)
can, possum
capable, compos
captive, captus
care, cura

careless, neglegens
to carry, ferre, portare, gestare, vehere; *to carry on*, gerere; *to carry away*, auferre
a cart, currus
Carthage, Carthago
Carthaginian, Carthaginiensis
to carve, scalpere
to cast, jacere
a cat, felis
to catch, capere
a cause, causa
it causes sorrow, paenitet or poenitet
cautious, cautus
to cease, cessare
certain, certus; *certainly*, certe; *a certain one*, quidam
a chain, catena
to charge, accusare, arguere, insimulare
to cheat, fallere
a cheese, caseus
to cherish, fovere
a cherry, cerasum
to chew, mandere
children, liberi
to chisel, sculpere
to choose, eligere
Christ, Christus; *before Christ*, ante Christum natum
Cicero Cicero
the Cimbrians, Cimbri
Cincinnatus, Cincinnatus
a circle, orbis
a citizen, civis
a city, urbs
to clang, clangere
to clank, crepare
a claw, ungula
clear, clarus, dilucidus
to cleave, findere
to climb up, scandere
to close, claudere
to clothe, amicire
clothing, vestes (pl.)
cloudy, nubilus
cold (noun), frigus; *to be cold*, algere, frigere
to collect, colligere, comportare
color, color
to comb, pectere

to come, venire; *to come to life again*, reviviscere; *to come off*, exire; *to come to the throne*, ad imperium accedere
a comet, cometes
to comfort, consolari
common, communis
commonly, plerumque
the commonwealth, res publica
to compare, comparare
in comparison with, prae
to complain, queri
to complete, conficere
to conceal, celare, occulere
concerning, de
it concerns, interest, refert
to condemn, damnare, condemnare; *to condemn to death*, capitis damnare
a condition, condicio
to confer on, tribuere
to confess, fateri, confiteri
to congratulate, gratulari
to conquer, vincere
conscience, conscientia
in consequence of, propter, causa
to consider, habere, putare
a consolation, solatium
constant, perpetuus
constantly, perpetuo
content, contented, contentus
continuous, continuus
to convict, coarguere, convincere
to cook, coquere
Corinth, Corinthus
corn, frumentum
to cost, stare, constare
counsel, consilium
to counsel, consulere
to count, numerare; *to count it a praise*, laudi ducere
the country, rus; *one's (own) country*, patria; *from the country*, rure; *in the country*, ruri; *into the country*, rus; *a country house*, villa
a course, cursus
a court, judicium
to cover, tegere
coward(ly), ignavus
to crawl, repere
to creak, crepare
to create, creare

credit, fides
to creep, repere, serpere
a crime, facinus, scelus
Croesus, Croesus
a crop, seges
to crop, carpere
to cross, transire
crowded, frequens
to cry out aloud, clamitare
a cubit, cubitum
to cultivate, exercere, colere
a cure, curatio
to cure, mederi
to curse, maledicere
a custodian, custos
to cut, secare, scindere
Cyrus, Cyrus

D.

danger, periculum
the Danube, Danubius
to dare, audere
Dareus, Dareus
darkness, tenebrae
to dash, affligere
a daughter, filia
a day, dies; *in day-time*, interdiu
dead, mortuus
dear, carus; *my dearest*, carissime
death, mors
a decision, sententia
to decry, obtrectare
a deed, factum
to deem worthy, dignari
a defect, vitium
to defend, defendere
the defendant, reus
in a high degree, admodum
to deliberate, consultare
deliberation, deliberatio
deliciously, jucunde
delight, deliciae
to deliver, tradere
Delphi, Delphi
delta, delta
to demand, poscere
to demolish, vastare
to deny, negare
to depart, exire
to deprive, orbare, privare

to deserve, merere, mereri
a design, consilium
desirable, optabilis
desire, cupiditas
to desire, cupere, quaerere
desirous, cupidus
to despise, contemnere, spernere
destiny, fatum
to destroy, delere
to determine, constituere
to devise, invenire
to devote one's self, studere; *devoted to*, studiosus
to dictate, dictare
a dictator, dictator
to die, mori
different, varius, diversus
difficult, difficilis
to dig, fodere
diligence, diligentia
diligent, diligens
to dine, cenare; *having dined*, cenatus
dinner, cena, coena
Dionysius, Dionysius
to dip, imbuere; *to dip in*, mergere
disagreeable, injucundus
to disavow, diffiteri
to discern, cernere
to discharge, fungi, defungi
a disease, morbus
a disgrace, ignominia
disgraceful, turpis
it disgusts, piget
to be distant, distare
to disturb, sollicitare
to divide, dividere
divine, divinus
to do, facere; *to do good*, prodesse; *to do harm*, nocere
a dog, canis
domestic, domesticus
a doubt, dubium
to draw, trahere, haurire [potus
to drink, bibere, potare; *that has drunk*,
to drive, impellere, agere, pangere; *to drive away*, pellere, expellere; *to drive into exile*, in exsilium agere
a drone, fucus
to (become) dry, arescere
to be due, deberi

Duilius, Duilius
dumb, mutus
during, per
a duty, officium
to dwell, habitare
to dye, imbuere

E.

each, quisque; *each one*, quisque, unusquisque
eager, cupidus
an eagle, aquila
the ear, auris
the earth, terra, tellus
easily, facile; *more easily*, facilius
the east, oriens
easy, facilis
to eat, edere
to eclipse, obscurare
to educate, educare
an effect, effectus
an egg, ovum
Egypt, Aegyptus
an Egyptian, Aegyptius
eight, octo
the eighteenth, duodevicesimus, octavus decimus
the eightieth, octogesimus
eighty, octoginta
either..or, aut..aut
elder, major natu
an element, elementum
an elephant, elephantus, elephas
eloquent, eloquens
to embrace, amplecti
an empire, imperium
an end, finis
to endure, ferre
an enemy, hostis
to enjoy, frui; *to enjoy fully*, perfrui
enough, sat, satis
to entice, allicere
envy, invidia
to envy, invidere
an epistle, litterae
equal, par; *to be equal*, aequare
especially, praecipue
to estimate (by), aestimare (ex)
an Ethiopian, Aethiops
Europe, Europa

even, par, aequus
even, etiam; *even if*, etiamsi
evening, vesper; *in the evening*, vesperi
every, omnis; *every body*, *every one*, quisque; *every thing*, omnia; *every year*, quotannis
everywhere, ubique
it is evident, constat
an evil, malum
an example, exemplum
to excel, excellere
to excite, lacessere
to exercise, experiri
exile, exsilium
an expense, sumptus
the eye, oculus; *to shut the eyes*, conivere

F.

a fable, fabula
faith, fides
faithful, fidelis
to fall, cadere; *to fall upon*, incessere
a falsehood, mendacium
famous, clarus
far (adv.), multo
to fashion, fingere
a father, pater; *the father of a family*, paterfamilias
a fault, vitium
to favor, favere, indulgere
fear, metus
to fear, timere
a feather, pluma
feeble, imbecillus
to feed, pascere, pasci; *to feed upon*, vesci
to feel, sentire
to fell, caedere
a female, femina
to fence in, saepire
few, *a few*, pauci
a field, ager
the fiftieth, quinquagesimus
to fight, dimicare, pugnare
to fill up, complere, explere, implere
to find, reperire; *to find (out)*, invenire; *to find fault with*, reprehendere; *to find guilty*, damnare, condemnare
a finger-ring, anulus
fire, ignis

first, primus
a fish, piscis
fit, idoneus
five, quinque
to fix, figere
fixed, fixus
to flee or *fly*, fugere, profugere
flesh, caro
a flight, fuga; *to put to flight*, fugare
to be flogged, vapulare
to flow, fluere
a flower, flos
a fly, musca
to fly out, evolare
to follow, sequi
a follower, comes
food, victus
a fool, stultus
foolish, stultus
a foot, pes
a footstep, vestigium
for (prep.), pro, prae, per, ob, in; *for* (conj.), enim, nam
to forbid, vetare
forbidden, nefas
force, vis; *forces*, copiae
to forge, cudere
to forget, oblivisci
in former times, olim
formerly, olim
to forsake, deserere
a fort, castrum
the fortieth, quadragesimus
fortunate, felix
forty, quadraginta
the forum, forum
to found, condere
four, quattuor
the fourth, quartus
a fox, vulpes
a fraud, fraus
free, expers   [rare
to free, solvere, liberare; *to set free*, libe-
freedom, libertas
a friend, amicus
friendly, amicus
friendship, amicitia
from, a, ab, abs, de, e, ex
frugality, parsimonia
fruit, (frux), fructus, poma

fruit-bearing, frugifer
fruitful, frugifer
to fulfil, perfungi
full, plenus
furthest, ultimus
future, faturus

G.

a gate, porta
Gaul, Gallia
a Gaul, Gallus
a general, imperator
a generation, saeculum
gentle, mollis
a gentleman, ingenuus
a German, Germanus
Germany, Germania
to get, parare, comparare, nancisci
a gift, donum
to gird, cingere
a girl, puella
to give, dare, praebere, tribuere; *to give out*, edere; *to give as a present*, dono dare, donare; *to give up*, profundere
to glide, labi
glorious, decorus
glory, gloria, fama
to glow, fervere
to gnaw, rodere
to go, ire, vadere; *to go to sleep*, obdormiscere
God, Deus; *a god*, deus
gold, aurum, *of gold*, aureus
golden, aureus
good, bonus; *a good*, bonum; *to do good*, prodesse
to govern, regere
government, administratio
grain, frumenta
a grammar, liber grammaticus
a grandfather, avus
granted that, ut; *granted that not*, ne
grass, gramen
a grave, sepulcrum, sepulchrum
to graze, pascere
great, magnus; *so great*, tantus; *greater*, major; *greatest*, maximus, summus
greatly, magnopere
Greece, Graecia
Greek, Graecus

grief, dolor, luctus
it grieves, piget
to grind, pinsere, molere
a grindstone, cos
the ground, humus; *from the ground*, humo; *on the ground*, humi
to grow, crescere; *to grow angry*, irasci; *to grow old*, senescere
to growl, fremere
to be on one's guard, cavere

H.

Hadrumetum, Hadrumetum
a hair, pilus, capillus
the hand, manus; *in the hands of*, penes
to hand down, tradere
handsome, pulcher
to hang, haerere, pendere
Hannibal, Hannibal
to happen, fieri, accidere; *it happens*, [accidit
happily, feliciter
happiness, felicitas
happy, beatus, felix
hardly, vix
a hare, lepus
to do harm, nocere
harmless, innoxius
Hasdrubal, Hasdrubal
to hate, odisse
hateful, odiosus
to have, habere; esse, w. Dat.; *to have pity*, misereri; *to have rather*, malle
he, she, it, is; *he who*, qui
to heal, sanare, mederi
health, valetudo
to hear, audire
the heart, cor
heaven, caelum, coelum
heavy, gravis
help, auxilium
to help, juvare, adjuvare
Henry, Henricus
Hephaestion, Hephaestion
highly, magni
Himera, Himera
himself, herself, itself, ipse
to hinder, impedire, officere
a hindrance, impedimentum
to hire, conducere
his, her, its (own), suus

history, historia
to hold, habere ; *(a triumph)* agĕre
a hole, antrum
holidays, feriae
holy, sacer
home, patria; domus; *at home*, domi; *from home*, domo
Homer, Homerus
honey, mel
an honor, honor, gloria
a hoof, ungula
a hook, hamus
a hoop, trochus
hope, spes
to hope for, sperare
a horn, cornu
a horse, equus
a horseman, eques
hot, calidus ; *to be hot*, calere ; *to become hot*, calescere
a house, aedes, domus
how, quomodo, quemadmodum, quam; *how great*, quantus ; *how long*, quamdiu ; *how many?* quot? *how much*, quantum
however, tamen ; *however much*, quamvis, quantumvis
to hum, consonare
human, humanus
a hundred, centum ; *a hundred thousand*, centum milia
hunger, fames
to be hungry, esurire
a hunter, venator
hurtful, noxius

I.

I, ego, egomet
ice, gelu
if, si ; (interrog. part.) -ne, -num, an; *if not* (interrog. part.) nonne ; *if only*, modo, si modo, dum, dummodo
ignorant, ignarus, inscius, nescius
ill, aegrotus, aeger
an image, imago, instar
to imitate, imitari
immeasurable, immensus
immense, immensus
immortal, immortalis
impatience, impatientia

to import, importare
it is of importance, interest
to improve the memory, memoriam augere
in, in ; *to be in*, inesse
to inclose, saepire
income, vectigal
inconstant, inconstans
increase, incrementum
to increase, augere, crescere
incredible, incredibilis
indeed, quidem
to indulge, indulgere
indulgence, indulgentia
industrious, assiduus
an injury, injuria
innocent, innocens
innumerable, innumerabilis, innumerus
an insect, insectum
integrity, integritas
to be intent on other matters, alias res agere
to interpret, vertere
into, in
to invent, invenire
to invite, invitare
irksome, molestus
iron (noun), ferrum
an island, insula
Italy, Italia

J.

Jerusalem, Hierosolyma
a jest, jocus; *jests*, joca
to join, jungere, serere; *to join to*, adjungere
a joke, jocus; *in joke*, joco; *jokes*, joca
a journey, iter
joy, gaudium
a judge, judex ; *a better judge*, peritior
to judge, judicare
Julius, Julius
just, justus
justly, jure

K.

to keep off, arcere
to kill, interficere
a kind, genus, instar; *a kind of*, quidam
to kindle, accendere
a king, rex

a kingdom, regnum
to knead, depsere
a knife, culter
to know, cognoscere, scire; *not to know*, nescire
knowledge, scientia
known, notus

L.

labor, labor
a Lacedaemonian, Lacedaemonius
a lake, lacus
a lamb, agnus
to lament, plangere
the land, terra
the language, lingua, vox
large, magnus
last, ultimus
to last, durare
late, serus; *too late*, serus; *later*, serius
Latin, Latinus
to laugh, ridere
law, jus, lex
to lay hold of, capessere; *to lay eggs*, ova parere
laziness, pigritia
to lead, ducere; *to lead one's life*, vitam agere
a leader, dux
a leaf, folium
to leap, salire
to learn, discere; *to learn to know*, noscere
learning, doctrina
to leave, linquere; *to leave (behind)*, relinquere
length, longinquitas
less (adj.), minor
less (adv.), minus
to lessen, minuere, levare
lest, ne
to let, sinere, locare, collocare
a letter (of the alphabet), litera, litterae; *a letter*, epistola, epistula
to level, aequare
liberty, libertas
a library, bibliotheca
to lick, lambere
to lie down, cubare
life, vita

light, levis
light, lux, lumen
it lightens, fulminat
like (adj.), similis, instar
like (adv.), sicut
to like, amare
a line of life, genus vitae
a lion, leo
little, parvus, pauca, paulum
to live, vivere; *to live upon*, vesci
a load, onus
long (adj.), longus
to look, spectare; *to look to*, spectare
a lord, dominus
to lose, amittere, perdere
a loss, damnum
a lot, sors
very loudly, vehementer
love, amor
to love, amare, diligere
luxury, luxuries, luxuria
Lycurgus, Lycurgus
lying, mendacium

M.

a Macedonian, Macedo
a magistrate, magistratus
Mago, Mago
a magnet, magnes
to make, facere, efficere, creare, reddere; *to be made*, fieri; *to make one's self master of*, potiri; *to make a noise*, strepere; *to make a treaty*, foedus icere
man, a man, homo, vir
manner, modus; *in no manner*, nullo modo; *in this manner*, sic
many, multus, multi, plures; *very many*, complures, plerique
Marius, Marius
it is the mark, proprium est
a market, mercatus, forum
market(day), nundinae
to marry (of the woman) nubere
a master, dominus; *a master (teacher)*, magister, rector
a match for, par
matter, materia, materies
it matters, interest, refert
a mattock, ligo
a meadow, pratum

a meal, cena
to measure, metiri
Media, Media
a medicine, medicina
to meet, subire
memory, memoria
men, homines
to mend, sarcire
a merchant, mercator
midday, meridies
to migrate, migrare
a mile, mille passuum
military affairs, res militaris
a military camp, castra
milk, lac
to milk, mulgere
Miltiades, Miltiades
the mind, animus
mindful, memor
to mingle, miscere
a miser, avarus
a misfortune, calamitas
to be mistaken, errare
to mix, miscere
modesty, modestia
money, pecunia
a month, mensis
the moon, luna
more, plus, amplius; *more than*, amplius
morning, mane
mortal, mortalis
most, plurimus, plerique; *most (of all)*, maxime
a mount, mountain, mons
to mourn, lugere
a mouse, mus
the mouth, os
to move, movere
much (adj.), multus; *much* (adv.), multum, multo
muddy, turbidus
a multitude, multitudo
Mummius, Mummius
I must, debeo; *it must needs*, necesse est
mute, mutus
my, meus; *my all*, omnia mea

N.

naked, nudus
a name, nomen; *a good name*, bona fama
to name, nominare, vocare
a narrative, narratio
one's native land, country, patria
nature, natura
naval, maritimus
navigation, navigatio
near (adv.), prope
near (prep.), apud, circa; *near to*, juxta
nearest, proximus
nearly, fere
necessary, necessarius
to (be in) need, carere, egere, indigere
there is need, opus est
it is needful, opus est, oportet
needless, supervacuus
to neglect, neglegere, negligere
to neigh to, adhinnire
neither (of the two), neuter
neither..nor, neque..neque, nec..nec
a net, rete
never, numquam, nunquam
nevertheless, tamen
next, proximus; *next best*, proximus bonis
the night, nox; *at night*, noctu
a nightingale, luscinia
nightly, nocturnus
night-time, tempus nocturnum
the (river) Nile, Nilus
no, nullus, non; *no one*, nullus, nemo
noble, nobilis
nobody, nemo
a noise, strepitus; *to make a noise*, strepere
none, nullus; *none of us*, nemo nostrum
noon, meridies
nor, nec
the north, septentrio
not, non, nonne, -ne; *not any, not one*, nullus
nothing, nihil, nihilum; *nothing but*, nihil nisi
to nourish, alĕre
now, nunc, modo
nowhere, nusquam

noxious, noxius
Numa, Numa
Numantia, Numantia
a *number*, numerus; a *great number*, multitudo
Numitor, Numitor

O.

an *oath*, religio
to *obey*, obedire, oboedire, parere
to *obscure*, obscurare
to *obtain*, adipisci
an *occupation*, negotium
the *ocean*, oceanus, mare
Octavia, Octavia
of, e, ex, de
an *office*, honor, munus
often, saepe; *oftener*, saepius; *oftenest*, saepissime
old, antiquus, vetus; *older*, major natu; *old age*, senectus; *an old man*, senex
on, in, de, super
once, semel
one, unus
only, unus; tantum, nonnisi, modo
to *open*, patefacere, aperire
to be *of opinion*, arbitrari
or, aut, vel, an; *or not*, annon, necne
an *oracle*, oraculum
by *order*, jussu; *in order that*, ut, quo; *in order that not*, ne
to *order*, jubere
other, alius; *the other (of two)*, alter; *belonging to others, of others*, alienus
I ought, debeo; *it ought*, oportet
our, noster
out of, e, ex
over, de, super, supra
to *overcome*, vincere
to *owe*, debere
own, proprius
an *ox*, bos

P.

a *pace*, passus
pain, dolor
to *paint*, pingere
a *painter*, pictor
Palatine, Palatinus
a *parent*, parens

parricide, parricidium
a *part*, pars
partaker, particeps
to *pass*, to *pass by* or *on*, praeterire; to *pass one's life*, vitam agere
passages in books, loci
passion, cupiditas
past (prep.), praeter
patience, patientia
a *patient*, homo aeger
patiently, patienter
peace, pax
a *peacock*, pavo
a *pear*, pirum
to *peel*, glubere
people, homines; *the common people*, plebs, plebes
to *perceive*, sentire
Perdiccas, Perdiccas
perfectly, plane
Pergamum, Pergamum
Pericles, Pericles
to *perish*, interire
to *permit*, sinere
a *Persian*, Persa
a *Phenician*, Phoenix
Philip, Philippus
a *physician*, medicus
to *pierce*, pungere
to *have pity*, misereri
a *place*, locus; *places*, loca
to *place*, statuere, ponere
the planet Saturn, stella Saturni
a *plant*, planta
to *plant*, serere
Plato, Plato
to *play*, ludere
pleasing, gratus
to *pledge*, spondere
to *plow*, arare
to *pluck*, carpere, vellere; to *pluck out*, evellere
to *plunder*, spoliare
to *plunge*, mergere
a *poet*, poeta
Pompey, Pompeius
poor, pauper
the populace, plebs, plebes
a *possession*, bonum
to *pound*, pinsere

pounds, pondo
to pour, fundere
poverty, paupertas
power, vis; *in the power of,* penes
a practice, exercitatio
praise, laus
to praise, laudare
to pray, orare
prayers, preces
a precept, praeceptum
to prefer, malle
to prepare for, parare
in presence of, coram, apud
a present, donum; *to give as a present,* dono dare, donare
to be present, interesse
to press, premere
a price, pretium; *at a very high price,* plurimo (pretio)
principally, praecipue
of printing, typographicus
probable, veri similis
profane, profanus
to prohibit, vetare
proper, idoneus
property, res familiaris
proud, superbus
provided, dum, dummodo
providence, providentia
to provoke, lacessere
prudent, prudens
public, publicus
to publish, edere
to pull, vellere
a pumice-stone, pumex
to punish, punire
a pupil, discipulus
to purchase, emere
pure, purus
to put off, exuere; *to put on,* induere; *to put out,* exstinguere; *to put to flight,* fugare
Pythagoras, Pythagoras

Q.

a quadruped, quadrupes
to quake for fear, pavere
a great quantity, vis
a queen, regina
a question, quaestio; *the question is,* quaeritur

quicker, citius
quickly, celeriter; *more quickly,* citius
to quit, relinquere
quoth I, inquam

R.

to rage, furere
rain, pluvia
to rain, pluere; *it rains,* pluit
to raise an army, exercitum comparare
rare, rarus
to have rather, malle
a razor, novacula
to reach, pervenire
to read, legere
readily, facile
ready, paratus
real, verus; *reality,* res vera
to reap, metere, demetere
for this reason, idcirco
to recall, revocare
to receive, accipere
to recline at table, accumbere
to recover, convalescere
recreation, recreatio
to redeem, redimere
to refrain, abstinere
to regard, existimare
regular, justus
to reign, regnare
to rejoice, gaudere
to relate, narrare
to release, liberare
to relieve, levare
relying, fretus
to remain, manere
a remedy, remedium
to remember, recordari, reminisci, meminisse
to remind, commonefacere, commonere, admonere
to remove, migrare
Remus, Remus
rented, conductitius
to repose, quiescere, requiescere
a republic, the republic, res publica
reputation, fama
to require, desiderare, postulare
to rest, quiescere, requiescere
to restore, reddere

to *restrain*, arcere, compescere
to *return*, redire
to *reveal*, indicare
the Rhine, Rhenus
rich, dives
riches, divitiae
to *ride*, equitare
a *rider*, eques
right (noun), fas, jus
to *ripen*, maturescere
to *rise*, oriri
a *river*, flumen, fluvius
a *road*, via
to *roast*, torrere
to *rob*, spoliare
to *roll*, volvere
Roman, Romanus
Rome, Roma
Romulus, Romulus
Roscius, Roscius
round, rotundus
to *rout*, fundere
to *rub*, fricare
to *ruin*, perdere
to *rule*, regĕre
a *ruler*, rector
to *run*, currere; to *run about*, cursare
to *rush (forth)*, ruere

S.

sacred, sacer
sad, tristis
Saguntum, Saguntum
for the sake of, causa
Salamis, Salamis
to *be for sale*, licere
salt (noun), sal
salubrious, saluber
the same, idem
to *sanction*, sancire
to *satiate*, satiare
Saturn, Saturnus; *the planet Saturn*, Saturni stella
to *say*, dicere; *I say*, ajo, inquam
a *saying*, dictum; *witticisms*, sales
the scale (of a fish), squama
a *scar*, cicatrix
a *scholar*, discipulus
a *school*, schola
a *science*, scientia

Scipio, Scipio
to *scrape*, radere
to *scratch*, scabere
the sea, mare; *sea-*, maritimus
a *season*, tempus anni
the second, secundus; *a second time*, iterum
to *see*, videre, cernere, adspicere
to *seek*, petere; *to seek (after, for)*, quaerere
to *seem*, videri
seldom, raro
to *sell*, vendere
the senate, senatus
to *send*, mittere
a *sentence*, sententia
to *separate*, sejungere, dividere
serious, serius
a *servant*, servus
servitude, servitus
to *set*, statuere; (*of the sun*), occidere; to *set free*, liberare; *to set out*, proficisci
seven, septem; *seven hundred*, septingenti
several, complures; plures
to *sew*, suere
a *shade, a shadow*, umbra
to *shake*, quatere
it shames, pudet
sharing, particeps
to *sharpen*, acuere
more sharply, acrius
to *shear*, tondere
a *sheep*, ovis
a *shepherd*, pastor
to *shine*, micare, lucere, fulgere
a *ship*, navis
short, brevis
I should, debeo
to *show one's self*, se praestare, se praebere
to *shut*, claudere; *to shut the eyes*, conivere; *to shut out*, excludere
Sicily, Sicilia
sick, aeger
on this side, cis, citra
to *be silent*, tacere
silver (noun), argentum
silver (adj.), argenteus

similar, similis
since, cum
to sing, canere, cantare
a sister, soror
to sit, sedere; *to sit down*, sidere
six, sex
sixteen, sedecim
skillful, peritus
a skin, pellis
the sky, caelum, coelum
to slander, rodere
a slave, servus
slavery, servitus
to slay, enecare
to sleep, dormire
sleep, somnus
slothfulness, segnitia, segnities
small, parvus, exiguus; *smaller*, minor
to smear, linere
to snatch away, rapere
to sneeze, sternuere
snow, nix
to snow, ningere
so, tam, sic; *so that*, ut, quo; *so that not*, ut non
society, societas
Socrates, Socrates
the soil, humus
to be sold, venire
a soldier, miles
to solve, solvere
some, nonnulli; *some one*, quidam; *something*, aliquid
sometime, aliquando
sometimes, nonnunquam
a son, filius
to soothe, mulcere
sorrow, maeror; *it causes sorrow*, paenitet or poenitet
the soul, animus
to sound, sonare
to sow, serere
space, intervallum; *the space of 2 days*, biduum
Spain, Hispania
to spare, parcere
a Spartan, Spartanus
to speak, loqui; *to speak the truth*, verum dicĕre
a speaker's platform, rostra

a speech, lingua
speed, celeritas
to spend the winter, *summer*, hiemem, aestatem agere
a spider, aranea
to spin, nere
to spit, spuere
to spread, pandere, tendere
spring, ver
to sprinkle, conspergere
a spur, calcar
to stain, tingere
to stand, stare; *to stand around*, circumstare
a star, stella
the state, res publica, civitas
to stay, manere
to stay one's self on, niti
to steer, gubernare
to step, gradi
to be still, tacere
to sting, pungere
to stop, sistere
a stork, ciconia
a story, historia
a stranger, peregrinus
a street, platea, via
strength, vires
to strew, sternere
to strike, icere, pangere, ferire; *to strike a bargain*, pacisci
to strip, spoliare
to study, studere
to stuff, farcire
to subjugate, domare
to suck, sugere
to sue for peace, pacem petere
to suffer, pati, sinere
suitable, aptus
suited, aptus
the summer, aestas
to summon, arcessere, evocare, reum facere
the sun, sol
to support, fulcire
suppose, ut, cum, licet
to be sure, certe
to surround, cingere, circumdare
a swallow, hirundo
to swear, jurare; *having sworn*, juratus

to sweep, verrere
sweet (to the taste), dulcis
to swell, turgere
to swim, natare
a switch, virga
Syracuse, Syracusae

T.

to take, capere, sumere; *to take away*, demere, tollere, eripere; *to take fire*, exardescere; *to take out*, promere; *to take up*, tollere; *to take a walk*, ambulare
a talk, sermo
to tame, domare
Tarquin, Tarquinius
the Tarquinians, Tarquinii
to taste, gustare
to teach, docere
a teacher, magister
a tear, lacrima, lacryma
to tell, dicere
a temple, aedes
ten, decem
to testify, testari
the Teutons, Teutoni
than, quam
thanks, gratia
that (demonstr.), is; *that* (yonder), ille; *that* (relat.), qui; *that* (conjunct.), quod, ut, quo; *that not*, ne, quin
the (w. comp.), eo; *the..the*, quo..eo
therefore, idcirco, ergo
a thief, fur
thin, tenuis
a thing, res
to think, cogitare, censere, arbitrari, reri
the third, tertius
thirsty, sitiens
thirty, triginta
this (of mine), hic; *this here?* hicine?
those things which, quae
thou, tu
though, licet, cum, etsi
a thousand, mille
to threaten, imminere
three, tres; *three things*, tria; *three hundred*, trecenti
a throne, imperium; *to come to the throne*, ad imperium accedere

through, per
to throw, jacere; *to throw the javelin*, jaculari
to thrust, trudere
to thump, tundere
to thunder, tonare
thus, sic
thy, tuus
the Tiber, Tiberis
Tiberius, Tiberius
to tie, nectere
to till the field, agrum colere
time, tempus; *in former times*, olim; *at the same time*, simul; *a second time*, iterum; *in a short time*, brevi tempore
it tires, taedet
to, ad, in
to-day, hodie
together, simul, pariter
the tongue, lingua
too, quoque
a tooth, dens
to torment, angere
a tortoise, testudo
to torture, torquere
to touch, tangere
toward, adversum, erga, sub, versus; *toward the east*, orientem versus
there is a tradition, traditum est
Trajan, Trajanus
tranquil, tranquillus
treachery, insidiae
treason, proditio
the treasury, aerarium
a treaty, foedus
a tree, arbor
to tremble, tremere
a trial for life, judicium capitis
a triumph, triumphus
troops, copiae
troublesome, molestus
Troy, Troja
true, verus
truly, vere
the trunk of an elephant, proboscis
to trust, fidere, fidem habere
trusting, fretus
truth, veritas
to try, experiri

to turn, volvere, vertere; to turn back, reverti; to turn out, evadere
twenty, viginti
twice, bis
twice as much, altero tanto
two, duo
a tyrant, tyrannus

U.

unable, impotens
the unanimous decision of the judges, omnium judicum sententia
it is unbecoming, dedecet
uncertain, incertus
an uncle, avunculus
under, infra, sub, subter
to understand, intellegere
undeservedly, immerito; most undeservedly, immeritissimo
unequal, impar
to unfold, explicare
unfriendly, inimicus
unhappy, infelix
unlike, dissimilis, dispar
unmindful, immemor
unpleasant, ingratus
unto, erga
to be unwilling, nolle
unworthy, indignus
upon, in
upright, probus
up to, tenus
to urge, urgere
use, usus
to use, adhibere, uti, solere; to become used, suescere; to use care, curam adhibere
useful, utilis; to be useful, prodesse
utmost, summus

V.

in vain, frustra, supervacuus
to value, aestimare, censere; to value highly, magni aestimare
variety, varietas
various, varius
Veii, Veii
to verge, vergere
Verres, Verres
very, admodum; not very, parum

Vespasian, Vespasianus
to vex, angere
a vice, vitium
a victory, victoria
to view, spectare
violence, vis
Virginia, Virginia
virtue, virtus
virtuous, probus
to visit, visere
a voice, vox
to vomit, vomere
to vow, vovere
a voyage, iter

W.

to (take a) walk, ambulare
to walk in the footsteps, vestigia premere
a wall, murus
want, egestas
to want, velle
to be wanting, deficere
war, bellum
ware, merx
warm, calidus
to warn, monere
to wash, lavare, luere
water, aqua
weak, debilis
a weapon, telum
to wear, ferre; to wear out, terere; to wear skins, pellibus uti
it wearies, taedet
weary (of), fessus
to weave, texere
a wedding, nuptiae
to weep, flere
to weigh, pendere
in weight, pondo
well, bene; as well as, tam..quam; to be well, valere
what? quid?
when, si, cum
where, ubi
whereas, cum, licet
to whet, acuere
whether, -ne, num, utrum; whether..or utrum..an
a whet-stone, cos

which, qui; *which (of two)?* uter?
while, dum, donec
white, albus
who, qui, quis
whole, totus
wicked, improbus, pravus
wild, ferus
willing(ly), libens, libenter
to be willing, velle; *to be more willing*, malle
a window, fenestra
wine, vinum
winter, hiems
to wipe, tergere
wisdom, sapientia
wise, sapiens; *a wise man*, sapiens; *to be wise*, sapere
wisely, sapienter
to wish for, cupere, velle: *not to wish*, [nolle
with, apud, cum
within, intra
without, absque, sine, extra: *without share*, expers
a witness, testis
witty sayings, sales
a wolf, lupus
a woman, mulier, femina
wonderful, mirabilis, mirificus, mirus
to be wont, solere
a word, verbum
a work, opus; *military works*, opera

to work, laborare
the world, mundus; *the whole world*, orbis terrarum
worthy, dignus
to worship, colere
worst, pessimus
a wound, vulnus
wretched, miser
to write, scribere
a writer, scriptor
a wrong, nefas

X.

Xerxes, Xerxes

Y.

a year, annus; *every year*, quotannis
yearly, annuus
yesterday, heri
yet, autem
to yield, cedere; *to yield fruits*, fructus ferre
young, adulescens; *a young man*, adulescens, adolescens; *younger*, minor natu; *youngest*, minimus natu
a youth, adulescens, adolescens, juvenis
your, tuus, vester

Z.

Zama, Zama
Zeuxis, Zeuxis

Part Third.

READING LESSONS.

1. *Daedalus.*

Daedălus, clarissĭmus artĭfex Graecōrum, Labyrinthum in insŭla Creta aedificāvit. Id aedificĭum plurĭma conclavĭa habēbat. Postquam magnifĭcum illud opus perfectum est, artĭfex ille clarissĭmus in patrĭam suam reverti cupīvit, Minōs autem, rex Cretae, discessum ei recusāvit. Tum Daedălus hunc dolum excogitāvit: Alas fecit quattŭor, quarum pennae cera continebantur. Duas alas Icăro filĭo aptāvit, duas sibi ipsi. Postquam id fecit, cum filĭo evolāvit; ipse dux erat, Icărus sequebātur. Sed Icărus soli nimis appropinquat[1], cera liquescit, alae solvuntur, ipse in mare dejectus morĭtur. Ab eo mare vocātum est Icarĭum. Pater incolŭmis in Graecĭam pervēnit.

[1] Historical Present

2. *Judicium Paridis.*

Nuptĭae Pelĕi et Thetĭdis celebrabantur. Omnes dii (di) deaeque adĕrant, una Eris, dea discordĭae, ad nuptĭas non invitāta erat. Qua[1] re Eris irāta discordĭam inter deas movēre constitŭit. Ităque malum aurĕum subĭto inter convīvas jecit, cui inscriptum erat: Pulcherrĭmae. Statim omnes deae de malo aurĕo certabănt. Postrēmo Mercurĭus Junōnem et Minervam et Venĕrem in Idam montem ad Trojam situm duxit. Parĭdi, Priămi filĭo, judicĭum mandātum est. Cum Paris id negotĭum suscepisset, Juno dixit: Mihi tribŭe malum; eris rex potentissĭmus. Tum Minerva (dixit): Mihi tribŭe malum; eris vir sapientissĭmus. Postrēmo Venus: Mihi tribŭe malum; eris conjunx femĭnae pulcherrĭmae. Venĕri Paris malum tribŭit. Idcŏ Minerva et Juno Parĭdi omnibusque Trojānis postĕa inimīcae fuĕrunt. Paris autem, consilĭo Venĕris motus,

in Graeciam navi profectus est. Ibi pulcherrima femina erat Helēna, uxor Menelāi, qui in urbe Sparta regnābat. Cum is illo tempŏre aliquando ab urbe abesset, Helĕna a Paride rapta est.
¹the Relative instead of the Demonstrative

3. Bellum Trojanum.

1. Propter Helĕnam raptam¹ bellum Trojānum motum est. Menelāus omnium Graeciae regum auxilium implorāvit. In portum Aulĭdis cum navĭbus et militĭbus convenērunt Ulixes, rex Ithăcae, Ajax et Teucer frater, Salaminiōrum duces, Nestor, Pyli rex, Diomĕdes, Argivōrum rex, et cum Patrŏclo Achilles, dux Myrmidŏnum. Agamemno, Menelāi frater, imperātor universi exercĭtus erat. Omnes ad navigandum parāti erant; sed ventis adversis prohibebantur. Diāna enim dea Agamemnŏni irascebātur, quod in venando cervam deae sacram necavĕrat. Calchas vates Agamemnŏni suāsit, ut filiam suam Iphigeniam immolāret, quod alio modo dea non placarētur². Postquam Agamemno consilio vatis parŭit, omnes Graeci, qui adĕrant, naves conscendērunt et in Asiam profecti sunt.

¹*In consequence of the abduction of Helena.* ²*could not be reconciled.*

2. Graeci, cum in Asiam pervenissent, in litŏre castra posuērunt, ut Trojam obsidĕrent. Troja erat urbs valde munīta, et Trojāni fortes defensōres urbis erant. Rex Trojanōrum erat Priāmus, fortissĭmus autem omnium Trojanōrum erat Hector, Priāmi filius, cujus fortitūdo etiam a Graecis laudabātur. Postrēmo, postquam Hector ab Achille interfectus est, Achillem autem Paridis sagitta interfēcit, decimo anno obsidiōnis Troja expugnāta est. Graeci enim magnum equum aedificavĕrant, cujus in ventre viri fortissĭmi se occultābant. Graeci naves in mare deduxĕrant et profecti erant. Qua¹ ex re magna laetitia erat in urbe Troja, cum dolus Graecōrum non timerētur. Trojāni, postquam equum in urbem traxērunt, conviviis delectabantur. Nocte autem Graeci ex equo egrediuntur², custōdes urbis necant et socios, qui in insŭla Tenĕdo erant, signo convŏcant. Plurĭmi Trojanōrum interficiuntur, aedificia urbis cremantur. Sic Troja dirŭta est.

¹Relative instead of the Demonstrative ²Observe the liveliness of the Historical Presents.

4. Ulixes in specu Polyphemi.

1. Postquam Troja capta est, Graeci in patrĭam revertērunt. Tŭ hĭs erat Ulixes, qui multas calamitātes passus est et diu errāvit; post multos errōres tandem in patrĭam pervēnit. In errorĭbus suis multas urbes vidit et multōrum homĭnum mores cognōvit. Errōres Ulixis Homērus, praestantissĭmus omnĭum Graecōrum poëtārum, egregĭo carmĭne descripsit. Primo anno Ulixes, postquam navem conscendĭt et Troja profectus est, in Sicilĭam venit. Ibi cum duodĕcim comitĭbus, qui eum sequebantur, in terram escendit. Insŭla Sicilĭa autem illo tempŏre non ab hominĭbus habitabātur, sed a feris gigantĭbus, qui Cyclōpes appellabantur.

2. Ulixes et comĭtes ejus ad specum Polyphēmi venērunt, qui erat ferocissĭmus omnĭum Cyclōpum. Is autem eo tempŏre non adĕrat in specu, sed oves in montĭbus pascēbat. Ulixes et comĭtes ejus in specum progressi lac et cascos invenērunt. Postquam diis sacrificavērunt, casēos edĕre incipĭunt. Intĕrim de[1] montĭbus Polyphēmus ligna portans cum ovĭbus revertit. Postquam saxo maxĭmo et gravissĭmo janŭam specus clausit, oves mulgēbat. Deinde lignis, quae in specum portavĕrat, ignem fecit. Hoc igne specus subĭto illustrātus est. Tum demum Polyphēmus Ulixem et comĭtes ejus conspexit.

[1] *down from*

3. Polyphēmus, cum eos conspexisset, interrogāvit: Estis mercatōres an praedōnes? Omnes gravi[1] voce gigantis terrīti sunt. Ulixes respondit: Graeci sumus, tempestāte a cursu nostro in hanc insŭlam dejecti[2]; te rogāmus, ut nos hospitĭo excipĭas, ut mos est Graecōrum. Si id fecĕris, gratissĭmi tibi erĭmus; si nos laesĕris, Juppĭter, defensor hospĭtum, te punĭet. Ita locūtus est Ulixes. Sed Polyphēmus ridens: Deos vestros, inquit, non metŭo, cum ego robustĭor et potentĭor sim[3], quam illi. Cum haec dixisset, duos comĭtes magna vi ad pariĕtem jecit et laceravit, ut cenam sibi parāret.

[1] *deep* [2] *driven* [3] Subjunctive governed by cŭm, *since*

4. Polyphēmus, postquam insequenti die idem fecit, e specu egressus est, ut pecŏra pascĕret; Ulixem autem et comĭtes ejus ita clausĕrat, ut e specu egrĕdi iis non licēret[1].

Cum Polyphēmus abesset, illi deliberābant, quo modo se ab illo gigante liberārent, metuentes, ne omnes lacerarentur, nisi dolo effugissent. Ulixis consilium omnĭbus sociis² probātum est. Cum Cyclops vespēre in specum revertisset, Ulixes pocŭlum vino, quod secum portavĕrat, implēvit et Polyphēmo praebŭit: Bibe, inquit, Polyphēme, hoc vinum optĭmum est. Cyclops, cum bibisset: Verum est, inquit, quod dixisti, hoc vinum optĭmum est. Praebe mihi altĕrum pocŭlum vini. Quo nomĭne appellāris, parve homo, qui mihi tam bonum vinum praebes? Tum Ulixes, postquam pocŭlum implēvit: O Polyphēme, inquit, rarum nomen mihi est, appellor Nemo. Polyphēmus, cum id audivisset, risit: Carissĭme Nemo, inquit, quod mihi tam bonum vinum praebuisti, hoc praemĭo te afficiam: Te postrēmum omnĭum ad cenam mihi parābo.

¹could not ²by all companions

5. Postquam id dixit, altus somnus eum complexus est, quod plurĭma pocŭla vini bibĕrat. Ulixes autem jam antĕa palum, quem in specu invenĕrat, acuĕrat et candentem fecĕrat. Hunc candentem palum in unum ocŭlum Polyphēmi intrusit et ita Cyclōpem excaecāvit. Is, postquam dolōrem sensit, omnĭum Cyclōpum auxilĭum implorāvit. Cyclōpes, cum ad specum venissent, interrogavērunt, quis cum necāre conarētur. Polyphēmus respondit: Nemo vi et dolo me necāre conātur. Cyclōpes, cum id audivissent, dixērunt: Si nemo te necare conātur, auxilĭum nostrum non est necessarĭum. Tum Cyclōpes domum avertĕrunt. Ita Polyphēmus nomĭne deceptus est. Ulixes autem et socĭi ejus hoc prudenti consilĭo e specu liberāti et servāti sunt.

6. Ulixes, cum in navi tutus esset, magna voce clamāvit: O Polyphēme, cum interrogātus eris, quis te excaecavĕrit, responde: Ulixes id fecit. Et nunc vale! Postquam id dixit, in altum mare navigāvit. Polyphēmus autem patrem suum Neptūnum, domĭnum maris, orāvit, ut filĭum ulciscerētur et Ulixem punīret. Neptūnus, cum filĭi preces audivisset, effēcit, ut Ulixes multos annos per multas terras errāret. In hoc longo errōre Ulixes cum comitĭbus suis multas calamitātes passus est. Postrēmo ad Phaeāces, beātos et benevŏlos

homĭnes, pervēnit, quorum rex eum hospitĭo recēpit. Inde in Ithăcam, patrĭam suam, navi vectus est. Sic Ulixes, postquam multōrum homĭnum urbes vidit et vitam moresque eōrum cognōvit, in patrĭam revertit. Adventu ejus et Penelŏpe uxor et Telemăchus filĭus valde delectātus est.

5. Dareus et Scythae.

Darēus, Hystaspis filĭus, rex Persārum, cum magno exercĭtu Scythas invāsit. Scythae semper fugiēbant. Postrēmo inopĭa in exercĭtu Darēi orta est. Eo tempŏre legātus Scythārum advēnit, qui avem, ranam, murem, quinque sagittas Darēo tradĭdit. Darēus laetus exclamāvit: Hostes nobis se tradunt! Tum unus ex comitĭbus regis, qui prudentĭa et sapientĭa omnes, qui adĕrant, superābat, dixit: Ne id speravĕris[1]. Scythae enim hoc dicunt: Nisi, ut aves, per aëra (aërem) avolabĭtis, aut in aquam immergētis, ut ranae, aut in terra vos occultabĭtis, ut mures, hae sagittae vos interficĭent. Scythae tum demum bellum incepērunt, et Darēus vix cum parva parte exercĭtus evāsit.

[1] the second person of the Perfect Subjunct. in a prohibition: *do not expect that*

6. Romulus.

Postquam Romŭlus Remum fratrem interfēcit, nova urbs Roma appellāta est. Ipse autem Romŭlus erat rex fortissĭmus. Ităque multa bella suscēpit et multos popŭlos, qui circa Romam habitābant, regno suo adjēcit. Cum autem in nova urbe paucae muliĕres essent, Romāni finitimōrum populōrum filĭas in matrimonĭum ducĕre cupiēbant. Sed Romāni ab his popŭlis ita contemnebantur, ut filĭae matrimonĭum Romanōrum repudiārent.

7. Sabinorum virgines rapiuntur.

Finitĭmus erat Romānis popŭlus Sabinōrum. Romŭlus eos invitāvit, ut in novam urbem venīrent, ludos spectātum. Magna multitūdo eōrum in urbem profecta est; etĭam uxōres et filĭae venērunt. Cum omnes, qui adĕrant, ludos spectārent, subĭto juvĕnes Romāni virgĭnes Sabīnas rapuērunt. Patres et matres virgĭnum fugērunt, sortem filiārum querentes. Raptae autem virgĭnes a viris suis ita tractabantur, ut eos amāre incipĕrent. Attămen Sabīni, postquam magnum exercĭtum paravērunt, ad bellum profecti et Romānos aggressi sunt. Cum Sabīni cum Romānis congressi essent, raptae virgĭnes in Sabinōrum acĭem irruentes patres suos rogavĕrunt, ut pacem cum Romānis facĕrent. Ităque pax facta est, et Sabīni in urbem recepti cum Romānis se conjunxērunt.

8. Tarquinius Superbus.

Tarquinĭus Superbus, septĭmus Romanōrum rex, maxĭma crudelitāte ad regnum pervēnit; nam socĕrum suum Servĭum Tullĭum, qui eo tempŏre regnābat, per satellītes suos interfecĕrat. Tarquinĭus, cum ad regnum pervenisset, eādem crudelitāte, qua regnum sibi pepercrat, Romānos tractāvit. Jura senātus et popŭli violāvit et propter superbĭam illud cognōmen accēpit. Ităque Romāni eum ejicĕre constituērunt. Cum Ardĕam ille obsidēret, Romāni portas clausērunt et ab urbe eum prohibuērunt.

9. Horatius Cocles.

Tarquinĭus cum filĭis ad Porsĕnam, regem Etrurĭae, fugit eumque orāvit, ut popŭlum Romānum punīret, quod regem ejecisset. Porsĕna voluntāti Tarquinĭi obsecūtus (est et) magnum exercĭtum parāvit, ut Roma potirētur. Mox ad urbem venit, quam Romāni firmis praesidĭis saepsĕrant. Magna pars urbis Tibĕri flumĭne munīta erat. Pontem, qui in¹ flumĭne factus erat, pauci Romāni custodiēbant. Ităque Porsĕna in pontem impĕtum fecit. Cum cetĕri Romāni fugĕrent, unus vir, Horatĭus Cocles, impĕtum hostĭum sustinŭit et effēcit, ut urbs servarētur. Ille solus hostes retinŭit, postquam suos adhortātus est, ut pontem rescindĕrent. Romāni maxĭmo studĭo fecērunt, quod ille jussĕrat. Horatĭus, cum sonĭtum rescissi pontis audivisset, in fluvĭum desĭlit et incolŭmis ad suos pervēnit. Ita unīus viri fortitudīne Roma servāta est.
¹over

10. Mucius Scaevola.

Mucĭus Scaevōla, vir fortissĭmus, gladĭo armātus in castra Porsĕnae, qui Tarquinĭum in regnum restituĕre conabātur, profectus est, ut regem, si invenisset, interficĕret. Cum in castra venisset, forte accĭdit, ut militĭbus stipendĭum impertirētur. Cum Mucĭus, qui regem non novĕrat, non interrogavisset, quis rex esset, ne interrogando se ipse aperīret, eum, qui militĭbus stipendĭum impertiēbat, pro rege interfēcit. Magnus tumultus ortus est. Mucĭum milĭtes ad regem traxērunt. Is statim consilĭum suum regi aperŭit. Rex, cum id audivisset, dixit: Quis te ad hoc facĭnus adduxit? Gravissĭmis poenis afficiēris, nisi id mihi dices. Mucĭus autem dextram manum in igne, qui ibi erat, torrŭit, cum dicĕret: Quo modo punīes me, qui omnĭa pati statuĕrim¹, ut patrĭam meam liberārem? Rex admirātus tantam fortitudĭnem eum non punīvit. Utĭnam, inquit rex, Etrusci tam fortes essent! Mucĭus, cum id audivisset, dixit: Quia fortitudĭnem meam honoravisti, tibi aperĭam, quod scire cupiēbas. Trecenti juvĕnes Romāni conjuravērunt, ut te interficĕrent. Forte ego eōrum primus fui, cetĕri me sequentur. Porsĕna, postquam cognōvit, in quanto pericŭlo esset, pacem cum Romānis facĕre constitŭit.

¹Subjunct. after the Relative

11. *Pyrrhus*.

1. Romāni, postquam Samnītes et omnes fere Italĭae gentes superavĕrunt, Tarentīnis bellum indixērunt, quod legātis Romanōrum injurĭam fecissent. Tarentīni Pyrrhum, regem Epīri, rogavērunt, ut sibi contra Romānos auxilĭo venīret. Pyrrhus, vir fortissĭmus et belli peritissĭmus, magna laetitĭa affectus est, quod a Tarentīnis ad id bellum invitabātur. Qui cum magnum exercĭtum paravisset, navĭbus in Italĭam profectus est. Viginti elephantos secum duxit: in tergis elephantōrum erant turres militĭbus implētae. Primum proelĭum fuit apud urbem Heraclēam. Romāni, quamquam maxĭma fortitudĭne pugnavērunt, tamen superāti sunt. Equi enim Romanōrum, adspectu elephantōrum terrīti, totam acĭem Romanōrum perturbavērunt. Ita factum est, ut Romāni, qui antĕa semper superiōres (victōres) fuĕrant, superarentur. Mille quingenti Romāni interfecti sunt, mille octingentos Pyrrhus cepit. Rex autem, quamquam victorĭam a Romānis reportavĕrat, tamen fortitudĭnem eōrum admirātus (est et) pacem cum iis facĕre cupīvit.

2. Cinĕas, legātus Pyrrhi, cum Romam venisset, in senātum ductus est. Legātus id fecit, quod ei a Pyrrho mandātum erat. Cum multi patrum condiciōnes regis accipĕre cupĕrent, unus ex iis, qui erat caecus, surrexit. O Romāni, inquit Appĭus Claudĭus, usque ad hunc diem dolŭi, quod caecus sum; sed hodĭe opto, ut non solum caecus, sed etĭam surdus sim, ne ista imprŏba consilĭa audĭam, quae modo audīvi. Condiciōnes regis accipĕre turpe est. Cetĕri patres, cum id audivissent, consilĭo caeci illīus senis obsecūti (sunt et) condiciōnes Pyrrhi repudiavērunt. Legātus, postquam ad regem revertit, omnĭa dixit, quae Romāni ei mandavĕrant. Tum a rege interrogātus, qualis sibi senātus visus esset, legātus respondit: Ille senātus tam magnifĭcus est, ut senatōres mihi non cives, sed reges esse videantur.

3. Post paucos dies legāti Romanōrum ad Pyrrhum venērunt, ut captīvos commutārent. In his legātis erat Fabricĭus, vir maxĭma probitāte insignis. Hunc rex magno dono sibi conciliāre studēbat, Fabricĭus autem id non accēpit. Postĕro die rex cum Fabricĭo colloquĭum habŭit. Maxĭmus elephantus adĕrat, ut eum terrēret. Tum Fabricĭus (dixit): O Pyrrhe, neque heri pecunĭa tua me ita delectāvit, ut eam cupĕrem, neque hodĭe elephantus tuus me terret. Pyrrhus, cum id audivisset, constantĭam Fabricĭi admirātus est. Insequenti anno Fabricĭus exercitŭi Romāno praeĕrat. Pyrrhus habēbat medĭcum, cui in omnĭbus rebus fidem tribuēbat; is autem regi non erat fidēlis. Nam ad Fabricĭum epistŭlam scripsit, in qua haec erant (scripta): Si magnum munus mihi tribūtum erit, Pyrrhum, hostem vestrum, venēno necābo. Fabricĭus curāvit, ut rex epistŭlam, quam ille scripsĕrat, accipĕret. Pyrrhus, cum hanc epistŭlam accepisset, probitātem Fabricĭi admirātus (est et) dixit: Ille est Fabricĭus, qui difficilĭus ab honestāte, quam sol a cursu avertītur.

12. Arminius.

Varus, postquam cum exercĭtu Romāno in Germanĭam venit, Germānos pessĭmo modo tractābat. Multa vectigalĭa a Germānis, qui neque aurum neque argentum possidēbant, postulāvit; idem imperāvit, ut Germāni legĭbus Romanōrum parērent et lingŭa Latīna in judiciis uterentur. His et multis aliis rebus Germanōrum anĭmos ita laesit, ut a Romanōrum dominatiōne se liberāre constituĕrent. Tum Arminĭus, princeps Cheruscōrum, postquam magnas copĭas parāvit, hoc modo Germanĭam liberāvit: Varus cum magno exercĭtu in silvam Teutoburgiensem profectus erat, ut seditiōnem, quae orta esse dicebātur, exstinguĕret. Cum in hanc regiōnem venisset, milītes multis imbrĭbus et maxĭmis tempestatĭbus fatigāti erant. Subīto Arminĭus cum Germānis impĕtum in legiōnes Romanōrum fecit. Acerrĭma pugna orītur. Romāni, laborĭbus fatigāti, impĕtum Germanōrum non sustinuērunt; plurĭmi eōrum in pugna, alii in fuga a Germānis interfecti, relĭqui capti sunt. Varus autem ipse neque captus neque necātus est, sed, cum Germāni victorĭam a Romānis reportavissent, gladĭo suo se ipse interfēcit. Sic unīus viri prudentĭa et fortitudĭne Germanĭa a dominatiōne Romanōrum liberāta est. Imperātor Augustus, cum nuntĭum magnae illīus cladis exercĭtus Romāni accepisset, maxĭmo dolōre exclamāvit: Vare, Vare, redde mihi legiōnes! Germanĭa autem ab illo tempŏre libĕra erat.

13. De morte Epaminondae.

Epaminondas, dux Thebanōrum, cum vicisset Lacedaemonĭos apud Mantinēam, ipse gravi vulnĕre ictus ex acĭe cessit. Cum anĭmum recepisset, interrogāvit, salvusne esset clipĕus. Cum amīci ejus flentes respondissent: "Salvus est;" interrogāvit, essentne fusi hostes. Cum id quoque, ut cupiēbat, audivisset, hastam, qua erat transfixus, evellit. Ita, postquam multum sanguĭnem fudit, laetus victorĭa anĭmam efflāvit.

14. De Romanorum disciplina militari.

Titus Manlĭus Torquātus aliquando imperavĕrat, ne milĭtes extra ordĭnem contra hostes pugnārent. Ejus filĭus autem, a duce equĭtum hostĭum ad certāmen provocātus, eum aggressus et victorĭam adeptus est. Reversum deinde filĭum pater laudāvit quidem propter fortitudĭnem, sed immodestĭam ejus supplicĭo ultus est.

15. De Apelle.

Apelles, clarissĭmus antiquitātis pictor, aliquando Alexandrum in equo sedentem pinxĕrat. Cum autem regi imāgo, praecipŭe equi, non ita placēret, ut artĭfex speravĕrat, equus Alexandri introductus est. Qui cum pictum equum conspexisset, ei adhinnīvit, quasi verus equus esset. Tum Apelles: "Equus, inquit, tuus, o rex, peritĭor artis pingendi vidētur esse quam tu." Nemo autem ab Apelle saepĭus pictus est quam Alexander; eundem nemo saepĭus ex aere et marmŏre finxit[1] quam Lysippus, aequālis Apellis.

[1] e marmŏre fingĕre, to carve an image in marble.

16. Senes et mors.

Quam dulcis vita sit, haec fabŭla docet: Duo senes, qui in silva ligna cecidĕrant et caesa domum portābant, et onĕre et via fatigāti fasces deposuĕrunt et paulum acquievērunt. Senectūtis et inopĭae mala secum[1] considerantes mortem clara voce invocavērunt, ut se ab omnĭbus malis liberāret. Mors, cum senum preces audivisset, statim venit eosque interrogāvit, cur se vocavissent. Adspectu ejus territi respondērunt: Nihil optāmus, sed quaesivīmus tantum alĭquem, qui levāret nobis fasces.

[1] with themselves.

17. Judicium Philippi.

Philippus, rex Macedŏnum, cum judex esset inter duos homĭnes malos, altĕri, ut e Macedonĭa fugĕret, altĕri, ut eum persequerētur, imperāvit. Hi statim fecērunt, quod jussi erant; ille fugit, hic eum persecūtus est. Ita Macedonĭa eōdem tempŏre a duōbus homĭnĭbus malis liberāta est.

18. De Socrate.

Socrătes injurĭa ab Atheniensĭbus capĭtis damnātus est. Cum in custodĭa esset, Crito, quocum familiarissĭme vixĕrat, ad eum venit: Socrătes, inquit Crito, injurĭam accĭpis, me igĭtur sequĕre et e carcĕre elabĕre; omnĭa ad fugam parāta sunt. Socrătes autem: Praestat, inquit, injurĭam accipĕre et accepisse, quam injurĭam facere et fecisse. Hic manēbo et legĭbus obtempĕrans id patĭar, quod jam multi et clari viri ante me passi sunt et post me patientur. Cum Crito eum interrogavisset, num quid habēret, quod libĕris vel amīcis mandāret, Socrătes respondit: Illis impĕra, ut praeceptis meis parĕant et injuriărum quidem, non beneficiōrum popŭli Athenicnsis obliviscantur.

19. De Mida.

Midae, regi Phrygĭae, Bacchus quondam dixit: Quid optas? Omnĭa praestābo. Tum ille respondit: Effĭce, ut omnĭa, quae tetigĕro, aurum fiant. Deus precĭbus ejus obsecūtus est. Statim Midas tetĭgit ramum; subĭto ramus erat aurĕus; sustŭlit lapĭdem, lapis erat aurĕus; exsultābat rex. Intĕrim ministri affĕrunt cibos jucundos; rex laetus consīdit, sed cheu omnes cibi, quos tangit, mutantur in aurum. Tum stultitĭam suam intellexit; nam famem explēre non potĕrat et fame exanimātus esset, nisi Bacchus eum illa facultāte rursus liberavisset.

20. Agricolae Lyciae in ranas mutantur.

Latōna, postquam in insŭla Delo Apollĭnem et Diānam pepĕrit, fugĕre inde a Junōne coacta est. In sinu igĭtur portans infantes in Lycīae fines venit. Longo ibi labōre et solis aestu fatigāta siti cruciabātur. Forte lacum modĭcum in valle situm et ad ripas ejus homĭnes agrestes conspexit. Laeta accessit jamque, ut aquam haurīret, genĭbus tetigĕrat terram, cum rustīca illa turba id vetŭit. Terrĭta Latōna: Cur, inquit, prohibētis me ab aqua? Commūnis est usus aquārum; ut enim neque solem neque aëra natūra cuīquam proprĭum fecit, ita ne aquam quidem. Etsi autem ad publīca munĕra venīo, supplex tamen, ut ea mihi detis, rogo. Non ego membra volo lavāre, sed sitim explēre, qua cruciāta vix vocem edĕre possum. Hi quoque vos movĕant, qui parva e sinu meo bracchĭa tendunt. Quem haec blanda deae verba movēre non debēbant? Illi tamen orantem prohībent, minantur, nisi discēdat, convicĭa etĭam addunt. Neque id fecisse satis habent, sed ipsum lacum etĭam pedĭbus manibusque turbant. Tum vero illa obliviscĭtur sitis et indignāta plenăque irārum: In aeternum vos, inquit, in hoc lacu vivātis. Evēnit, quod dea optavĕrat. Vix enim haec verba locūta erat, cum illi miro quodam aquārum desiderĭo capti modo totum corpus submergunt, modo capĭta profĕrunt, modo in summo lacu natant, interdum ad ripam consistunt paullōque post in aquas desilĭunt. Ita agricŏlae Lycĭae in ranas sunt mutāti.

21. De Tantalo.

Tantălus, Jovis filĭus, tam carus fuit diis, ut Juppĭter ei consilĭa sua credĕret cumque ad epŭlas deōrum admittĕret. At ille, quae apud Jovem audivĕrat, cum mortalĭbus communicābat. Ob eam perfidĭam dicĭtur apud infĕros in aqua collocātus esse semperque sitīre. Nam quotĭens aquam sumĕre volŭit, aqua recēdit. Tum etĭam mala ei super caput pendent; sed quotĭens ea carpĕre conātus est, rami vento moti recēdunt.

22. De Theseo.

Paucis annis ante adventum Thesĕi Athenienses cum Minōe, rege Cretae, bellum gessĕrant. Postĕa autem a Minōe victi pacem fecĕrant, ea condicĭōne, ut singŭlis annis septēnos juvĕnes septēnasque virgĭnes in insŭlam Cretam mittĕrent. Hos Minos in Labyrintho clausit, quem Daedălus ita struxĕrat, ut nemo eōrum, qui ingressi erant, exĭtum reperīre posset. Theseus, cum audivisset, quanta calamitāte civĭtas Atheniensĭum tenerētur, ipse cum juvenĭbus et virginĭbus in insŭlam proficisci constituit. Postquam navis ad Cretam appulsa est, Ariadne, filĭa Minōis, Thesĕum docŭit, quo modo ex Labyrintho se expedīre posset. Theseus, cum Minotaurum, qui in Labyrintho erat, occidisset, Ariadnen secum abduxit. Cum autem eam dormientem in insŭla Naxo reliquisset, Liber deus postĕa eam conjugem fecit.

23. De Iphigenia.

Cum universus Graecōrum exercĭtus in portum Aulĭdis convenisset, tempestas eos ob iram Diānae retinēbat. Agamemno enim, dux illīus expeditiōnis, cervam deae sacram vulneravĕrat superbiusque in Diānam locūtus erat. Calchas, Graecōrum vates, ab Agamemnōne interrogātus, qua ratiōne dea placāri posset: Ira deae, inquit, placāri non potĕrit, nisi filĭam tuam Iphigenīam immolavĕris. Ob eam causam Ulixes mittĭtur, ut eam in portum Aulĭdis abdūcat. Iphigenīa, cui Ulixes matrimonĭum Achillis promisĕrat, ut eam ad profectiōnem impellĕret, cum sequĭtur. Cum vero pater eam immolatūrus esset, Diāna virgĭnem miserāta per nubes in terram Taurĭcam detŭlit ibīque templi sui sacerdōtem fecit. Pro Iphigenīa cerva a Diāna missa immolāta est.

24. De Codro.

Erant inter Athenienses et Dores vetĕres simultātes. Dores, qui pro injurīis acceptis eos bello ulcisci[1] volēbant, de eventu belli oracŭla consuluērunt. Responsum est: Dores victōres erunt Atheniensĭum, nisi regem eōrum occīdent. Cum ad bellum essent profecti, militĭbus praeceptum est, ut regem vivum capĕrent. Atheniensĭum rex eo tempŏre Codrus erat. Is, cum hostĭum consilĭum cognovisset, regĭam vestem exŭit et in castra hostĭum ingressus est. Ibi cum in turba milĭtum alĭquem falce vulneravisset, ab eo interfectus est. Dores, cum regis corpus agnovissent, sine proelĭo discessērunt. Atque ita Athenienses virtūte regis, qui pro salūte patrĭae morti se obtulĕrat, bello liberāti sunt.

[1] to punish

25. De libris Sibyllinis.

Ab antĭquis scriptorĭbus de libris Sibyllīnis haec memorĭae prodīta sunt. Mulĭer quaedam, cujus nomen non est notum, ad Tarquinĭum Superbum regem adīit, novem libros ferens. Divīna in iis incrant oracŭla. Cum Tarquinĭus eam interrogavisset, quantum pretĭum esset librōrum, mulĭer nimĭum poposcit. Rex autem eam derīsit. Tum illa, postquam tres libros ex novem cremāvit, regem interrogāvit, num relĭquos sex eōdem pretĭo emĕre vellet. Tarquinĭus multo magis risit. Mulĭer statim tres libros alĭos cremāvit atque denŭo placĭde interrogāvit, num tres relĭquos eōdem pretĭo emĕre vellet. Rex tum demum eos emĕre constitŭit, neque minōre pretĭo, quam quod erat petītum pro omnĭbus, eos emit. Sed illa mulĭer, postquam a Tarquinĭo digressa est, postea nusquam visa esse dicītur.   Libri tres Sibyllīni sunt appellāti.   Ad eos quasi ad oracŭlum Romāni adībant, cum deos immortālcs publīce consulĕre volēbant.

26. De Cyro et Tomyri.

Cyrus, postquam Asĭam subēgit, Scythis bellum intŭlit. Erat eo tempŏre Scythārum regīna Tomўris. Haec adventu hostĭum non terrebātur neque hostes, quos transĭtu flumīnis Araxis prohibēre potĕrat, prohibŭit. Ităque Cyrus copĭas trajēcit et in Scythĭam progressus castra posŭit. Postĕro die quasi fugĭens castra deserŭit magnamque cibōrum et vini vim in castris relīquit. Regīna, cui id nuntiātum erat, filĭum adulescentem cum tertĭa parte copiārum ad Cyri castra misit. Scythae, cum nullos invenissent hostes, ad vinum cibosque se vertunt et paullo post ebrĭi facĭle vincuntur.   Nam Cyrus per noctem cum copĭis suis revertĭtur omnesque Scythas cum regīnae filĭo interfĭcit.   Tomўris, quamquam tantum exercĭtum atque unum filĭum amisĕrat, lacrĭmas tamen cohibŭit et illud modo˘ reputāvit, quo modo filĭi mortem ulciscerĕtur.   Cum hostes recenti victorĭa exsultārent, pari fraude Tomўris Cyrum in insidĭas induxit. Fugit enim regīna atque ita effēcit, ut rex hostes usque ad angustĭas et montes insequerĕtur.   Ibi ducenta milĭa Persārum cum ipso rege trucidāvit. Caput Cyri in utrem quem sanguĭne implevĕrat, regīna conjēcit. Satĭa te, inquit regīna, sanguĭne, quem appetivisti.

27. De Marcio Coriolano.

Marcĭus, cui a captis Coriŏlis[1], Volscōrum oppĭdo, cognōmen erat Coriolānus, plebi odiōsus esse coepit.   Quare[2] expulsus ad Volscos, acerrĭmos Romanōrum hostes, se contŭlit et exercitŭi praefectus Romānos saepe vicit.   Ad urbem accessit neque ullis civĭum suōrum legationĭbus movēri potĕrat, ut patrĭae parcĕret. Tum Veturĭa mater et Volumnĭa uxor ad eum venērunt, quarum fletu et precĭbus commōtus est, ut exercĭtum reducĕret. Quod cum fecisset, a Volscis ut prodĭtor occīsus esse dicĭtur.

¹*from the taking of Corioli.*   ²*therefore*, Rel. for the Demonst.

28. De Herostrato.

Eādem nocte, qua in Macedonĭa Alexander Magnus natus est, in Asĭa templum Diānae Ephesĭae conflagrāvit. Nullum templum eo tempŏre clarĭus erat. Incensum est ab Herostrăto quodam; causam ipse confessus est. Volēbam, inquit, nomen meum immortāle reddĕre. Quamquam Ephĕsĭi nomen ejus abolēre conāti sunt, tamen etĭam nunc notum est.

29. De Stilpone philosopho.

Demetrĭus Poliorcētes, cum Megăram urbem vastavisset et cives ejus urbis omnĭa amisissent, Stilpōnem philosŏphum interrogāvit, quam jactūram fecisset¹. Nullam, inquit philosŏphus; virtūti enim nihil adimĕre potest bellum, neque quemquam ex militĭbus tuis vidi, qui sapientĭam rapĕret.

¹to suffer

30. De amicitia Orestis et Pyladis.

Orestis et Pylădis amicitĭa immortālem apud postĕros famam adepta est. Quid enim celebrātum magis, quam illōrum coram rege Thoante contentĭo, uter morerētur. Alter enim nitebātur ab altĕro depellĕre crimen et crimĭnis poenam in se transferre. Cum rex ignorāret, uter eōrum esset Orestes, Pylădes Orestem se vocābat, ut pro illo necarētur, Orestes autem poenam in se transferre studēbat.

31. De Solone et Croeso.

1. Solon Atheniensis, postquam civĭbus suis leges scripsit, decem annos peregrinātus est, ne leges mutāre cogerētur. Nam Atheniensĭbus ipsis non licēbat leges ab illo scriptas mutāre, cum juravissent, se decem annos legĭbus ejus usūros esse. Solon autem sperābat, Athenienses illo tempŏris spatĭo bonitātem legum ita intellectūros esse, ut de iis nihil mutāre cupĕrent. Solon, ob eam causam consilĭo peregrinandi capto, multas terras urbesque vidit et mores institutăque multōrum populōrum cognōvit.

2. Solon, cum Sardes ad Croesum, opulentissĭmum illum Lydĭae regem, venisset, hospitĭo ab eo exceptus est. Tertĭo

aut quarto die post, quam Solon advenĕrat. Croesus hospĭtem a ministris circumdūci cīque omnes opes regis ostendi jussit. Quas cum spectasset et magna admiratiōne affectus contemplātus esset, rursus ad regem se contŭlit, qui cum eo collŏqui cupiĕbat. Tum Croesus: Hospes Atheniensis, inquit, te virum sapientem esse et multas terras vidisse dicunt; dic mihi, quem vidĕris omnĭum homĭnum felicissĭmum. Croesus autem opinabātur, se ipsum omnĭum homĭnum felicissĭmum esse. At Solon, nulla usus adulatiōne: Felicissĭmum, inquit, vidi Tellum Atheniensem. Hoc responsum mirātus Croesus eum interrŏgat, cur Tellum felicissĭmum esse existĭmet. Tellus, inquit Solon, cui satis magnae opes erant, ut commŏde vivĕre posset, florente civitāte filĭos habēbat bonos honestosque. Idem splendidissĭme vita decessit; nam in proelĭo fortĭter pugnans, cum hostes in fugam vertisset, cecĭdit et eōdem loco, quo cecĭdit, ab Atheniensĭbus honorificentissĭme sepultus est.

3. Quae cum Solon dixisset, Croesus rursus eum interrogāvit, quem praeter Tellum vidisset felicissĭmum, sperans, se certe secundum fore. At Solon: Cleŏbim, inquit, et Bitōnem, Argīvos, quibus et victus facĭlis et tantae corpŏris vires erant, ut uterque praemĭa certamĭnum ferret. De iisdem etĭam haec memorĭae prodĭta sunt: Die festo Junōnis matrem eōrum curru ad templum vehi jus erat. Cum autem boves morarentur, juvĕnes ipsi ad jugum accessērunt et currum quadraginta quinque stadĭa ad templum vexērunt. Ita sacerdos in fanum vecta est. Qua pietāte juvĕnes omnĭum, qui adĕrant, ocŭlos in se convertērunt. Cum autem Argīvi, qui adĕrant, vires juvĕnum laudassent, muliĕres matrem praedicassent, quod tam pios filĭos habēret, mater, et facto filiōrum et sermōne homĭnum laeta, a dea precāta esse dicītur, ut Cleŏbi et Bitōni filĭis praemĭum daret pro pietāte, quod maxĭmum homĭni dari posset a dea. Juvĕnes, qui, postquam cum matre epulāti sunt, in fano somno se dedērunt, mane inventi sunt mortŭi. Qua re dea ostendit, melĭus esse hominĭbus mori quam vivĕre. Argīvi autem statŭas eōrum, cum optĭmi juvĕnes fuissent, Delphis constituērunt.

4. Cum Solon Cleŏbi et Bitōni secundum felicitātis locum tribuisset, Croesus irātus exclamāvit: Hospes Atheniensis,

meăne[1] felicĭtas tam parva tibi vidētur, ut privātos homĭnes mihi praepōnas? Tum Solon: O rex, inquit, nunc quidem dives es et rex multārum gentĭum; sed felĭcem te non praedicābo, priusquam audivĕro, te bonum vitae finem habuisse. Nam multi homĭnes jucunde quidem vivunt, sed non felicĭter vita decēdunt; is autem solus felix praedicāri potest, cui utrumque obtĭgit. Ităque nemo mortalĭum ante mortem beātus est. His verbis Solon iram regis ita concitāvit, ut neque donum ei daret neque benigne eum dimittĕret, eum stultum homĭnem esse judĭcans, qui praesentĭa bona pro nihĭlo putāret et nemĭnem ante mortem beātum esse judicāret.

[1] meăne; mĕă with the interrogative particle nĕ.

32. De Amasi et Polycrate.

1. Polycrătes, rex insŭlae Sami, cum Amāsi, Aegypti rege, hospitĭum fecit. Brevi tempŏre Polycrătis potentĭa ita aucta est, ut per totam Graecĭam celebrarētur. Quocunque enim duces ejus cum classĭbus proficiscebantur, ut finitĭmis popŭlis bellum inferrent, omnĭa iis felicĭter cedēbant. Ita multas insŭlas, multa etĭam continentis (terrae) oppĭda cepit.

2. Amāsis, cum nuntĭus ei allātus esset, Polycrătem ingenti felicitāte uti, non laetitĭa, sed magna cura affectus est. Ităque, cum prospĕra ejus fortūna in dies magis augerētur, haec ad eum scripsit: Amāsis Polycrăti salūtem dicit. Jucundum quidem est audīre, amīcum et hospĭtem felīcem esse; sed nimĭa tua felicĭtas mihi non placet. Equĭdem hanc fortūnae meae vicissitudĭnem cupĭo, ut ea, quae suscipĭo, partim prospĕre partim male mihi cedant. Idem amīcis et hospitĭbus meis obtingĕre cupĭo. Multos enim homĭnes novi, quibus, postquam omnes res bene gessērunt, postrēmo miserrĭmus vitae finis obtĭgit. Tu igĭtur consilĭum meum secūtus ipse hoc modo nimĭae tuae felicitāti obnitĕre: Cogĭta, quid omnĭum tuārum rerum pretiosissimārum tibi carissĭmum sit. Eam rem, cujus jactūram gravissĭme feres, abjĭce, ut inter homĭnes non amplĭus appareat. Quod si fecĕris, fortūnae vicissitudĭnem non expertus, idem itĕrum ac saepĭus fac, ut ita nimĭae tuae felicitāti ipse obnitāris.

3. Hac epistŭla lecta, Polycrātes, cum intellexisset, Amāsim bonum sibi consilĭum dedisse, toto anĭmo cogitāvit, cujus rei jactūram gravissīme ferret. Quod cum cogitasset, aurĕum anŭlum, quem omnĭum suārum rerum pretiosissĭmum et sibi carissĭmum esse arbitrabātur, in mare abjicĕre constitŭit. Ităque navem hominĭbus complēvit; postquam eam conscendit, nautas in altum mare navigāre jussit. Cum procul ab insŭla essent, rex anŭlum de digīto detraxit et omnĭbus, qui in navi erant, inspectantĭbus in mare abjĕcit. Quo facto¹ domum redĭit.

¹this being done.

4. Quinque vel sex diēbus post, quam Polycrātes-anŭlum in mare abjecĕrat, piscātor quidam magnum pulchrumque piscem cepit, quem, cum Polycrāti dono dare vellet, in domum regĭam portāvit. Qui¹ cum ad regem venisset: Hunc piscem, inquit, quem hodĭe cepi, in forum ferre nolŭi, etsi manu mea victum quaero. Quare tibi, rex, hunc piscem, qui te tuōque imperĭo dignus esse vidĕātur, fero donōque. Polycrātes, piscatōris liberalitāte magna laetitĭa affectus: Recte fecisti, inquit, atque gratĭas tibi ago; beneficĭi tui memor et gratus ad cenam te voco. Regis autem ministri, piscem secantes, in ventre ejus Polycrātis anŭlum invenērunt. Quem¹ cum vidissent, laeti ad Polycrātem se contulērunt, ut ei nuntiārent, anŭlum in ventre piscis repertum esse. Polycrātes, hoc miracŭlo obstupefactus, omnĭa, quae fecĕrat et quae postĕa ei accidĕrant, ad Amāsim regem diligentissīmo perscripsit.

¹Relative for the Demonstrative.

5. Polycrātis epistŭla lecta, Amāsis intellexit, fiĕri non posse, ut hospes fato eriperētur, cui omnĭa tam prospĕre cedĕrent, ut etĭam ea, quae in mare abjecisset, invenīret. Ităque nuntĭum Samum misit, qui dicĕret, hospitĭum ab Amāsi solūtum esse. Id autem ob eam causam Amāsis fecit, ne, si magna atque gravis calamĭtas Polycrāti accidisset, ipse hospĭtis calamitāte nimis dolēret. Factum est, quod ne fiĕret Amāsis timuĕrat; nam non ita multo post Polycrātes Persae cujusdam perfidĭa deceptus cruci affixus est.

33. Quomodo Croesus, Lydiae rex, a Cyro, Persarum rege, victus sit.

1. Eōdem tempŏre, quo Croesus in Lydĭa regnābat, Cyrus regnum Persārum condĭdit. Cum autem Persārum potentĭa magis magisque crescĕret, Croesus eam coërcēre constitŭit, priusquam nimis augerētur sibĭque periculōsa esset. Ităque dona ad oracŭlum Delphos misit atque Apollīnem consulŭit, num Persis bellum inferret. Pythĭa, sacerdos oracŭli Delphĭci, respondit, illum magnum regnum deletūrum esse, si Halym flumen transisset. Halys autem Croesi regnum a regno Persārum dividēbat. Quo oracŭli responso laetus Croesus, qui Cyri regnum se deletūrum esse opinarētur², itĕrum legātos Delphos misit, qui Apollĭni dona ferrent.

¹Relative for the Demonstrative   ²Subjunctive governed by qui = cum is, since he

2. Croesus, cum bellum Persārum paravisset, cum magno exercĭtu profectus Halym flumen transīit et Cappadocĭam, extremam regni Persārum partem, aggressus est. Castris ibi posĭtis, agros vastāvit multisque oppĭdis captis incŏlas in servitūtem redēgit. Cyrus, Persārum rex, nuntĭo allāto, Croesum bellum sibi intulisse, quam celerrĭme exercĭtum parāvit conjunctisque omnĭbus, qui inter Persĭdem Cappadociamque incolēbant, in Cappadocĭam profectus est. Qui cum eo venisset, contra Croesum castra posŭit. Ibi acerrĭme pugnātum est; multis utrimque occīsis, utrīque nocte appetente aequo proelĭo discessērunt.

3. Postquam aequo proelĭo discessērunt, Croesus, qui putāret, se proptereā non discessisse superiōrem, quod Cyrus copiārum numĕro sibi praestāret, majōres copĭas colligĕre decrēvit. Ităque, cum postĕro die Cyrus eum non aggrederētur, Sardes redīre constitŭit. Sardes autem reversus ad Amāsim, Aegypti regem, quocum foedus et societātem fecĕrat, et ad cetĕros socios nuntĭos misit, qui eos bellum parāre et proxĭmo vere Sardes convenīre jubērent; nam ineunte vere Persis itĕrum bellum inferre anĭmum induxĕrat. Milĭtes autem mercenarĭos, quos contra Cyrum secum duxĕrat, dimīsit, non verĭtus, ne Cyrus, qui non vicisset, exercĭtum suum contra Sardes ducĕret.

4. At Cyrus, certĭor factus, Croesum magnam copiārum partem dimisisse, statim Sardes proficisci constitŭit. Ităque exercĭtum tam celerĭter in Lydĭam duxit, ut ipse adventus sui nuntĭus Croeso venīret. Qua re Croesus magna cura affectus tamen Lydos ex urbe in proelĭum eduxit. Lydi autem, qui eo tempŏre a nullo Asĭae populo fortitudĭne superabantur, ex equis[1] pugnābant hastasque longas gerēbant. Proelĭum commissum est in magno campo ante urbem sito, per quem et alĭi fluvĭi et Hermus fluēbant.

[1] *on horseback*

5. Cyrus, cum Lydĭae regem equitătu multum valēre cognovisset, dolo usus est, ut equĭtes ad pugnandum inutīles essent. Camēlis, qui in exercĭtu ejus erant, ut frumentum, vasa aliăque impedimenta portārent, ea detraxit et armātos milĭtes imposŭit, quibus imperāvit, ut in Croesi equĭtes ferocĭter inveherentur; pedĭtes vero camēlos sequi jussit et post pedĭtes omnes suos equĭtes instruxit. Copĭis ita instructis praecēpit, ut nullīus, qui resistěret, vitae parcěrent, Croesum vero ne occiděrent, etiamsi captus resistěret. Camēlos autem ob eam causam Croesi equitĭbus opposŭit, ut equi inusitāto eōrum adspectu terrerentur ităque[1] equĭtes, quibus Croesus plurĭmum potěrat, ad pugnandum inutĭles essent. Et factum est, quod Cyrus fore speravěrat. Proelĭo commisso, equi, ubi camēlos adspexērunt, statim se retro vertērunt. Neque tamen Lydi in tanta perturbatiōne spem victorĭae abjecērunt, sed, Cyri dolo cognĭto, ab equis desiluērunt et pedĭbus cum Persis conflixērunt. Multis utrimque occīsis, postrēmo Lydi, qui copiārum numĕro a Persis superabantur, in fugam versi sunt. Ităque factum est, ut in urbem compulsi a Persis obsiderentur.

[1] *ităque = et ita*

6. Croesus, obsidiōnem diuturnam fore sperans, alĭos nuntĭos misit, qui socĭos adhortarentur, ut quam celerrĭme sibi auxilĭum ferrent, quod ab hostĭbus obsiderētur. Ii enim, qui antěa missi erant, socĭos proximo vere Sardes convenīre jussěrant. Priusquam autem socĭi regi auxilĭo venīre possent, urbs expugnāta et Croesus ab hostĭbus captus est.

7. Sardes autem hoc modo a Persis expugnātae sunt. Postquam hostes quattuordĕcim dies urbem frustra obsedērunt,

Cyrus equĭtes per castra misit, qui militĭbus edicĕrent, magna dona ei datum iri, qui primus in murum ascendisset. Postquam id frustra a multis tentătum est, miles quidam murum ascendĕre conătus est ab ea parte arcis, in qua custōdes non erant posĭti. Cum enim ibi maxĭme ardŭa esset, Lydi non timēbant, ne ab ea parte impĕtus fiĕret. Eōdem autem loco miles ille vidĕrat alĭquem Lydōrum descendĕre, ut galĕam, quae decidĕrat, recipĕret, eamque reportāre. Quod cum vidisset, eōdem modo ascendit. Cum multi alĭi eum secūti in murum ascendissent, urbs capta atque direpta est. Croesus vivus captus est, postquam quattuordĕcim annos regnāvit.

8. Croesum captum Persae ad regem adduxĕrunt. Cyrus cum vinctum rogo impōni jussit cumque eo quattuordĕcim Lydōrum filĭos. Croeso autem in rogo stanti et tanta calamitāte oppresso illud Solōnis (dictum) in mentem venisse dicĭtur, nemĭnem ante mortem beātum esse. In cogitationĭbus defixus post longum silentĭum ex imo pectŏre vocem edĭdit et ter Solōnem vocāvit. Qua voce audīta, Cyrus interprĕtes cum interrogāre jussit, quis ille esset, quem vocāret. Qui cum accessissent et interrogassent, Croesus initĭo nihil respondit; deinde autem, cum interrogando urgerētur: Is est, inquit, quōcum collŏqui omnĭbus regĭbus melĭus est, quam magnas opes habēre. Interprĕtes, cum illud responsum non intellexissent, rursus interrogavērunt, quid dicĕret. Tum demum Croesus, identĭdem interrogātus, eis narrāvit, Solōnem Atheniensem, virum sapientem, qui longinquas peregrinatiōnes suscepisset, olim ad se venisse, ut mores institūtaque Lydōrum cognoscĕret. Cum omnes suas divitĭas ei ostendisset, se ex eo quaesivisse, nonne beātus esset; at Solōnem, eas pro nihĭlo putantem, dixisse, finem vitae respiciendum esse; ante mortem nemĭnem beātum esse. Cyrus, cum ab interpretĭbus audivisset, quae Croesus dixĕrat, eum servāre constitŭit. Ităque celerĭter ignem exstingŭi et Croesum eosque, qui cum eo rogo imposĭti erant, dedūci jussit.

9. Croesum ad se adductum sic allocūtus est: Quis tibi homĭnum, Croese, persuāsit, ut regnum meum aggrederēris et hostis mihi quam amīcus esse malles? Tum ille: Quod feci,

inquit, tibi prospĕre, mihi male cessit. Causa autem belli fuit deus quidam Graecōrum, qui me impŭlit, ut bellum tibi inferrem. Nemo enim tam stultus est, ut bellum paci praepōnat, cum in bello filii a patrĭbus, in pace patres a filiis sepeliantur. Sed ut haec ita fiĕrent, a diis constitūtum esse existĭmo.

10. Croesum ad hunc modum locūtum Cyrus vincŭlis liberāri et sibi assidĕre jussit; rex ipse et omnes, qui adĕrant, magnum ei honōrem tribuĕrunt. Croesus autem, in cogitationĭbus defīxus, aliquamdīu silēbat; cum subĭto: Licetne, inquit, rex, dicĕre, quod mihi in mentem venit? Tum ille, cum Cyrus eum cohortātus esset, ut sine ulla dubitatiōne dicĕret, quae vellet, interrogāvit: Quid ista magna homĭnum turba tanto studīo facit? Urbem tuam, inquit Cyrus, dirĭpit et opes tuas aufert. Tum Croesus: Neque meam, inquit, urbem dirĭpit, neque meas opes aufert, sed tua diripiunt et aufĕrunt; jam enim nihil¹ omnīum harum rerum meum est. Postquam autem dii immortāles me tibi servum tradidērunt, aequum esse puto tibi suadēre, quod tibi utīle sit. Persae quidem superbi, sed inŏpes sunt. Quod si passus eris, eos omnes opes ablātas sibi retinēre, hoc tibi accīdet: Quo plures opes habēbunt, eo magis tibi timendum erit, ne tibi insidĭas parent. Quamobrem tibi suadĕo, ut hoc meum consilĭum sequāris. Ex satellitĭbus tuis custōdes apud portas dispōne, ut exeuntĭbus militĭbus opes aufĕrant, simulantes, decĭmam partem praedae diis tribuendam esse. Quod si fecĕris, non resistent, te justa facĕre putantes, odiumque eōrum effugĭes.

¹jăm..nĭhil, *no longer..anything*

11. Croesi consilĭum, quŏd prudentissĭmum esse vidēbātur, secūtus Cyrus satellĭtes statim ad portas se conferre jussit, ut militĭbus praedam auferrent. Croesum autem laudĭbus ornātum his verbis allocūtus est: Croese, qui consilĭo tuo mihi plurĭmum profuĕris, dic, quid tibi gratum facĕre possim. O rex, inquit ille, abs te peto, ut patiāris, me deo Graecōrum, cui semper maxĭmum honōrem tribui, haec vincŭla mittĕre eumque interrogare, num ei mos sit, eos fallĕre, a quibus colātur. Cum Cyrus interrogasset, cur deum ita incusāret, Croesus narrāvit, se, cum Delphos Apollĭni dona misisset, ejus responso

impulsum esse, ut bellum Persis inferret. Qua re narrāta, rursus idem petīvit, quod antĕa petivĕrat. Cyrus ridens: Et hoc, inquit, te facĕre sinam et alĭa, quae a me petivĕris. Venĭa impetrāta, Croesus alĭquos Lydōrum Delphos misit, qui Apollĭni vincŭla tradĕrent.

12. Lydis Croesi jussu Delphos profectis Pythĭa sic respondit: Injurĭa Croesus deum incūsat. Apollo enim praedixĕrat, illum magnum regnum delctūrum esse, si Halym transisset. Croesus autem, si prudenter facĕre voluisset, itĕrum interrogāre debēbat, Lydōrum an Cyri regnum deus dixisset. Ităque cum. responso non intellecto, itĕrum non interrogavĕrit, sibi ipsi culpam tribŭat. Lydi Sardes reversi responsum Pythĭae Croeso renuntiavērunt. Quo responso lato, Croesus intellexit, culpam sibi, non deo attribuendam esse.

34. De Cyro puero.

1. Astyăgi, ultĭmo Medōrum regi, fĭlĭa erat, cui nomen erat Mandăne. Rex olim somnĭum vidit, quo perterrĭtus magos, somniōrum interprĕtes, consulŭit. Magi, cum omnĭa deliberavissent, a fĭlĭa imperĭo illīus pericŭlum fore dixērunt. Ităque rex fĭlĭam non nobīli cuĭdam Medōrum, qui illustri regis familĭa dignus esset, sed Persae cuĭdam uxōrem dedit. Is tranquillo ingenĭo et nobīli apud Persas genĕre erat. Cum enim Medi Persas in diciōne sua tenērent, nobilissĭmi Persārum mediocrĭbus Medis vix pares habebantur. Ităque non timendum erat, ne Astyăgis imperĭo a fĭlĭa pericŭlum esset.

2. Primo anno post, quam fĭlĭam nobīli illi Persae uxōrem dedĕrat, Astyăges alĭud somnĭum vidit, quo non minus perterrĭtus est. Ităque magos rursus consulŭit, qui ei suasērunt, ut, si Mandăne fīlĭum peperisset, eum occidĕret, ne is regno Astyăgis potirētur. Ităque Astyăges, ubi Mandănen filĭum peperisse compĕrit, cum statim ad se portāri jussit. Quo facto Harpăgum, homĭnem amīcum et omnĭum Medōrum fidelissĭmum, cui in omnĭbus rebus confidēbat, ad se vocāvit eumque puĕrum secum ferre et occidĕre jussit.

3. Harpăgus, cum ipse puĕrum occidĕre nollet, unum ex Astyăgis pastorĭbus, qui in montĭbus greges pascēbat, ad se

venīre jussit eīque mandāvit, ut Astyăgis jussu puĕrum in montĭbus deserto loco exponĕret, ut quam celerrĭme morerētur; quem si non occidisset, sed alĭquo modo servasset, ipsi pessĭme moriendum esse denuntiāvit; sibi autem regem imperasse, ut expositum puĕrum vidēret.

4. Id facĕre ab Harpăgo jussus pastor puĕrum portans eādem via, qua venĕrat, domum redīit. Casu autem accidĕrat, ut eōdem die, quo pastor in urbem profectus erat, uxor ejus filĭum parĕret. Qui cum domum redisset, uxor interrogāvit, cur ad Harpăgum vocātus esset. Tum ille: O mulĭer, inquit, postquam in domum Harpăgi veni, vidi audivīque, quae nunquam vidisse et audivisse vellem. Vidi ibi puĕrum, auro et pretiōsa veste ornātum, quem Harpăgus me quam celerrĭme domum meam portāre et deserto loco exponĕre jussit, mortem minātus, si non fecissem, quod mihi imperasset. Ita factum est, ut puĕrum domum portārem. Mirātus autem, quod puer auro pretiosāque veste ornātus esset, in itinĕre ex ministro, qui me ex urbe domum redeuntem comitātus est, cognōvi, puerum esse Mandănes filĭum.

5. Pastor, cum haec dixisset, puĕrum uxōri ostendit, quae, cum vidēret, puĕrum pulchrum esse, omnĭbus precĭbus petīvit, ne eum exponĕret. Tum ille negāvit, se alĭter facĕre posse; exploratōres enim ab Harpăgo missos ventūros esse, ut expositum puĕrum vidērent; si non fecisset, quod Harpăgus imperasset, sibi pessĭme moriendum fore. Mulĭer, cum conjŭgi persuadēre non posset, ut puĕrum servāret: Quonĭam tibi, inquit, persuadēre non possum, ne puĕrum expōnas, et quia necesse est, expositum puĕrum ostendi, dolo usus mandātum hoc modo confĭce: Pepĕri mortŭum puĕrum; eum cape et expōne; Mandănes autem filĭum ut nostrum educēmus. Ita et tu non videbĕris neglexisse, quod domĭnus tibi mandāvit, et nos filĭum habebĭmus.

6. Pastor, cum mulĭer ei optĭme suasisse vidērētur, consilĭum ejus statim secūtus est. Filĭum Mandănes uxōri tradīdit, suum vero mortŭum, postquam auro et pretiōsa veste alterīus puĕri ornāvit, in montĭbus loco deserto exposŭit. Tertĭo die post, quam puĕrum exposŭerat, pastor in urbem se contŭlit,

ut Harpăgo dicĕret, se parātum esse puĕrum expositum ostendĕre. Harpăgus satellĭtum suōrum fidelissĭmos misit, qui eum vidērent et sepelīrent. Mandănes autem filĭum, qui postĕa Cyrus appellātus est, ut suum pastor educāvit.

7. Cum Cyrus, cui pastor alĭud nomen dedĕrat, puer decem annōrum esset, res quaedam accĭdit, qua cognĭtus est. Aliquando puer ille ludēbat in vico, in quo pastor habitābat. Puĕri cum eo ludentes pastōris filĭum regem creāvērunt. Is, rex creātus, alĭos puerōrum domos aedificāre, alĭos satellĭtes esse jussit; idem nuntĭos constituit, qui res, de quibus cum rege agendum erat, sibi nuntiārent. Ita suum cuīque negotĭum dedit. Unus ex puĕris, nobĭlis inter Medos viri filĭus, Cyri jussis non parēbat. Ităque Cyrus a satellitĭbus eum comprehendi et ad se addūci jussit. Quo facto Cyrus eum verberāvit. Ille vero valde dolens, quod id passus erat, in urbem ad patrem redĭit, ut de pastōris filĭo quererētur. Pater irātus statim ad regem se contŭlit, filĭum secum ducens, ut umĕros ejus verberĭbus sauciātos ei ostendĕret. O rex, inquit, a servo tuo, pastōris filĭo, haec indigna passi sumus.

8. Astyăges nobĭli illi Medo, quem praeter¹ cetĕros colēbat et diligēbat, pollicĭtus, se pastōris filĭum punitūrum esse, pastōrem cum filĭo ad se arcessīvit. Qui cum ad regem venissent, Astyăges irāto anĭmo Cyrum intŭens: Tu, inquit, qui es pastōris filĭus, ausus es filĭum nobilissĭmi Medi, quem omnĭum maxĭme colo et dilĭgo, tam indigne tractāre? Tum Cyrus: Equĭdem, o rex, non injuste feci. Nam puĕri vici nostri mecum ludentes me regem creavērunt, quod iis aptissĭmus vidēbar esse. Cetĕri puĕri omnes jussa faciēbant, hic unus mihi non parēbat; ob eam causam eum verberāri jussi. Quae cum ita sint, judĭca, num injuste fecĕrim et poena dignus sim.

¹praeter cetĕros, *more than the rest*

9. Haec dum puer loquĭtur, Astyăges, os vultumque puĕri acerrĭme contemplātus, eum Mandānes filĭum esse suspicātus est. Huc accedēbat, ut tempus, quo filĭum Mandānes exponi jussĕrat, cum aetāte puĕri convenīre viderētur. Quibus rebus commōtus, rex in cogitationĭbus defixus aliquamdĭu tacēbat. Cum se recepisset, pollicĭtus, se in¹ puĕrum ita factūrum esse,

ut ille de se queri non posset, nobĭlem illum Medum dimīsit, ut pastōrem secrēto de filĭo interrogāret. Medo dimisso, rex Cyrum a ministris in alĭam regĭae domus partem duci jussit. Quo abducto, pastōrem rex interrogāvit, a quo puĕrum accepisset. Ille respondit, eum suum filĭum esse. Astyăges autem, cum eum falsa dicĕre suspicarētur, illum prudentem esse negāvit, si non prius confitēri vellet, quam tormentis coactus esset; dumque haec loquĭtur, satellitĭbus signo dato impĕrat, ut homĭnem comprehendant. Tum demum pastor, cum rex tormenta ei minātus esset, rem, ut erat, narrāvit et sibi venīam a rege petīvit.
¹with

10. Astyăges, cum hoc modo cognovisset, Cyrum servātum esse, eosdem magos convocāvit, qui ei tristĭa illa de Mandānes filĭo somnĭa interpretāti erant. Qui cum advenissent, rex sic allocūtus est: Abhinc decem annos mihi suasistis, ut filĭum Mandānes exponĕrem, cum dicerētis, eum, si vivĕret, regno meo potitūrum esse. Consilĭum vestrum secūtus puĕrum Harpăgo tradidĕram, ut eum exponĕret expositumque occidĕret. At Harpăgus eum servāvit, et servātus puer vivit. Puĕri ejus vici, in quo a pastōre quodam educabātur, cum eo ludentes regem eum creavērunt, atque illo rex creātus omnĭa fecit, quae veri reges facĭunt; nam et satellĭtes constitŭit et aliis alĭa¹ negotĭa tribŭit. Nunc dicĭte, quid de hac re judicētis. Magi, cum diu multumque secum reputassent, respondērunt: Cum puer jam rex fuĕrit, bono es anĭmo²; iterum enim rex non erit. Quo responso laetus Astyăges: Ego quoque, inquit, judĭco, somnĭum jam non respiciendum esse, quonĭam puer rex fuit; nihilomĭnus autem omnĭa bene deliberāte, ut sciam, quid mihi tutissĭmum sit. Nihil prorsus vidēmus, inquĭunt magi, quod tibi timendum sit. Ităque te cohortāmur, ut bono sis anĭmo et puĕrum in Persĭdem ad parentes mittas. His verbis laetus Astyăges Cyrum ad se vocāvit et sic allocūtus est: O puer, vanum somnĭum me commōvit, ut injurĭam tibi inferrem, sed deōrum benignitāte servātus es. Nunc igĭtur in Persĭdem abi; ministros tecum mittam, qui te comitentur. Quo cum venĕris, patrem et matrem invenĭes, qui nobilĭore genĕre sunt, quam pastor ejusque uxor, qui te educavērunt.

¹alĭis alĭa negotĭa, *to some one, to some another business* ²*of good cheer*

11. Astyăges haec locūtus Cyrum dimīsit; Harpăgum autem gravi poena affēcit, quia non fecĕrat, quod facĕre jussus erat. Cyrus, cum ad parentes venisset, benigne ab iis exceptus est. Postquam autem cognovērunt, quis esset, magna laetitĭa affecti sunt; nam putavĕrant, eum mortŭum esse, simŭlac natus esset. Ille rem exposŭit; se ipsum antĕa nihil scivisse ait, in itinĕre autem omnĭa comperisse. Ipse enim putavĕrat, se filĭum pastōris esse, in itinĕre autem veram rem a comitĭbus cognovĕrat.

35. Quomodo Cyrus Persarum regnum condiderit.

1. Cum Cyrus, aequalĭum suōrum fortissĭmus omnibusque Persis carissĭmus, adolevisset, Harpăgus injurĭam a rege sibi illātam ulcisci constitŭit. Ităque Cyro ampla munĕra misit, ut eum sibi amīcum, regi inimīcum reddĕret; simulque autem cum nobilissĭmis Medōrum collocūtus iis persuāsit, melĭus esse, Cyrum regnāre pro Astyăge, qui crudelitāte sua multōrum in se odĭum convertisset. Conjuratiōne ita praeparāta, Harpăgus Cyro, qui in Persīde erat, consilĭum suum hoc modo aperŭit: In lepŏris ventre epistŭlam occultāvit, in qua scripta erant, quae fĭeri vellet. Lepōrem fidelissĭmo cuĭdam servo, qui pastorālem cultum induĕrat, ut venător esse viderētur, tradĭdit eumque in Persīdem ad Cyrum misit. Harpăgus autem eum, cum lepŏrem tradĕret, Cyro dicĕre jussĕrat, necessarĭum esse, Cyrum sua manu lepōrem aperīre neque ullum homĭnem adesse, cum id facĕret.

2. Cyrus, cum lepōrem accepisset, arbĭtris (testĭbus) remōtis ventrem ejus aperŭit. Ventre aperto, epistŭlam invēnit, in qua haec scripta erant: Cyre, dii tibi benigni sunt; nam benignitāte deōrum servātus es. Nunc igĭtur ulciscĕre et persequĕre injurĭam ab Astyăge tibi illātam, qui te infantem expōni jussit, ut perīres. Mea autem et deōrum benignitāte vivis, quia non feci, quod rex mihi imperavĕrat, sed te servāvi et pastōri cuĭdam educandum tradĭdi. Quodsi consilĭum meum secūtus eris, omnĭum Astyăgis terrārum imperĭum obtinēbis. Persuāde igĭtur Persis, ut ab Astyăge deficĭant, et exercĭtum duc in Medĭam. Si ego ab Astyăge dux contra te factus ero, exercĭtum meum cum tuo conjungam. Idem facĭet quilĭbet nobilĭum Medōrum, cum dux factus erit.

3. Cyrus, epistŭla lecta, secum deliberāvit, quo modo Persis persuadēre posset, ut ab Astyăge deficĕrent. Qua re deliberāta, hoc ei optĭmum esse videbātur. Simŭlans, se ab Astyăge Persārum ducem factum esse, Persas convocāvit eosque constitūta die cum falcĭbus adesse jussit. Postquam omnes Persae constitūto tempŏre cum falcĭbus convenērunt, Cyrus eos locum quendam spinōsum uno die purgāre jussit. Cum id fecissent, iis imperāvit, ut postridĭe lauti adessent. Intercă omnes ovĭum et boum greges patris sui in unum locum conduxit, ut optĭmis cibis Persas excipĕret. Cum postridĭe convenissent, eos in prato considĕre jussit, ut laetitĭae et hilaritāti se darent. Cyrus, ubi eos vino cibōque se largĭter invitantes[1] vidit, interrogāvit, utra meliōra illis viderentur, quae pridĭe habuissent, an quae hodĭe habērent. Cum Persae respondissent, magnum discrīmen esse: pridĭe enim se omnĭa mala habuisse, at hodĭe omnĭa bona. Tum Cyrus: Persae, inquit, sic res se habet: Si me sequi volētis, haec et plurĭma alĭa bona vobis obtingent omnĭumque servilĭum labōrum expertes erĭtis; sin autem me sequi nolētis, plurĭmi labōrēs hesternis simĭles vos opprĭment. Agĭte, consilĭum meum sequimĭni, ut libĕri sitis. Equĭdem deōrum voluntāte ad id[2] natus esse mihi vidĕor, ut haec bona vobis parem, quos neque aliis rebus neque fortitudĭne Medis inferiōres esse judĭco. Quae cum ita sint, vos admonĕo, ut ab Astyăge deficiātis.

[1] se largīter invitāre, *to enjoy one's self* [2] *for this purpose*

4. Persae, Medōrum imperĭum aegre ferentes, postquam ducem invenērunt, libenter sibi libertātem paravērunt. Astyăges, certĭor factus, Cyrum id agĕre, ut regnum sibi eripĕret, nuntĭum misit, qui eum advocāret. Cyrus eum regi renuntiāre jussit, se prius adventūrum esse, quam illi gratum esset. Quo nuntĭo relāto, Astyăges bellum adversus Cyrum summa vi parāvit et Harpăgum ducem fecit, oblītus, quam injurĭam ei fecisset. Omnĭbus rebus parātis, Medi ad bellum profecti sunt. Proelĭo commisso, alĭi, Harpăgi consilĭi non conscĭi, fortĭter pugnavērunt, alĭi ad Persas defecērunt, plerīque autem fuga salūtem petivērunt.

5. Ita factum est, ut Medi a Persis devincerentur. Astyăges, cum nuntĭus ei allātus esset, rem[1] male gestam esse, omnes

Medos in urbe relictos, et juniōres et seniōres, quam celerrĭme arma capĕre jussit, ut itĕrum proelĭum cum Persis committerētur. Medi itĕrum fusi fugatīque sunt; rex ipse, maxĭma Medōrum parte occīsa, cum vivus in hostĭum potestātem venisset, regno suo privātus est. Ab eo tempŏre Persae imperĭum Asĭae tenēbant.

fight

———

VOCABULARY

TO THE FOREGOING READING LESSONS.

A.

ā
ăb } (with ablat.), *from, away from, by*

abdūcō, -ĕrĕ, abduxī, abductŭm, *to carry away, to take with*

ăbĕō, -īrĕ, -iī, -ĭtŭm, *to go away*

ăbhinc, *ago*

abjĭcĭō, -ĕrĕ, abjēcī, abjectŭm, *to throw down;* spem abjicĕre, *to give up hope*

ăbŏlĕō, -ĕrĕ, ăbŏlēvī, ăbŏlĭtŭm, *to abolish*

abs (w. abl.), *from*

absŭm, ăbessĕ, ăfŭī, *to be absent, to be away*

accēdō, -ĕrĕ, accessī, accessŭm, *to go near, approach;* ad jugum accedĕre, *to put one's self to the yoke;* huc accēdit, *to this it is added*

accĭdit, *it happens*

accĭpĭō, -ĕrĕ, accēpī, acceptŭm, *to receive, accept*

ăcĕr, -rĭs, -rĕ, *keen, sharp, bitter;* ăcerrĭmŭs, *ardent;* acrĭter, *sharply*

Achillēs, -ĭs (m.), *Achilles, the celebrated Grecian hero*

ăcĭēs, -ēī (f.), *a (line of) battle*

acquĭescō, -ĕrĕ, acquĭēvī, acquĭētŭm, *to rest*

ăcŭō, -ĕrĕ, ăcŭī, ăcūtŭm, *to sharpen, whet*

ăd (w. acc.), *at, to, near*

addō, -ĕrĕ, -ĭdī, -ĭtŭm, *to add*

addūcō, -ĕrĕ, adduxī, adductŭm, *to lead, to induce*

ădĕō, -īrĕ, ădiī, ădĭtŭm, *to go to*

ădhinnĭō, -īrĕ, -īvī, -ĭtŭm, *to neigh to*

adhortŏr, -ārī, -ātŭs sŭm, *to exhort*

ădĭmō, -ĕrĕ, ădēmī, ademptŭm, *to take away*

ădĭpiscŏr, -ī, ădeptŭs sŭm, *to obtain*

adjĭcĭō, -ĕrĕ, adjēcī, adjectŭm, *to add*

admīrātĭō, -ōnĭs (f.), *admiration*

admīrŏr, -ārī, -ātŭs sŭm, *to admire*

admittō, -ĕrĕ, admīsī, admissŭm, *to admit*

admŏnĕō, -ĕrĕ, -ŭī, -ĭtŭm, *to admonish*

ădŏlĕō, -ĕrĕ, ădŏlēvī, adultŭm, *to grow up*

adspectŭs, -ūs (m.), *appearance, a sight*

adspĭcĭō, -ĕrĕ, adspexī, adspectŭm, *to see*

adsŭm, ădessĕ, adfŭī, *to be present*

ădūlātĭō, -ōnĭs (f.), *flattery*

ădūlescens, -tĭs (m.), *a youth, a young man*

advĕnĭō, -īrĕ, advēnī, adventŭm, *to arrive*

adventŭs, -ūs (m.), *a coming, an arrival*

adversŭs, -ă, -ŭm, *adverse, unfavorable*

advŏcō, -ārĕ, -āvī, -ātŭm, *to summon*

aedĭfĭcĭŭm, -ī (n.), *a building*

aedĭfĭcō, -ārĕ, -āvī, -ātŭm, *to build*

aegrē, *with grief, reluctantly*

Aegyptŭs, -ī (f.), *Egypt*

aequālĭs, - (m.), *a contemporary*

aequŭs, -ă, -ŭm, *equal, fair;* aequo proelĭo, *with equal success*

āĕr, āĕrĭs (m.), *the air*

aes, aerĭs (n.), *brass*

aestŭs, -ūs (m.), *heat*

aetās, -ātĭs (f.), *age*

aeternŭs, -ă, -ŭm, *eternal;* in aeternum, *forever*

affectŭs, -ă, -ŭm, *struck*

afférō, -rĕ, attŭlī, allātŭm, to bring to; (cibos) afferre, to serve (dishes)

afficiō, -ĕrĕ, affēcī, affectŭm, to treat, affect; praemio afficĕre, to bestow a reward; poena afficĕre, to afflict with punishment; laetitĭa afficĕre, to gladden; cura afficĕre, to cast down

affīgō, -ĕrĕ, affīxī, affīxŭm, to fasten to

Agămemnō, -ŏnĭs (m.), Agamemnon, commander in chief of the Grecian forces before Troy

ăgĕ, come

aggrĕdĭŏr, -ī, aggrĕssŭs sŭm, to attack

agnoscō, -ĕrĕ, agnōvī, agnĭtŭm, to acknowledge, recognize

ăgō, -ĕrĕ, ēgī, actŭm, to do, to transact; id agĕre, to have in mind; grātĭās ăgĕrĕ, to return thanks

ăgrestĭs, -ĕ, rustic; homo agrestis, a peasant

agrĭcŏlă, -ae (m.), a farmer, peasant

agrĭcultūră, -ae (f.), agriculture

Ājax, -ācĭs (m.), Ajax

ājō, I say

ălă, -ae (f.), a wing

Ălexandĕr, -rī (m.), Alexander

ălĭquamdĭū, some time

ălĭquandō, some time

ălĭquĭs, ălĭquă, ălĭquĭd, ălĭquŏd, some one, some, any one

ălĭtĕr, otherwise

ălĭŭs, -ă, -ŭd, other, another

allŏquŏr, -ī, allŏcūtŭs sŭm, to address

altĕr, -ă, -ŭm, second, the other (of two), one of two

altŭs, -ă, -ŭm, high, deep

ămārŭs, -ă, -ŭm, bitter

Amāsĭs, - (m.), Amasis

ămīcĭtĭă, -ae (f.), friendship

ămīcŭs, -ī (m.), a friend

ămittō, -ĕrĕ, ămīsī, ămissŭm, to lose

ămō, -ārĕ, -āvī, -ātŭm, to love, like

amplĭŭs, further; non amplĭus, no longer

amplŭs, -ă, -ŭm, splendid

ăn, or

angustĭae, -ārŭm (pl. f.), a narrow passage

ănĭmŭs, -ī (m.), the mind, soul, spirit; animos laedĕre, to hurt the feelings

annŭs, -ī (m.), a year

antĕ (w. acc.), before

antĕă, before

antīquĭtās, -ātĭs (f.), antiquity

antīquŭs, -ă, -ŭm, ancient

ănŭlŭs, -ī (m.), a finger-ring

Ăpellēs, -ĭs (m.), Apelles, a distinguished Greek painter

ăpĕrĭō, -īrĕ, ăpĕrŭī, ăpertŭm, to disclose; se aperīre, to betray one's self

Ăpollō, -ĭnĭs (m.), Apollo

appārĕō, -ĕrĕ, -ŭī, -ĭtŭm, to appear, to make one's appearance

appellō, -ārĕ, -āvī, -ātŭm, to name, call

appellō, -ĕrĕ, appŭlī, appulsŭm, to land

appĕtō, -ĕrĕ, appĕtīvī (-ĭī), appĕtītŭm, to seek; nocte appetente, at night fall

Appĭŭs, -ă, -ŭm, Appian

apprŏpinquō, -ārĕ, -āvī, -ātŭm, to approach

aptō, -ārĕ, -āvī, -ātŭm, to fit

aptŭs, -ă, -ŭm, adapted, fitted for

ăpŭd (w. acc.), among, with, at; near

ăquă, -ae (f.), water

Ăraxēs, -ĭs (f.), the river Araxes

arbĭtĕr, -rī (m.), an arbiter; a witness

arbĭtrŏr, -ārī, -ātŭs sŭm, to believe, think, regard

accessō, -ĕrĕ, accessīvī, accessītŭm, to summon

Ardĕă, -ae (f.), Ardea

ardŭŭs, -ă, -ŭm, arduous, steep

argentŭm, -ī (n.), silver

Argīvī, -ōrŭm (pl. m.), the Argives

Ărĭadnē, -ēs (f.), Ariadne

armātŭs, -ă, -ŭm, armed

Armĭnĭŭs -ī (m.), Arminius

ars. -tĭs (f.), an art

artĭfex, -ĭcĭs (m.), an artist

arx, -cĭs (f.), a citadel

ascendō, -ĕrĕ, ascendī, ascensŭm, to ascend, to climb up

Ăsĭă, -ae (f.), *Asia*
assĭdō, -ĕrĕ, assēdī, (no sup.), *to sit down*
Astyăgēs, -Is (m.), *Astyages*
ăt, *but, on the contrary*
Athēnĭensĭs, - (m.), *an Athenian*
atquĕ, *and*
attămĕn, *still*
attrĭbŭō, -ĕrĕ, attrĭbŭī, attrĭbŭ-tŭm, *to attribute; to put on*
audĕō, -ĕrĕ, ausŭs sŭm, *to dare, venture*
audĭō, -īrĕ. -īvī, -ītŭm, *to hear*
aufĕrō, auferrĕ, abstŭlī, ablātŭm, *to carry away*
augĕō, -ĕrĕ, auxī, auctŭm, *to increase*
Augustŭs, -ī (m.), *Augustus, the first emperor of Rome*
Aulĭs, -ĭdĭs (f.), *Aulis*
aurĕŭs, -ă, -ŭm, *of gold, golden*
aurŭm, -ī (n.), *gold*
autĕm (follows the first word in the sentence or clause), *but, yet*
auxĭlĭŭm, -ī (n.), *help, assistance;* auxĭlĭŭm ferrĕ, *to afford, render assistance*
āvertō, -ĕrĕ, āvertī, āversŭm, *to avert*
ăvĭs, - (f.), *a bird*
ăvŏlō, -ārĕ, -āvī, -ātŭm, *to fly away*

B.

Bacchŭs, -ī (m.), *Bacchus*
bĕātŭs, -ă, -ŭm, *happy, blessed*
bellŭm, -ī (n.), *war*
bĕnĕ, *well*
bĕnĕfĭcĭŭm, -ī (n.), *a benefit*
bĕnĕvŏlŭs, -ă, -ŭm, *benevolent*
bĕnignĭtās, -ātĭs (f.), *goodness*
bĕnignŭs, -ă, -ŭm, *favorable, kind*
bĭbō, -ĕrĕ, bĭbī (no sup.), *to drink*
Bĭtōn, -ōnĭs (m.), *Biton*
blandŭs, -ă, -ŭm, *flattering, gentle*
bŏnĭtās, -ātĭs (f.), *excellence*
bŏnŭm, -ī (n.), *a good, possession*
bōs, bŏvĭs (m.), *an ox*
bracchĭŭm, -ī (n.), *the arm*
brĕvĭs, -ĕ, *short*

C.

cădō, -ĕrĕ, cĕcĭdī, cāsŭm, *to fall*
caecŭs, -ă, -ŭm, *blind*
caedō, -ĕrĕ, cĕcĭdī, caesŭm, *to fell;* lignɑ caedĕre, *to cut wood;* caesa, *cuttings* [*fortune*
călămĭtās, -ātĭs (f.), *a calamity, mis-*
Calchās, -ae (m.), *Calchas*
cămēlŭs, -ī (m.), *a camel*
campŭs, -ī (m.), *a plain, field*
candens, -tĭs, *red-hot*
căpĭō, -ĕrĕ, cēpī, captŭm, *to take, catch, seize, to take prisoner*
Cappadŏcĭă, -ae (f.), *Cappadocia*
captīvŭs, -ī (m.), *a captive*
căpŭt, -ĭtĭs (n.), *the head;* căpĭtĭs damnārĕ, *to condemn to death*
carcĕr, -ĭs (m.), *a prison*
carmĕn, -ĭnĭs (n.), *a poem*
carpō, -ĕrĕ, carpsī, carptŭm, *to pluck*
cārŭs, -ă, -ŭm, *dear;* cārissĭmĕ, *my dearest*
cāsĕŭs, -ī (m.), *a cheese*
castră, -ōrŭm (pl. n.), *a military camp*
cāsŭs, -ūs (m.), *an accident, chance;* cā-ū, *by chance*
causă, -ae (f.), *a cause*
cēdō, -ĕrĕ, cessī, cessŭm, *to retire;* felicĭter cedĕre, *to go on, turn out, happily*
cĕlĕbrō, -ārĕ, -āvī, -ātŭm, *to celebrate*
cĕlĕr, -ĭs, -ĕ, *swift;* quam celerrĭme, *as quick as possible*
cēnă, -ae (f.), *dinner, meal.* Written also: coenă
cēră, -ae (f.), *wax*
certāmĕn, -ĭnĭs (n.), *a contest* (in games); *a combat*
certĕ, *to be sure, certainly*
certō, -ārĕ, -āvī, -ātŭm, *to contend, strive*
certŭs, -ă, -ŭm, *certain;* certĭōrem făcĕre, *to inform*
cervă, -ae (f.), *a hind*
cētĕrī, -ae, -a, *the rest, other*
Chĕruscī, -ōrŭm (pl. m.), *the Cherusci*

cĭbŭs, -Ī (m.), *food;* cibos afferre, *to serve dishes*
Cĭnĕăs, -ae (m.), *Cineas*
circă (w. acc.), *around, near*
circumdūcō, -ĕrĕ, circumduxī, circumductŭm, *to lead around*
cīvĭs, - (m.), *a citizen*
cīvĭtās, -ātĭs (f.), *a state*
clădēs, -ĭs (f.), *a defeat*
clāmō, -ārĕ, -āvī, -ātŭm, *to cry out*
clārŭs, -ă, -ŭm, *famous;* clara vox, *a loud voice*
classĭs, - (f.), *a fleet, the navy*
Claudĭŭs, -Ī (m.), *Claudius, a Roman consul*
claudō, -ĕrĕ, clausī, clausŭm, *to shut, close*
Clĕŏbĭs, - (m.), *Cleobis*
clĭpĕŭs, -Ī (m.), *a shield*
Coclēs, -ĭtĭs (m.), *Cocles*
Cōdrŭs, -Ī (m.), *Codrus*
cŏercĕō, -ĕrĕ, -ŭī, -ĭtŭm, *to restrain*
cōgĭtātĭō, -ōnĭs (f.), *thought*
cōgĭtō, -ārĕ, -āvī, -ātŭm, *to think, reflect*
cognōmĕn, -ĭnĭs (n.), *a surname*
cognōscō, -ĕrĕ, cognōvī, cognĭtŭm, *to know, recognize; to make the acquaintance*
cōgō, -ĕrĕ, cōĕgī, cōactŭm, *to compel, force*
cŏhĭbĕō, -ĕrĕ, -ŭī, -ĭtŭm, *to restrain*
cŏhortŏr, -ārī, -ātŭs sŭm, *to exhort*
collĭgō, -ĕrĕ, collēgī, collectŭm, *to collect*
collŏcō, -ārĕ, -āvī, -ātŭm, *to put, place*
collŏquĭŭm, -Ī (n.), *a conversation*
collŏquŏr, -Ī, collŏcūtŭs sŭm, *to converse*
cōlō, -ĕrĕ, cŏlŭī, cultŭm, *to cultivate, to honor;* Dĕŭm cŏlĕrĕ, *to worship God, revere God*
cŏmĕs, -ĭtĭs (m.), *a companion*
cŏmĭtŏr, -ārī, -ātŭs sŭm, *to accompany*
committō, -ĕrĕ, commĭsī, commĭsŭm, *to commit;* proelĭŭm commĭttĕrĕ, *to fight a battle*
commŏdē, *conveniently, at one's ease*
commŏvĕō, -ērĕ, commōvī, commōtŭm, *to move, rouse*
commūnĭcō, -ārĕ, -āvī, -ātŭm, *to impart*
commūnĭs, -ĕ, *common*
commūtō, -ārĕ, -āvī, -ātŭm, *to change, exchange*
compellō, -ĕrĕ, compŭlī, compulsŭm, *to drive*
compĕrĭō, -īrĕ, compĕrī, compertŭm, *to learn*
complectŏr, -Ī, complexŭs sŭm, *to embrace*
complĕō, -ĕrĕ, complēvī, complētŭm, *to fill up*
comprĕhendō, -ĕrĕ, comprĕhendī, comprĕhensŭm, *to seize*
conciliō, -ārĕ, -āvī, -ātŭm, *to win, reconcile*
concĭtō, -ārĕ, -āvī, -ātŭm, *to arouse*
conclāvĕ, -ĭs (n.), *a room*
condĭcĭō, -ōnĭs (f.), *a condition*
condō, -ĕrĕ, condĭdī, condĭtŭm, *to found*
condūcō, -ĕrĕ, conduxī, conductŭm, *to lead*
confĕrō, conferrĕ, contŭlī, collātŭm, *to confer;* sē conferrĕ, *to betake one's self*
confĭcĭō, -ĕrĕ, confēcī, confectŭm, *to accomplish*
confīdō, -ĕrĕ, confīsŭs sŭm, *to trust, confide*
confĭtĕŏr, -ērī, confessŭs sŭm, *to confess*
conflăgrō, -ārĕ, -āvī, -ātŭm, *to burn down*
conflīgō, -ĕrĕ, conflixī, conflictŭm, *to fight*
congrĕdĭŏr, -Ī, congressŭs sum, *to engage*
conĭcĭō, -ĕrĕ, conĭēcī, conĭectŭm, *to throw*
conjungō, -ĕrĕ, conjunxī, conjunctŭm, *to unite*
conjunx, *see* conjux

conjūrātĭŏ, -ōnĭs (f.), *a conspiracy*
conjūrō, -ārĕ, -āvī, -ātŭm, *to conspire*
conjux, -ŭgĭs (m.), *a husband;* (f.), *a wife*
cōnŏr, -ārī, -ātŭs sŭm, *to try*
conscendō, -ĕrĕ, conscendī, conscensŭm (naves), *to embark*
conscĭŭs, -ă, -ŭm, *knowing, aware*
consīdĕrō, -ārĕ, -āvī, -ātŭm, *to consider*
consīdō, -ĕrĕ, consēdī, consessŭm, *to alight; to sit down*
consĭlĭŭm, -ī (n.), *advice, plan*
consistō, -ĕrĕ, constĭtī, constĭtŭm, *to stand*
conspĭcĭŏ, -ĕrĕ, conspexī, conspectŭm, *to see*
conspīrō, -ārĕ, -āvī, -ātŭm, *to conspire*
constantĭă, -ae (f.), *constancy*
constĭtŭō, -ĕrĕ, constĭtŭī, constĭtŭtŭm, *to set up, determine, appoint*
consŭlō, -ĕrĕ, consŭlŭī, consultŭm, *to counsel, care for;* consŭlĕrĕ ălĭquĕm, *to consult some one*
contemnō, -ĕrĕ, contempsī, contemptŭm, *to despise*
contemplŏr, -ārī, -ātŭs sŭm, *to contemplate*
contentĭŏ, -ōnĭs (f.), *strife*
contĭnens, -tĭs (f.), *a continent*
contĭnĕō, -ĕrĕ, contĭnŭī, contentŭm, *to hold together*
contrā (w. acc.), *against*
convĕnĭō, -īrĕ, convĕnī, conventŭm, *to meet; to agree*
convertō, -ĕrĕ, convertī, conversŭm, *to turn;* odīum in se convertere, *to incur the hatred;* ocŭlos in se convertĕre, *to attract the attention*
convīcĭă, -ōrŭm (pl. n.), *abusive language*
convīvă, -ae (m.), *a guest*
convīvĭŭm, -ī (n.), *a feast*
convŏcō, -ārĕ, -āvī, -ātŭm, *to call together*
cōpĭae, -ārŭm (pl. f.), *troops, forces*
cōrăm (w. abl.), *in presence of*

Cŏrinthŭs, -ī (f.), *the city of Corinth*
Cŏrĭŏlānŭs, -ī (m.), *Coriolanus*
Cŏrĭŏlī, -ōrŭm (pl. m.), *Corioli*
corpŭs, -ŏrĭs (n.) *a body*
crēdō, -ĕrĕ, credĭdī, credĭtŭm, *to believe, confide*
crĕmō, -ārĕ, -āvī, -ātŭm, *to burn*
crĕō, -ārĕ, -āvī, -ātŭm, *to create, elect, make*
crescō, -ĕrĕ, crēvī, crētŭm, *to grow, increase*
Crētă, -ae (f.), *Crete*
crīmĕn, -ĭnĭs (n.), *a crime*
Crĭtō, -ōnĭs (m.), *Crito*
Croesŭs, -ī (m.), *Croesus, celebrated for his riches*
crŭcĭō, -ārĕ, -āvī, -ātŭm, *to torture*
crūdēlĭtās, -ātĭs (f.), *cruelty*
crux, crŭcĭs (f.), *a cross*
culpă, -ae (m.), *a fault, blame*
cultŭs, -ūs (m.), *garb*
cŭm (w. abl.), *with*
cŭm (conjunct.), *when, as, though, whereas, since*
cŭpĭō, -ĕrĕ, cŭpīvī, cŭpītŭm, *to wish, desire, covet*
cūr, *why*
cūră, -ae (f.), *care;* cura afficĕre, *to cast down*
cūrō, -ārĕ, -āvī, -ātŭm, *to take care, to care for*
currŭs, -ūs (m.), *a carriage*
cursŭs, -ūs (m.), *a course*
custōdĭă, -ae (f.), *a prison*
custōdĭō, -īrĕ, -īvī, -ītŭm, *to guard, watch*
custōs, -ōdĭs (m.), *a guard*
Cyclops, -ŏpĭs (m.), *a Cyclop*
Cȳrŭs, -ī (m.), *Cyrus*

D.

Daedălŭs, -ī (m.), *Daedalus*
damnō, -ārĕ, -āvī, -ātŭm, *to condemn*
Dārēŭs, -ī (m.), *Dareus, a Persian king*
dē (w. abl.), *of, from, down from, concerning*
dĕă, -ae (f.), *a goddess*

dĕbĕŏ, -ērĕ, -ŭī, -ĭtŭm, *to owe; I ought, must, should*
dēcēdŏ, -ĕrĕ, dēcessī, dēcessŭm, *to depart;* vītā dēcēdĕrĕ, *to depart from life*
dĕcĕm, *ten*
dēcernŏ, -ĕrĕ, dēcrēvī, dēcrētŭm, *to determine*
dĕcĭdŏ, -ĕrĕ, dĕcĭdī, (no sup.), *to fall down*
dĕcĭmŭs, -ă, -ŭm, *the tenth*
dēcĭpĭŏ, -ĕrĕ, dēcēpī, dēceptŭm, *to deceive*
dēdūcŏ, -ĕrĕ, dēduxī, dēductŭm, *to bring down*
dēfensŏr, -ōrĭs (m.), *a defender*
dēfĕrŏ, -rĕ, dētŭlī, dēlātŭm, *to bring*
dēfĭcĭŏ, -ĕrĕ, dēfēcī, dēfectŭm, *to rebel against*
dēfixŭs, -ă, -ŭm, *lost*
dĕindĕ, *then, afterwards, next*
dējĭcĭŏ, -ĕrĕ, dējēcī, dējectŭm, *to throw down, to drive*
dēlectŏ, -ārĕ, -āvī, -ātŭm, *to delight*
dēlĕŏ, -ērĕ, dēlēvī, dēlētŭm, *to destroy*
dēlībĕrŏ, -ārĕ, -āvī, -ātŭm, *to deliberate*
Dēlōs, -ī (f.), *Delos*
Delphī, -ōrŭm (pl. m.), *Delphi*
Delphĭcŭs, -ă, -ŭm, *Delphic*
Dēmētrĭŭs, -ī (m.), *Demetrius*
dēmūm, *at length*
dēnuntĭŏ, -ārĕ, -āvī, -ātŭm, *to warn*
dēnŭŏ, *again, anew*
dēpellŏ, -ĕrĕ, dēpŭlī, dēpulsŭm, *to remove*
dēpōnŏ,-ĕrĕ, dēpŏsŭī, dēpŏsĭtŭm, *to lay down*
dērīdĕŏ, -ērĕ, dērīsī, dērīsŭm, *to laugh at*
descendŏ, -ĕrĕ, descendī, descensŭm, *to come down*
dēscrībŏ, -ĕrĕ, dēscripsī, dēscriptŭm, *to describe*
dēsĕrŏ, -ĕrĕ, dēsĕrŭī, dēsertŭm, *to abandon*

dēsertŭs, -ă, -ŭm, *desert*
dēsīdĕrĭŭm, -ī (n.), *longing*
dēsĭlĭŏ, -īrĕ, dēsĭlŭī, dēsultŭm, *to leap down*
dētrăhŏ,-ĕrĕ, dētraxī, dētractŭm, *to draw from*
dĕŭs, -ī (m.), *a god;* Dĕŭs, *God*
dēvincŏ, -ĕrĕ, dēvīcī, dēvictŭm, *to vanquish*
dextĕr, dext(ĕ)ră, dext(ĕ)rŭm, *right*
Dĭānă, -ae (f.), *Diana*
(dĭcĭŏ), -ōnĭs (f.), *dominion*
dīcŏ, -ĕrĕ, dixī, dictŭm, *to say*
dictŭm, -ī (n.), *a saying, word*
dĭēs, -ēī (m. & f. in the sing., m. in the plur.), *a day;* dĭēs festŭs, *a holiday;* in dĭēs, *from day to day*
diffĭcĭlĕ, *with difficulty*
dĭgĭtŭs, -ī (m.), *a finger*
dignŭs, -ă, -ŭm, *worthy, deserving*
dīgrĕdĭŏr, -ī, dīgressŭs sŭm, *to depart*
dīlĭgentĕr, *carefully*
dīlĭgŏ,-ĕrĕ,dīlexī,dīlectŭm,*to love*
dīmittŏ, -ĕrĕ, dīmīsī, dīmissŭm, *to dismiss, disband*
Dĭŏmēdēs, -īs (m.), *Diomedes*
dīrĭpĭŏ, -ĕrĕ, dīrĭpŭī, dīreptŭm, *to plunder*
dīrŭŏ, -ĕrĕ, dīrŭī, dīrŭtŭm, *to destroy, demolish*
discēdŏ,-ĕrĕ, discessī, discessŭm, *to leave, depart*
discessŭs, -ūs (m.), *departure*
discĭplīnă, -ae (f.), *a discipline*
discordĭă, -ae (f.), *discord*
discrīmĕn, -ĭnĭs (n.), *a difference*
dispōnŏ, -ĕrĕ, dispŏsŭī, dispŏsĭtŭm, *to dispose*
dĭŭ, *for a long time, long*
dĭŭturnŭs, -ă, -ŭm, *long-continued*
dīvĕs, -ĭtĭs, *rich*
dīvĭdŏ, -ĕrĕ, dīvīsī, dīvīsŭm, *to divide, separate*
dīvīnŭs, -ă, -ŭm, *divine*
dīvĭtĭae, -ārŭm (pl. f.), *riches*
dŏ, dărĕ, dĕdī, dătŭm, *to give;* dōnŏ dărĕ, *to give as a present;* sē dărĕ, *to give one's self up*

dŏcĕō, -ērĕ, dŏcŭī, doctŭm, to teach
dŏlĕō, -ērĕ, -ŭī, -ītŭm, to grieve for
dŏlŏr, -ōrĭs (m.), pain, grief
dŏlŭs, -ī (m.), a trick, craft; dŏlō, craftily
dŏmĭnātĭō, -ōnĭs (f.), dominion
dŏmĭnŭs, -ī (m.), a master, a lord
dŏmŭs, -ūs (f.), a house; dŏmī, at home; dŏmŭm, home; dŏmō, from home
dōnō, -ārĕ, -āvī, -ātŭm, to present with, to give (as a present)
dōnŭm, -ī (n.), a gift, present; dōnō dărĕ, to give as a present
Dōrēs, -ĭŭm (pl. m.), the Dorians
dormĭō, -īrĕ, -īvī, -ītŭm, to sleep
dŭbĭtātĭō, -ōnĭs (f.), hesitation
dŭcentī, -ae, -ă, two hundred
dūcō, -ĕrĕ, duxī, ductŭm, to lead, bring, take; in matrimonĭum ducĕre, to marry
dulcĭs, -ĕ, sweet
dŭm, while, as long as
dŭō, -ae, -ō, two
dŭōdĕcĭm, twelve
dux, dŭcĭs (m.), a leader, guide

E.

ē (w. abl. and only before consonants), from, of, out of
ēbrĭŭs, -ă, -ŭm, drunk
ēdĭcō, -ĕrĕ, ēdixī, ēdictŭm, to make known
ĕdō, -ĕrĕ, ĕdī, ēsŭm, to eat
ēdō, -ĕrĕ, ēdĭdī, ēdĭtŭm, to give out; vocem edĕre, to utter a cry
ēdūcō, -ārĕ, -āvī, -ātŭm, to bring up, educate
ēdūcō, -ĕrĕ, ēduxī, ēductŭm, to lead out
effĭcĭō, -ĕrĕ, effēcī, effectŭm, to make, accomplish
efflō, -ārĕ, -āvī, -ātŭm, to breathe out; anĭmum efflāre, to breathe one's last
effŭgĭō, -ĕrĕ, effŭgī, (no sup), to escape

ĕgō, I; ĕgŏmĕt, I
ēgrĕdĭŏr, -ī, ēgressŭs sŭm, to go out
ēgrĕgĭŭs, -ă, -ŭm, excellent
ĕheu, alas
ējĭcĭō, -ĕrĕ, ējēcī, ējectŭm, to drive from, out
ēlābŏr, -ī, ēlapsŭs sŭm, to escape
ĕlĕphantŭs, -ī (m.), an elephant
ĕmō, -ĕrĕ, ĕmī, emptŭm, to buy, purchase
ĕnĭm, for
ĕō, thither
Ĕpāmĭnondās, -ae(m.), Epaminondas
Ĕphĕsĭŭs, -ă, -ŭm, Ephesian
Ēpīrŭs, -ī (f.), Epirus
ĕpĭstŭlă, -ae (f.), a letter
ĕpŭlae, -ārŭm (pl. f.), a meal
ĕpŭlŏr, -ārī, -ātŭs sŭm, to eat
ĕquĕs, -ĭtĭs (m.), a horseman, rider
ĕquĭdĕm, I for my part
ĕquĭtātŭs, -ūs (m.), cavalry
ĕquŭs, -ī (m.), a horse, steed; ex equis, on horseback
ērĭpĭō, -ĕrĕ, ērĭpŭī, ēreptŭm, to deliver from, to wrest from
Ĕrĭs, -ĭdĭs (f.), Eris, goddess of discord
errō, -ārĕ, -āvī, -ātŭm, to err, wander
errŏr, -ōrĭs (m.), a wandering
escendō, -ĕrĕ, escendī, escensŭm, to land
essĕ, to be; see sŭm
ĕt, and, even; ĕt..ĕt, both..and
ĕtĭam, also, too, even
ĕtĭamsī, even if, although
Etrūrĭă, -ae (f.), Etruria
Etruscŭs, -ī (m.), an Etruscan
etsī, although, though
ēvādō, -ĕrĕ, ēvāsī, ēvāsŭm, to escape
ēvellō, -ĕrĕ, ēvellī, ēvulsŭm, to pluck out
ēvĕnĭō, -īrĕ, ēvēnī, eventŭm, to happen; ēvĕnĭt, it happens
ēventŭs, -ūs (m.), an event, a result
ēvŏlō, -ārĕ, -āvī, -ātŭm, to fly out, fly up
ex (w. abl.), from, of, out of
exănĭmō, -ārĕ, -āvī, -ātŭm, to kill

excaecō, -āre, -āvī, -ātum, to make blind
excĭpĭō, -ĕre, excēpī, exceptum, to take, receive; hospitĭo excipĕre, to receive as a friend; optĭmis cĭbis excipĕre, to treat to the best dishes
exclāmō, -āre, -āvī, -ātum, to cry out
excōgĭtō, -āre, -āvī, -ātum, to think out, devise
exĕō, -īre, -iī, -ĭtum, to depart
exercĭtŭs, -ūs (m.), an army
existĭmō, -āre, -āvī, -ātum, to regard, believe
exĭtŭs, -ūs (m.), a going out
expĕdĭō, -īre, -īvī, -ītum, to bring out
expĕdĭtĭō, -ōnĭs (f.), an expedition
expellō, -ĕre, expŭlī, expulsum, to banish
expĕrĭŏr, -īrī, expertŭs sŭm, to experience
expers, -tĭs, free from
explĕō, -ēre, explēvī, explētum, to fill; famem, sitim explēre, to lay the hunger, thirst
explōrātŏr, -ōrĭs (m.), a searcher
expōnō, -ĕre, expŏsuī, expŏsĭtum, to set out, expose, explain
expugnō, -āre, -āvī, -ātum, to capture, take by storm
exstinguō, -ĕre, exstinxī, exstinctum, to quench
exsultō, -āre, -āvī, -ātum, to exult
extrā (w. acc.), without, out of; extra ordĭnem, outside of the ranks
extrēmŭs, -ă, -ŭm, outermost
exŭō, -ĕre, exŭī, exūtum, to put off

F.

Fābrĭcĭŭs, -ī (m.), Fabricius
fābŭlă, -ae (f.), a play, a fable
facĭlĭs -ĕ, easy; facĭlis victus, a good income
facĭnŭs, -ŏris (n.), a deed, crime
facĭō, -ĕre, fēcī, factum, to make; injurĭam facĕre, to offer an insult
factum, -ī (n.), a deed
facultās, -ātĭs (f.), ability

fallō, -ĕre, fĕfellī, falsum, to cheat, deceive
falsŭs, -ă, -ŭm, false; falsă, -ōrum (pl. n.), falsehood
falx, -cĭs (f.), a sickle
fāmă, -ae (f.), fame
fāmēs, -ĭs (f.), hunger
famĭlĭă, -ae (f.), a family
famĭlĭărissĭmē, on very friendly terms
fānum, -ī (n.), a temple
fascĭs, - (m.), a bundle
fatīgō, -āre, -āvī, -ātum, to weary
fātum, -ī (n.), destiny
fēlĭcĭtās, -ātĭs (f.), happiness
fēlix, -ĭcĭs, happy
fēmĭnă, -ae (f.), a woman
fĕrē, almost
fĕrō, ferre, tŭlī, lātum, to bear, carry; praemĭum ferre, to bear away the palm, gravĭter ferre, to be grieved at
fĕrox, -ōcĭs, fierce
fĕrŭs, -ă, -ŭm, wild
festŭs, -ă, -ŭm, festal
fĭdēlĭs, -ĕ, faithful
fĭdēs, -ĕī (f.), faith, belief; fĭdem habere, tribuĕre, to trust
fīlĭă, -ae (f.), a daughter
fīlĭŭs, -ī (m.), a son
fingō, -ĕre, finxī, fictum, to carve an image
fīnĭs, - (m.), an end; fīnēs, -ĭum, (pl. m.), a territory
fĭnĭtĭmŭs, -ă, -ŭm, neighboring
fīō, fĭĕrī, factus sŭm, to become, turn out, happen, be made; fĭĕri non potest, it cannot be possible
firmŭs, -ă, -ŭm, strong, firm
fit, it happens
flĕō, flēre, flēvī, flētum, to weep
flētŭs, -ūs (m.), tears
flōrĕō, -ēre, -uī, (no sup.), to flourish
flūmĕn, -ĭnĭs (n.), a river
flŭō, -ĕre, fluxī, fluxum, to flow
flŭvĭŭs, -ī (m.) a river
foedŭs, -ĕris (n.), a treaty
fŏrĕ, to be about to be
fortĕ, perchance

fortis, -ĕ, *brave*
fortĭtĕr, *bravely*
fortĭtūdŏ, -ĭnĭs (f.), *bravery, courage*
fortūnā, -ae (f.), *fortune, luck;* prospĕrā fortūnā, *good fortune*
fŏrŭm, -ī (n.), *the market*
frātĕr, -rĭs (m.), *a brother*
fraus, -dĭs (f.), *a fraud*
frūmentŭm, -ī (n.), *corn*
frustrā, *in vain*
fŭgā, -ae (f.), *flight*
fŭgĭŏ, -ĕrĕ, fūgī, fŭgĭtŭm, *to flee or fly*
fŭgŏ, -ārĕ, -āvī, -ātŭm, *to put to flight*
fundŏ, -ĕrĕ, fūdī, fūsŭm, *to rout;* sanguĭnem fundĕre, *to pour forth blood*

G.

gălĕā, -ae (f.), *a helmet*
gens, -tĭs (f.), *a nation*
gĕnū, -ūs (n.), *the knee*
gĕnŭs, -ĕrĭs (n.), *a kind, race;* nobĭle genus, *a noble family*
Germānĭā, -ae (f.), *Germany*
Germānŭs, -ī (m.), *a German*
gĕrŏ, -ĕrĕ, gessī, gestŭm, *to carry on*
gĭgās, -antĭs (m.), *a giant*
glădĭŭs, -ī (m.), *a sword*
Graecĭā, -ae (f.), *Greece*
Graecŭs, -ă, -ŭm, *Greek*
grātĭae, -ārŭm (pl. f.), *thanks*
grātŭs, -ă, -ŭm, *pleasing; thankful*
grăvĭs, -ĕ, *heavy, severe;* vox gravis, *a deep voice*
grăvĭtĕr, *with vexation;* gravĭter ferre, *to be grieved at*
grex, grĕgĭs (m.), *a flock*

H.

hăbĕŏ, -ĕrĕ, -ŭī, -ĭtŭm, *to have;* sīc sē rēs hăbĕt, *this is the matter;* satis habēre, *to be satisfied*
hăbĭtŏ, -ārĕ, -āvī, -ātŭm, *to inhabit; to live*
Hălys, -yŏs (m.), *the Halys*
Harpăgŭs, -ī (m.), *Harpagus*
hastā, -ae (f.), *a spear*

haurĭŏ, -īrĕ, hausī, haustŭm, *to draw*
Hectŏr, -ŏrĭs (m.), *Hector*
Hĕlĕnā, -ae (f.), *Helena*
Hĕraclĕā, -ae (f.), *Heraclea*
hĕrī, *yesterday*
Hermŭs, -ī (m.), *the Hermus*
Hĕrostrătŭs, -ī (m.), *Herostratus*
hesternŭs, -ă, -ŭm, *of yesterday*
hĭc, haec, hŏc, *this (of mine);* haec, *the following;* hīc (adv.), *here*
hĭlărĭtās, -ātĭs (f.), *cheerfulness*
hŏdĭĕ, *to-day*
Hŏmĕrŭs, -ī (m.), *the Greek poet Homer*
hŏmŏ, -ĭnĭs (m.), *man, a man;* hŏmĭnēs (pl. m.), *people*
hŏnestās, -ātĭs (f.), *honesty*
hŏnestŭs, -ă, -ŭm, *honorable*
hŏnŏr, -ŏrĭs (m.), *an honor*
hŏnōrĭfĭcŭs, -ă, -ŭm, *honorable*
hŏnōrŏ, -ārĕ, -āvī, -ātŭm, *to honor*
Hŏrātĭŭs, -ī (m.), *Horace*
hospēs, -ĭtĭs (m.), *a friend, guest*
hospĭtĭŭm, -ī (n.), *friendship;* hospĭtĭo excipĕre, *to receive as a friend*
hostĭs - (m.), *an enemy*
hŭmĕrŭs, -ī (m.), *the shoulder*
Hystaspēs, -ĭs (m.), *Hystaspes*

I.

ĭbī, *there, here*
Īcărĭŭs, -ă, -ŭm, *Icarian*
Īcărŭs, -ī (m.), *Icarus*
īcŏ, -ĕrĕ, īcī, ictŭm, *to strike*
Īdā, -ae (f.), *mount Ida*
ĭdĕm, ĕădĕm, ĭdĕm, *the same*
ĭdentĭdĕm, *again and again*
ĭdĕŏ, *for the reason, on that account*
ĭgĭtŭr, *therefore, then*
ignĭs, - (m.), *fire*
ignōrŏ, -ārĕ, -āvī, -ātŭm, *not to know*
illĕ, illă, illŭd, *that (yonder)*
illustrĭs, -ĕ, *illustrious*
illustrŏ, -ārĕ, -āvī, -ātŭm, *to illuminate*
ĭmāgŏ, -ĭnĭs (f.), *an image, likeness*
imbĕr, -rĭs (m.), *a shower*

immergō, -ĕrĕ, immersī, immersŭm, *to plunge*
immŏdestĭă, -ae (f.), *disobedience*
immŏlō, -ārĕ, -āvī, -ātŭm, *to sacrifice*
immortālĭs, -ĕ, *immortal*
impĕdīmentŭm, -ī (n.), *a hindrance;* impĕdīmentă, -ōrŭm, *baggage*
impellō, -ĕrĕ, impŭlī, impulsŭm, *to impel*
impĕrātŏr, -ōrĭs (m.), *a commander-in-chief, an emperor*
impĕrĭŭm, -ī (n.), *empire, rule*
impĕrō, -ārĕ, -āvī, -ātŭm, *to command, order*
impertĭō, -īrĕ, -īvī, -ītŭm, *to distribute, give*
impĕtrō, -ārĕ, -āvī, -ātŭm, *to obtain*
impĕtŭs, -ūs (m.), *assault*
implĕō, -ĕrĕ, implēvī, implētŭm, *to fill, fill up*
implōrō, -ārĕ, -āvī, -ātŭm, *to implore*
impōnō, -ĕrĕ, impŏsŭī, impŏsĭtŭm, *to put, place, lay on, impose*
imprŏbŭs, -ă, -ŭm, *wicked*
īmŭs, -ă, -ŭm, *deepest*
In (w. acc.), *into, on, against;* (w. abl.), *in, on, upon, among*
incendō, -ĕrĕ, incendī, incensŭm, *to burn, set on fire*
incĭpĭō, -ĕrĕ, incēpī, inceptŭm, *to begin*
incŏlō, -ĕrĕ, incŏlŭī, incultŭm, *to inhabit*
incŏlŭmĭs, -ĕ, *safe*
incūsō, -ārĕ, -āvī, -ātŭm, *to accuse*
indĕ, *thence* [*declare*
indĭcō, -ĕrĕ, indixī, indictŭm, *to*
indignātŭs, -ă, -ŭm, *wrathful*
indignŭm, -ī (n.), *a wrong;* indignē, *undeservedly*
indignŭs, -ă, -ŭm, *unworthy*
indūcō, -ĕrĕ, induxī, inductŭm, *to entice;* anīmum inducĕre, *to make up one's mind*
induō, -ĕrĕ, induī, indūtŭm, *to put on*

ĭnĕō, -īrĕ, ĭnĭī, ĭnĭtŭm, *to begin*
infans, -tĭs (m. & f.), *a babe, child*
infĕrĭŏr, -ŭs, *inferior, lower*
infĕrō, -rĕ, intŭlī, illātŭm, *to carry into;* bellŭm inferrĕ ălīcŭī, *to wage war upon somebody;* injūrĭŭm inferrĕ, *to do an injury, wrong*
infĕrŭs, -ă, -ŭm, *below, lower;* apud infĕros, *in the lower world*
ingĕnĭŭm, -ī (n.), *disposition*
ingens, -tĭs, *immense*
ingrĕdĭŏr, -ī, ingressŭs sŭm, *to enter*
īnīmīcŭs, -ă, -ŭm, *unfriendly, opposed;* inīmīcŭs, -ī (m.), *an enemy*
īnĭtĭŭm, -ī (n.), *a beginning;* inĭtĭō, *in the beginning*
injūrĭă, -ae (f.), *an injury, wrong;* injūrĭă, *unjustly;* injurĭam facĕre, *to offer an insult*
injustŭs, -ă, -ŭm, *unjust;* injuste facĕre, *to do wrong*
ĭnŏpĭă, -ae (f.), *want; scarcity of provisions*
ĭnops, -ŏpĭs, *poor*
inquăm, *I say, quoth I*
inscrībō, -ĕrĕ, inscripsī, inscriptŭm, *to write upon*
insĕquens, -tĭs, *following*
insĕquŏr, -ī, insĕcūtŭs sŭm, *to follow*
insĭdĭae, -ārŭm (pl. f.), *an ambush*
insignĭs, -ĕ, *distinguished*
inspectō, -ārĕ, -āvī, -ātŭm, *to view*
instĭtūtŭm, -ī (n.), *an institution*
instrūmentŭm, -ī (n.), *an implement*
instrŭō, -ĕrĕ, instruxī, instructŭm, *to draw up in order*
insŭlă, -ae (f.), *an island*
insŭm, ĭnessĕ, infŭī, *to be in*
intellĕgō, -ĕrĕ, intellexī, intellectŭm, *to understand, see, comprehend*
intĕr (w. acc.), *among, between*
interdŭm, *sometimes*
intĕrĕă, *meanwhile*
interfĭcĭō, -ĕrĕ, interfēcī, interfectŭm, *to kill*
intĕrĭm, *meanwhile*

interprĕs, -ĕtis (m.), *an interpreter*
interprĕtŏr, -ārī, -ātŭs sŭm, *to explain*
interrŏgŏ, -ārĕ, -āvī, -ātŭm, *to ask, question, inquire*
intrŏ, -ārĕ, -āvī, -ātŭm, *to enter*
intrŏdūcŏ, -ĕrĕ, introduxī, introductŭm, *to lead in*
intrūdŏ, -ĕrĕ, intrūsī, intrūsŭm, *to thrust in*
intŭĕŏr, -ērī, -ītŭs sŭm, *to look at, behold*
ĭnūsĭtātŭs, -ă, -ŭm, *extraordinary, uncommon*
ĭnūtĭlĭs, -ĕ, *useless, unfit*
invādŏ, -ĕrĕ, invāsī, invāsŭm, *to attack*
invĕhŏr, -ī, invectŭs sŭm, *to ride into*
invĕnĭŏ, -īrĕ, invĕnī, inventŭm, *to find*
invītŏ, -ārĕ, -āvī, -ātŭm, *to invite;* se largīter invitāre, *to enjoy one's self*
invŏcŏ, -ārĕ, -āvī, -ātŭm, *to invoke*
Īphĭgĕnīă, -ae (f.), *Iphigenia*
ipsĕ, -ă, -ŭm, *himself, herself, itself*
īrā, -ae (f.), *anger*
īrascŏr, -ī, īrātŭs sŭm, *to grow or to be angry*
īrātŭs, -ă, -ŭm, *angry*
irrŭŏ, -ĕrĕ, -ī, (no sup.), *to rush*
ĭs, ĕă, ĭd, *that; he, she, it*
istĕ, -ă, -ŭd, *that (of yours)*
ĭtă, *so, thus, in this way*
Ītălĭă, -ae (f.), *Italy*
ităquĕ, *therefore*
ĭtĕr, ĭtĭnĕrĭs (n.), *a journey, way*
ĭtĕrŭm, *again*
Ĭthăcă, -ae (f.), *Ithaca*

J.

jăcĭŏ, -ĕrĕ, jēcī, jactŭm, *to throw*
jactūră, -ae (f.), *a loss;* jacturam facĕre, *to suffer a loss*
jăm, *already;* with negatives, *longer*
jănŭă, -ae (f.), *a door*
jŭbĕŏ, -ērĕ, jussī, jussŭm, *to order*

jūcundē, *pleasantly*
jūcundŭs, -ă, -ŭm, *pleasant, delicious*
jūdex, -ĭcĭs (m.), *a judge*
jūdĭcĭŭm, -ī (n.), *a court, judgment*
jūdĭcŏ, -ārĕ, -āvī, -ātŭm, *to judge, consider*
jŭgŭm, -ī (n.), *a yoke*
jūnĭŏr, (without n.), *younger*
Jūnŏ, -ōnĭs (f.), *Juno*
Juppĭtĕr, Jŏvĭs (m.), *Jupiter, Jove*
jūrŏ, -ārĕ, -āvī, -ātŭm, *to swear;* jūrātŭs. -ă, -ŭm, *having sworn*
jūs, jūrĭs (n.), *right, law*
jussū, *by order*
jussŭm, -ī (n.), *an order*
justŭs, -ă, -ŭm, *just, proper;* justa facĕre, *to do right*
jŭvĕnĭs, - (m.), *a youth*

L.

lăbŏr, -ōrĭs (m.), *labor, exertion*
Lăbўrinthŭs, -ī (m.), *the Labyrinth*
lăc, lactĭs (n.), *milk*
Lăcĕdaemŏnĭŭs, -ī (m.), *a Lacedaemonian*
lăcĕrŏ, -ārĕ, -āvī, -ātŭm, *to tear in pieces*
lăcrĭmă, -ae (f.), *a tear*
lăcŭs -ūs (m.), *a lake*
laedŏ, -ĕrĕ, laesī, laesŭm, *to violate, hurt*
laetĭtĭă, -ae (f.), *joy, delight*
laetŭs, -ă, -ŭm, *merry, joyful*
lăpĭs, -ĭdĭs (m.), *a stone*
largĭtĕr, *very much*
Lătīnŭs, -ă, -ŭm, *Latin*
Lātŏnă, -ae (f.), *Latona*
laudŏ, -ārĕ, -āvī, -ātŭm, *to praise*
laus, -dĭs (f.), *praise*
lautŭs, -ă, -ŭm, *in a fine dress*
lăvŏ, -ārĕ, lāvī, lăvātŭm (lautŭm, lōtŭm), *to wash*
lēgātĭŏ, -ōnĭs (f.), *an embassy*
lēgātŭs, -ī (m.), *an ambassador*
lĕgĭŏ, -ōnĭs (f.), *a legion*
lĕgŏ, -ĕrĕ, lēgī, lectŭm, *to read*
lĕpŭs, -ŏrĭs (m.), *a hare*
lĕvŏ, -ārĕ, -āvī, -ātŭm, *to uplift*

lex, lēgĭs (f.), *a law*
lĭbentĕr, *with pleasure, freely, willingly*
lībĕr, -ă, -ŭm, *free*
Lībĕr, -ī (m.), *Bacchus*
lĭbĕr, -rī (m.), *a book*
lībĕrălĭtās, -ātĭs (f.), *liberality*
lībĕrī, -ōrŭm (pl. m.), *children*
lībĕrō, -ārĕ, -āvī, -ātŭm, *to (set) free, liberate, deliver*
lĭcĕt, *it is allowed, lawful, I am free;* lĭcŭĭt *or* lĭcĭtŭm est, lĭcērĕ
lignŭm, -ī (n.), *wood*
linguă, -ae (f.), *the tongue, a language*
lĭquescō, -ĕrĕ, lĭcŭī, (no sup.), *to melt*
lītŭs, -ŏrĭs (n.), *a shore*
lŏcŭs, -ī (m.), *a place*
longinquŭs, -ă, -ŭm, *far*
longŭs, -ă, -ŭm, *long*
lŏquŏr, -ī, lŏcūtŭs sŭm, *to speak*
lūdō, -ĕrĕ, lūsī, lūsŭm, *to play*
lūdŭs, -ī (m.), *a play, game*
Lўcĭă, -ae (f.), *Lycia*
Lўcĭŭs, -ă, -ŭm, *Lycian*
Lўdĭă, -ae (f.), *Lydia*
Lўsippŭs, -ī (m.), *Lysippus*

M.

Mācĕdō, -ŏnĭs (m.), *a Macedonian*
Mācĕdŏnĭă, -ae (f.), *Macedonia*
măgĭs, *more*
magnĭfĭcŭs, -ă, -ŭm, *magnificent, grand*
magnŭs, -ă, -ŭm, *great, large, big;* magna voce, *with a loud voice*
măgŭs, -ī (m.), *a magician*
mălĕ, *badly*
mălō, mallĕ, mălŭī, (no sup.), *to be more willing, prefer*
mălŭm, -ī (n.), *an evil*
mălŭm, -ī (n.), *an apple*
mălŭs, -ă, -ŭm, *bad*
Mandānē, -ēs (f.), *Mandane*
mandātŭm, -ī (n.), *an order*
mandō, -ārĕ, -āvī, -ātŭm, *to order, commit, entrust*
mānĕ, *in the morning*
mănĕō, -ērĕ, mansī, mansŭm, *to stay, remain*
Manlĭŭs, -ī (m.), *Manlius*

Mantĭnēă, -ae (f.), *Mantinea*
mănŭs, -ūs (f.), *the hand*
Marcellŭs, -ī (m.), *Marcellus*
Marcĭŭs, -ī (m.), *Marcius*
mărĕ, -ĭs (n.), *the sea, ocean*
marmŏr, -ĭs (n.), *marble*
mātĕr, -rĭs (f.), *a mother*
mātrĭmōnĭŭm, -ī (n.), *a marriage*
maxĭmŭs, -ă, -ŭm, *greatest*
mĕdĭcŭs, -ī (m.), *a physician*
mĕdĭŏcrĭs, -ĕ, *ordinary*
Mēdŭs, -ī (m.), *a Median*
Mĕgără, -ae (f.), *Megara*
mĕlĭŏr, -ŭs, *better*
membrŭm, -ī (n.), *a member*
mĕmŏr, -ĭs, *mindful*
mĕmŏrĭă, -ae (f.), *memory*
Mĕnĕlāŭs, -ī (m.), *Menelaus*
mens, -tĭs (f.), *the mind*
mercātŏr, -ōrĭs (m.), *a merchant*
mercēnārĭŭs, -ă, -ŭm, *hired*
Mercŭrĭŭs, -ī (m.), *Mercury*
mĕtŭō, -ĕrĕ, mĕtŭī, (no sup.), *to fear*
mĕŭs, -ă, -ŭm, *my*
Mĭdās, -ae (m.), *Midas, king of Phrygia*
mīlĕs, -ĭtĭs (m.), *a soldier*
mīlĭtărĭs, -ĕ, *military*
mille, *a thousand;* mīllĭă, *thousands*
Mĭnervă, -ae (f.), *Minerva, the goddess of wisdom*
mĭnistĕr, -rī (m.), *a servant*
mĭnŏr, -ŭs, *less, smaller*
mĭnŏr, -ārī, -ātŭs sŭm, *to threaten*
Mĭnōs, -ōĭs (m.), *Minos, king in Crete*
Mĭnōtaurŭs, -ī (m.), *Minotaurus*
mĭnŭs (adv.), *less*
mīrācŭlŭm, -ī (n.), *a wonder*
mīrŏr, -ārī, -ātŭs sŭm, *to wonder at, to admire*
mīrŭs, -ă, -ŭm, *wonderful*
mĭsĕr, -ă, -ŭm, *wretched, miserable*
mĭsĕrŏr, -ārī, -ātŭs sŭm, *to pity*
mittō, -ĕrĕ, mĭsī, missŭm, *to send*
mŏdĭcŭs, -ă, -ŭm, *little*
mŏdō, *just now, only;* mŏdō..mŏdō, *now ..now*
mŏdŭs, -ī (m.), *way, manner;* hōc mŏdō, *in this manner;* quōmŏdō, *in what manner, how?*

mons, -tĭs (m.), *a mountain, mount*
mŏrĭŏr, -ī, mortŭus sŭm, *to die*
mŏrŏr, -ārī, -ātŭs sŭm, *to delay*
mors, -tĭs (f.), *death*
mortālĭs, -ĕ, *mortal*
mortŭŭs, -ă, -ŭm, *dead*
mōs, mōrĭs (m.), *custom*
mŏvĕō, -ērĕ, mōvī, mōtŭm, *to move, influence; discordĭam movēre, to produce discord;* bellum movēre, *to stir up war*
mox, *soon*
Mūcĭŭs, -ī (m.), *Mucius*
mulgĕō, -ērĕ, mulsī, mulsŭm, *to milk*
mŭlĭĕr, -ĭs (f.), *a woman*
multĭtūdŏ, -ĭnĭs (f.), *a multitude;* magnā multĭtūdŏ, *a very great number*
multō, *much;* non ita multo post, *a short time afterwards*
multŭs, -ă, -ŭm, *much, many*
mūnĭō, -īrĕ, -īvī, -ītŭm, *to fortify, protect*
mūnŭs, -ĕrĭs (n.), *a gift*
mūrŭs, -ī (m.), *a wall*
mūs, mūrĭs (m.), *a mouse*
mūtō, -ārĕ, -āvī, -ātŭm, *to change*
Myrmĭdŏnēs, -ŭm (pl. m.), *the Myrmidons*

N.

năm, *for*
narrō, -ārĕ, -āvī, -ātŭm, *to tell, relate*
nascŏr, -ī, nātŭs sŭm, *to be born, to rise;* Part. Fut. nascĭtūrŭs,-ă,-ŭm
nătō, -ārĕ, -āvī, -ātŭm, *to swim*
nātūră, -ae (f.), *nature*
naută, -ae (m.), *a sailor, seaman*
nāvĭgō, -ārĕ, -āvī, -ātŭm, *to sail*
nāvĭs, - (f.), *a ship;* nāvī, nāvĭbŭs, *by ship*
Naxŭs, -ī (f.), *Naxos*
nē, *not, that not, lest; granted that not;*
—nĕ (interrog. part.), *whether, if*
nē..quĭdĕm, *not even*
nĕcessārĭŭs, -ă, -ŭm, *necessary*
nĕcessĕ est, *it must needs*
nĕcō, -ārĕ, -āvī, -ātŭm, *to kill, slay*

neglĕgō,-ĕrĕ, neglexī, neglectŭm, *to neglect.* Written also neglĭgĕrĕ
nĕgō, -ārĕ, -āvī, -ātŭm, *to deny, say no*
nĕgōtĭŭm, -ī (n.), *an affair, matter, business*
nēmŏ, -ĭnĭs (m.), *nobody, no one;* nēmŏ nostrūm, *none of us*
Neptūnŭs, -ī (m.), *Neptune, the god of the sea*
nĕquĕ, *and not;* nĕquĕ..nĕquĕ, *neither..nor;* nĕquĕ tămĕn, *but not*
Nestŏr, -ŏrĭs (m.), *Nestor*
nĭhĭl, *nothing*
nĭhĭlōmĭnŭs, *nevertheless*
nĭhĭlŭm, -ī (n.), *nothing*
nĭmĭs, *too much, too*
nĭmĭŭm, *too much*
nĭmĭŭs, -ă, -ŭm, *overgreat*
nĭsī, *if not, unless, except*
nĭtŏr, -ī, nĭsŭs & nixŭs sŭm, *to endeavor*
nōbĭlĭs, -ĕ, *noble*
nōlō, nollĕ, nōlŭī, (no sup.), *to be unwilling, not to wish*
nōmĕn, -ĭnĭs (n.), *a name*
nōn, *not, no;* nōn sōlŭm..sĕd ĕtĭăm, *not only..but also*
nonnĕ (interrog. part.), *not, if not*
nostŏr, -ră, -rŭm, *our*
nōtŭs, -ă, -ŭm, *known*
nŏvĕm, *nine*
nōvī, nōvissĕ, *to know*
nŏvŭs, -ă, -ŭm, *new*
nox, noctĭs (f.), *the night*
nūbēs, -ĭs (f.), *a cloud*
nullŭs, -ă, -ŭm, *no*
nŭm (interrog. part.), *whether, if*
nŭmĕrŭs, -ī (m.), *a number*
nunc, *now*
nuntĭō, -ārĕ, -āvī, -ātŭm, *to bring word, announce*
nuntĭŭs, -ī (m.), *a messenger; news*
nuptĭae, -ārŭm (pl. f.), *a wedding*
nusquăm, *nowhere*

O.

ŏb (w. acc.), *on account of;* ŏb eam causăm, *on that account*
oblīviscŏr, -ī, oblītŭs sŭm, *to forget*

obnītŏr, -ī, obnixūs sŭm, to oppose
obsĕquŏr, -ī, obsĕcūtūs sŭm, to accede
obsĭdĕō, -ērĕ, obsēdī, obsessŭm, to besiege
obsĭdĭō, -ōnĭs (f.), a siege
obstŭpĕfactŭs, -ă, -ŭm, astonished
obtempĕrō, -ārĕ, -āvī, -ātŭm, to obey
obtĭnĕō, -ērĕ, obtĭnŭī, obtentŭm, to obtain
obtingō, -ĕrĕ, obtĭgī, (no sup.), to fall to one's lot
occīdō, -ĕrĕ, occīdī, occīsŭm, to slay, kill
occultō, -ārĕ, -āvī, -ātŭm, to hide, conceal
octingentī, -ae, -ă, eight hundred
ŏcŭlŭs, -ī (m.), the eye; ocŭlos in se convertĕre, to attract the attention
ŏdĭōsŭs, -ă, -ŭm, hateful
ŏdĭŭm, -ī (n.), hatred, enmity
offĕrō, -rĕ, obtŭlī, oblātŭm, to offer
ŏlĭm, in former times, formerly
omnĭs, -ĕ, all, every, entire; omnĭă, -ĭŭm (pl. n.), all things, every thing
ŏnŭs, -ĕrĭs (n.), a burden, load
ŏpēs, -ŭm (pl. f.), means, wealth
ŏpīnŏr, -ārī, -ātŭs sŭm, to think
oppĭdŭm, -ī (n.), a town
oppōnō, -ĕrĕ, oppŏ-ŭī, oppŏsĭtŭm, to oppose
opprĭmō, -ĕrĕ, oppressī, oppressŭm, to crush, overwhelm
optĭmē, best, in the best manner
optĭmŭs, -ă, -ŭm, best
optō, -ārĕ, -āvī, -ātŭm, to wish for, desire
ŏpŭlentŭs, -ă, -ŭm, wealthy
ŏpŭs, -ĕrĭs (n.), a work
ōrācŭlŭm, -ī (n.), an oracle
ordō, -ĭnĭs (m.), order, rank
Ōrestēs, -ĭs (m.), Orestes
ŏrĭŏr, -īrī, ortŭs sŭm, to rise, arise
ornō, -ārĕ, -āvī, -ātŭm, to adorn; laudĭbus ornāre, to bestow praise upon
ōrō, -ārĕ, -āvī, -ātŭm, to pray
ōs, ōrĭs (n.), the mouth; face

ostendō, -ĕrĕ, ostendī, ostensŭm, to show
ŏvĭs, - (f.), a sheep

P.

pālŭs, -ī (m.), a pale
pār, părĭs, equal
părātŭs, -ă, -ŭm, ready
parcō, -ĕrĕ, pĕpercī, parsŭm, to spare
parens, -tĭs (m. & f.), a parent
pārĕō, -ērĕ, -ŭī, -ĭtŭm, to obey, to submit
părĭēs, -ĕtĭs (m.), a wall
părĭō, -ĕrĕ, pĕpĕrī, partŭm, to bear; to secure; regnum parĕre, to secure the reign
Părĭs, -ĭdĭs (m.), Paris
părō, -ārĕ, -āvī, -ātŭm, to prepare for; to obtain; exercĭtum parāre, to raise an army
pars, -tĭs (f.), a part
partĭm, partly
parvŭs, -ă, -ŭm, little, small
pascō, -ĕrĕ, pāvī, pastŭm, to feed, to tend
pastŏr, -ōrĭs (m.), a shepherd
pastōrālĭs, -ĕ, pastoral
pătĕr, -rĭs (m.), a father, senator
pătĭŏr, -ī, passŭs sŭm, to suffer
pătrĭă, -ae (f.), one's country, one's native land
Pătrŏclŭs, -ī (m.), Patroclus
paucī, -ae, -ă, few, a few
paulŭm, little; paulo post, a little after
pāx, -cĭs (f.), peace
pectŭs, -ŏrĭs (n.), the breast, heart
pĕcūnĭă, -ae (f.), money
pĕcŭs, -ŏrĭs (n.), cattle
pĕdĕs, -ĭtĭs (m.), a foot-soldier
Pēleŭs, Pēlĕī (m.), Peleus, father of Achilles
pendĕō, -ērĕ, pĕpendī, pensŭm, to hang
Pēnĕlŏpē, -ēs (f.), Penelope
pennă, -ae (f.), a feather
pĕr (w. acc.), through, during
pĕrĕgrīnātĭō, -ōnĭs (f.), travel
pĕrĕgrīnŏr, -ārī, -ātŭs sŭm, to travel

pěrěō, -īrě, -ĭī, -ĭtŭm, *to perish*
perfĭcĭō, -ěrě, perfěcī, perfectŭm, *to finish*
perfĭdĭā, -ae (f.), *perfidy*
pěrīcŭlōsŭs, -ā, -ŭm, *dangerous*
pěrīcŭlŭm, -ī (n.), *danger*
pěrītŭs, -ā, -ŭm, *experienced;* pěrītĭŏr, *a better judge*
Persā, -ae (m.), *a Persian*
perscrībō, -ěrě, perscripsī, perscriptŭm, *to write*
persěquŏr, -ī, persěcūtŭs sŭm, *to pursue*
Persĭs, -ĭdĭs (f.), *Persia*
persuāděō, -ěrě, persuāsī, persuāsŭm, *to persuade, convince*
perterrěō, -ěrě, -ŭī, -ĭtŭm, *to frighten*
perturbātĭō, -ōnĭs (f.), *a disturbance*
perturbō, -ārě, -āvī, -ātŭm, *to disturb*
pervěnĭō, -īrě, pervěnī, perventŭm, *to arrive in;* ad regnum pervenīre, *to come to the throne*
pēs, pědĭs (m.), *a foot*
pessĭmē, *in the most calamitous way*
pessĭmŭs, -ā, -ŭm, *worst*
pětō, -ěrě, pětīvī, pětītŭm, *to seek, ask, entreat*
Phaeācēs, -ŭm (pl. m.), *the Phaeacians*
Phĭlippŭs, -ī (m.), *Philip, king of Macedonia*
phĭlŏsŏphŭs, -ī (m.), *a philosopher*
Phrўgĭā, -ae (f.), *Phrygia*
pictŏr, -ōrĭs (m.), *a painter*
pĭětās, -ātĭs (f.), *piety*
pingō, -ěrě, pinxī, pictŭm, *to paint*
piscātŏr, -ōrĭs (m.), *a fisherman*
piscĭs, - (m.), *a fish*
plŭs, -ā, -ŭm, *pious*
plăcěō, -ěrě, -ŭī, -ĭtŭm, *to please*
plăcĭdē, *gently* [concile
plăcō, -ārě, -āvī, -ātŭm, *to replēbs,* -ĭs or plěbēs, -ěī (f.), *the common people, populace*
plēnŭs, -ā, -ŭm, *full*
plērīquě, plēraequě, plērāquě, *very many, most*

plūrĭmŭs, -ā, -ŭm, *most, very much* or *many*
pōcŭlŭm, -ī (n.), *a bowl, cup*
poenā, -ae (f.), *punishment, penalty*
pŏētā, -ae (m.), *a poet*
Pŏlĭorcētēs, -ae (m.), *Poliorcetes*
pollĭcěŏr, -ērī, -ĭtŭs sŭm, *to promise*
Pŏlўcrătēs, -ĭs (m.), *Polycrates*
Pŏlўphēmŭs, -ī (m.), *Polyphemus*
pōnō, -ěrě, pŏsŭī, pŏsĭtŭm, *to place;* castrā pōněrě, *to pitch a camp*
pons, -tĭs (m.), *a bridge*
pŏpŭlŭs, -ī (m.), *a people, nation*
Porsěnā, -ae (m.), *Porsena*
portā, -ae (f.), *a gate*
portō, -ārě, -āvī, -ātŭm, *to carry*
portŭs, -ūs (m.), *a harbor*
poscō, -ěrě, pŏposcī, (no sup.), *to demand, to ask*
possĭděō, -ērě, possēdī, possessŭm, *to possess*
possŭm, possě, pŏtŭī, *to be able;* plurīmum posse, *to be very powerful*
post (w. acc.), *behind, after;* non multo post, *not long after*
postěā, *afterwards*
postěrī, -ōrŭm (pl. m.), *descendants, posterity*
postěrŭs, -ā, -ŭm, *following*
postquăm, *after, after that*
postrēmō, *finally*
postrēmŭs, -ā, -ŭm, *last, latest*
postrīdĭē, *on the following day*
postŭlō, -ārě, -āvī, -ātŭm, *to require*
pŏtens, -tĭs, *powerful, mighty*
pŏtentĭā, -ae (f.), *power*
pŏtĭŏr, -īrī, -ĭtŭs sŭm, *to take or acquire possession of, to make one's self master of*
praeběō, -ērě, -ŭī, -ĭtŭm, *to give, to hold out*
praeceptŭm, -ī (n.), *a precept*
praecĭpĭō, -ěrě, praecēpī, praeceptŭm, *to give orders*
praecĭpŭě, *principally, especially*
praedā, -ae (f.), *prey*
praedĭcō, -ārě, -āvī, -ātŭm, *to declare, to extol*

praedīcŏ, -ĕrĕ, praedixī, praedictūm, *to predict*
praedŏ, -ōnĭs (m.), *a robber*
praefectŭs, -ā, -ŭm, *in command*
praemĭŭm, -ī (n.), *a reward, prize*
praepărŏ, -ārĕ, -āvī, -ātŭm, *to prepare for*
praepōnŏ, -ĕrĕ, praepŏsŭī, praepŏsĭtŭm, *to prefer*
praesens, -tĭs, *present, actual*
praesĭdĭŭm, -ī (n.), *a defence*
praestans,-tĭs, *excellent, distinguished*
praestăt, *it is better*
praestŏ, -ārĕ, praestĭtī, (no sup.), *to afford; to surpass*
praesŭm, praeesse, praefŭī, *to be at the head of*
praetĕr (w. acc.), *beside, except; praeter ceterōs, more than the rest*
prātŭm, -ī (n.), *a meadow*
prĕcēs, -ŭm (pl. f.), *prayers*
prĕcŏr, -ārī, -ātŭs sŭm, *to pray*
prĕtĭōsŭs,-ā,-ŭm, *precious, valuable*
prĕtĭŭm, -ī (n.), *a price*
Prĭămŭs, -ī (m.), *Priamus*
prĭdĭē, *the day before*
prīmŭs, -ā, -ŭm, *the first*
princeps, -ĭpĭs (m.), *a chief, prince*
prĭŭs, *sooner*
prĭusquăm, *before that, before*
prīvātŭs, -ā, -ŭm, *private*
prīvŏ, -ārĕ, -āvī, -ātŭm, *to deprive*
prō (w. abl.), *for, instead of*
prŏbĭtās, -ātĭs (f.), *probity*
prŏbŏ, -ārĕ, -āvī, -ātŭm, *to approve*
prŏcŭl, *at a distance, far*
prŏdĭtŏr, -ōrĭs (m.), *a traitor*
prŏdŏ, -ĕrĕ, prŏdĭdī, prŏdĭtŭm, *to deliver;* memorĭae prodĭtum est, *there is a tradition*
proelĭŭm, -ī (n.), *a battle*
prŏfectĭŏ, -ōnĭs (f.), *a departure*
prōfĕrŏ, -rĕ, prŏtŭlī, prōlātŭm, *to extend*
prŏfĭcīscŏr, -ī, prŏfectŭs sŭm, *to set out;* ad bellum proficisci, *to go to war*
prōgrĕdĭŏr, -ī, progressŭs sŭm, *to proceed*

prŏhĭbĕŏ, -ērĕ, -ŭī, -ĭtŭm, *to hold back, keep from; to prevent*
prōmittŏ, -ĕrĕ, prōmīsī, prōmissŭm, *to promise*
proprĭŭs, -ā, -ŭm, *own*
proptĕr (w. acc.), *on account of, in consequence of*
proptĕrĕā, *for this reason*
prorsŭs, *wholly;* nōn prorsŭs, *not at all*
prospĕr, -ā, -ŭm, *prosperous*
prospĕrē, *successfully*
prōsŭm, prōdessĕ, prōfŭī, *to be useful*
prōvŏcŏ, -ārĕ, -āvī, -ātŭm, *to provoke*
proxĭmŭs, -ā, -ŭm, *next*
prūdens, -tĭs, *prudent, sensible*
prūdentĕr, *prudently*
prūdentĭā, -ae (f.), *prudence*
pūblĭcē, *publicly*
pūblĭcŭs, -ā, -ŭm, *public;* rēs pūblĭcă, *the commonwealth*
pŭĕr, -ī (m.), *a boy*
pugnŏ, -ārĕ, -āvī, -ātŭm, *to fight*
pulchĕr, -ră, -rŭm, *beautiful*
pūnĭŏ,-īrĕ,-īvī,-ītŭm, *to punish*
purgŏ, -ārĕ, -āvī, -ātŭm, *to clean*
pŭtŏ, -ārĕ, -āvī, -ātŭm, *to think, believe, consider*
Pylădēs, -ĭs (m.), *Pylades*
Pylŭs, -ī (m.), *Pylus*
Pyrrhŭs, -ī (m.), *Pyrrhus, king of Epirus*
Pythĭā, -ae (f.), *Pythia*

Q.

quădrāgintā, *forty*
quaerŏ, -ĕrĕ, quaesīvī, quaesītŭm, *to ask, to seek, to look out for*
quālĭs, -ĕ, *such as, what..? of what sort?*
quăm, *how, than;* quam celerrĭme, *as quick as possible*
quămobrem, *therefore*
quamquăm, *although*
quantŭs, -ā, -ŭm, *how great?*
quārĕ, *why*
quartŭs, -ā, -ŭm, *the fourth*
quăsī, *as, as if, as it were, so to speak*
quattŭŏr, *four*

quattŭŏrdĕcĭm, *fourteen*
-quĕ (to be appended to the word), *and*
quĕrŏr, -Ī, questŭs sŭm, *to complain*
quī, quae, quŏd, *who, which, that*
quĭă, *because*
quīdăm, quaedăm, quiddăm, quoddăm, *some one*
quīdĕm, *indeed*
quīlĭbĕt, quaelĭbĕt, quidlĭbĕt, quodlĭbĕt, *any one*
quingentī, -ae, -ă, *five hundred*
quinquĕ, *five*
quĭs, quid, *who, what?*
quisquăm, *any one;* quidquăm, *any thing* (w. negat.)
quŏ, *that, in order that, so that;* quo..ĕō, *the..the*
quŏcunquĕ, *wherever*
quŏd, *because, that*
quodsī, *(but) if*
quŏmŏdŏ, *how*
quondăm, *once, formerly*
quŏnĭăm, *since, in as much as*
quoquĕ, *also, too*
quŏtĭens, *how often?*

R.

rāmŭs, -ī (m.), *a branch*
rānă, -ae (f.), *a frog*
răpĭŏ, -ĕrĕ, răpŭī, raptŭm, *to abduct*
rārŭs, -ă, -ŭm, *rare*
rătĭŏ, -ōnĭs (f.) *reason;* quā rătĭōnĕ, *in what way*
rĕcēdŏ, -ĕrĕ, rĕcessī, rĕcessŭm, *to move backwards*
rĕcens, -tĭs, *recent*
rĕcĭpĭŏ, -ĕrĕ, rĕcēpī, rĕceptŭm, *to receive; to take back;* hospitĭo recipĕre, *to receive as a friend;* se recipĕre, *to collect one's thoughts;* animum recipĕre, *to recover*
rectē, *right, rightly;* rectē făcĕrĕ, *to do right*
rĕcūsŏ, -ārĕ, -āvī, -ātŭm, *to refuse*
reddŏ, -ĕrĕ, reddĭdī, reddĭtŭm, *to give back; to make*
rĕdĕŏ, -īrĕ, rĕdĭī, rĕdĭtŭm, *to return*

rēdĭgŏ, -ĕrĕ, rēdăgī, rĕdactŭm, *to reduce*
rēdūcŏ, -ĕrĕ, reduxī, rĕductŭm, *to reduce*
rēgīnă, -ae (f.), *a queen*
rēgĭŏ, -ōnĭs (f.), *a country, region*
rēgĭŭs, -ă, -ŭm, *kingly*
regnŏ, -ārĕ, -āvī, -ātŭm, *to reign*
regnŭm, -ī (n.), *dominion, kingdom*
rĕlinquŏ, -ĕrĕ, rĕlīquī, rĕlictŭm, *to leave (behind)*
rĕlĭquī, -ae, -ă, *the rest*
rĕmŏvĕŏ, -ērĕ, rĕmōvī, rĕmōtŭm, *to remove*
Rĕmŭs, -ī (m.), *Remus, the brother of Romulus*
rēnuntĭŏ, -ārĕ, -āvī, -ātŭm, *to report*
rĕpĕrĭŏ, -īrĕ, reppĕrī, rĕpertŭm, *to find*
rĕportŏ, -ārĕ, -āvī, -ātŭm, *to carry back, off;* victorĭam reportāre, *to get the victory* [*reject*
rĕpŭdĭŏ, -ārĕ, -āvī, -ātŭm, *to*
rĕpŭtŏ, -ārĕ, -āvī, -ātŭm, *to reflect upon*
rēs, rĕī (f.), *a thing, circumstance*
rescindŏ, -ĕrĕ, rescĭdī, rescissŭm, *to break down*
rĕsistŏ, -ĕrĕ, restĭtī, (no sup.), *to offer resistance*
respĭcĭŏ, -ĕrĕ, respexī, respectŭm, *to consider;* respĭcĕrĕ finĕm, *to keep the goal in view*
respondĕŏ, -ērĕ, respondī, responsŭm, *to answer, reply*
responsŭm, -ī (n.), *an answer*
restĭtŭŏ, -ĕrĕ, restĭtŭī, restĭtūtŭm, *to restore*
rĕtĭnĕŏ, -ērĕ, rĕtĭnŭī, rĕtentŭm, *to detain;* sibi retinēre, *to keep for one's self*
retrō, *back*
rĕvertŏr, -ī, rĕvertī (active), *to return*
rex, rēgĭs (m.), *a king*
rĭdĕŏ, -ērĕ, rīsī, rīsŭm, *to laugh*
rīpă, -ae (f.), *the bank (of a stream)*
rōbustŭs, -ă, -ŭm, *strong, robust*
rŏgŏ, -ārĕ, -āvī, -ātŭm, *to ask, beg, request*

rŏgŭs, -ī (m.), *a funeral pile*
Rōmă, -ae (f.), *Rome*
Rōmānŭs, -ă, -ŭm, *Roman*
Rōmŭlŭs, -ī (m.), *Romulus*
rūpēs, -ĭs (f.), *a rock*
rursŭs, *again*
rustĭcŭs, -ă, -ŭm, *rural, rustic*

S.

Săbīnŭs, -ă, -ŭm, *Sabine*
săcĕr, -ră, -rŭm, *sacred, holy*
săcerdōs, -ōtĭs (m. & f.), *a priest, priestess*
săcrĭfĭcŏ, -ārĕ, -āvī, -ātŭm, *to sacrifice*
saepĕ, *often, frequently*; saepĭŭs, *oftener*; saepissĭmē, *oftenest*
saepĭŏ, -īrĕ, saepsī, saeptŭm, *to inclose*
săgittă, -ae (f.), *an arrow*
Sălămīnĭŭs, -ī (m.), *an inhabitant of Salamis*
sălūs, -ūtĭs (f.), *safety, welfare*; salūtem dicĕre, *to greet*
salvŭs, -ă, -ŭm, *safe*
Samnītēs, -ĭŭm (pl. m.), *the people of Samnium*
Sămŭs, -ī (f.), *Samus*
sanguĭs, -ĭnĭs (m.), *blood*
săpĭens, -tĭs, *wise*
săpĭentĭă, -ae (f.), *wisdom*
Sardēs, -ĭŭm (pl. f.), *Sardes*
sătellēs, -ĭtĭs (m.), *a guard*; pl. *an escort*
sătĭŏ, -ārĕ, -āvī, -ātŭm, *to satiate, glut*
sătĭs, *enough, sufficiently*; satis habēre, *to be satisfied*
saucĭātŭs, -ă, -ŭm, *bruised*
saxŭm, -ī (n.), *a rock*
Scaevŏlă, -ae (m.), *Scaevola*
scĭŏ, -īrĕ, -īvī, -ītŭm, *to know*
scrībŏ, -ĕrĕ, scripsī, scriptŭm, *to write*
scriptŏr, -ōrĭs (m.), *a writer*
Scythă, -ae (m.), *a Scythian*
Scythĭă, -ae (f.), *Scythia*
sĕcŏ, -ārĕ, sĕcŭī, sectŭm, *to cut*
sēcrētō, *privately*
sĕcundŭs, -ă, -ŭm, *the second*

sĕd, *but*
sĕdĕŏ, -ērĕ, sēdī, sessŭm, *to sit*; in equo sedens, *on horseback*
sēdĭtĭŏ, -ōnĭs (f.), *sedition*
sempĕr, *always, ever, forever*
sĕnātŏr, -ōrĭs (m.), *a senator*
sĕnātŭs, -ūs (m.), *the senate*
sĕnectŭs, -ūtĭs (f.), *old age*
sĕnex, -ĭs (m.), *an old man*; sĕnĭŏr, *older*
sentĭŏ, -īrĕ, sensī, sensŭm, *to perceive, feel*
sĕpĕlĭŏ, -īrĕ, sĕpĕlīvī, sĕpultŭm, *to bury*
septēnī, -ae, -ă, *seven by seven, seven at a time*
septĭmŭs, -ă, -ŭm, *the seventh*
sĕquŏr, -ī, sĕcūtŭs sŭm, *to follow*
sermŏ, -ōnĭs (m.), *a talk*
servīlĭs, -ĕ, *slavish*
servĭtŭs, -ūtĭs (f.), *slavery, servitude*
Servĭŭs Tullĭŭs, -ī -ī (m.), *Servius Tullius*
servŏ, -ārĕ, -āvī, -ātŭm, *to save*
servŭs, -ī (m.), *a slave, servant*
sex, *six*
sī, *if, when*
Sĭbyllīnŭs, -ă, -ŭm, *Sibylline*
sīc, *in this manner, so, thus*
Sĭcĭlĭă, -ae (f.), *Sicily*
signŭm, -ī (n.), *a signal*
sĭlentĭŭm, -ī (n.), *silence*
sĭlĕŏ, -ērĕ, -ŭī, (no sup.), *to be silent*
silvă, -ae (f.), *a forest, wood*
sĭmĭlĭs, -ĕ, *like*
sĭmŭl, *at the same time*
sĭmŭlăc, sĭmŭlatquĕ, *as soon as*
sĭmŭlŏ, -ārĕ, -āvī, -ātŭm, *to feign*; sĭmŭlans, *under pretext*
sĭmultās, -ātĭs (f.), *a quarrel*
singŭlī, -ae, -ă, *one by one, one at a time*
sĭnŏ, -ĕrĕ, sīvī, sĭtŭm, *to let, suffer, permit*
sĭnŭs, -ūs (m.), *the bosom*
sĭtĭŏ, -īrĕ, -īvī, -ītŭm, *to be thirsty*
sĭtĭs - (f.), *thirst*

— 157 —

sĭtŭs, -ă, -ŭm, *situated*
sŏcĕr, -ī (m.), *a father-in-law*
sŏcĭĕtās, -ātĭs (f.), *alliance*
sŏcĭŭs, -ī (m.), *a companion, ally*
Sōcrătēs, -ĭs (m.), *Socrates*
sōl, -ĭs (m.), *the sun*
Sŏlōn, -ĭs (m.), *Solon*
sōlŭs, -ă, -ŭm, *alone*
solvō,-ĕrĕ, solvī, sŏlūtŭm, *to (dis)-solve, loosen;* hospitĭum solvĕre, *to withdraw one's friendship*
somnĭŭm, -ī (n.), *a dream*
somnŭs, -ī (m.), *sleep*
sŏnĭtŭs, -ūs (m.), *a sound*
sors, -tĭs (f.), *a lot*
Spartă, -ae (f.), *Sparta*
spătĭŭm, -ī (n.), *space*
spectō, -ārĕ, -āvī, -ātŭm, *to view, to look to, at*
spĕcŭs, -ūs (m.), *a cave, den*
spērō, -ārĕ, -āvī, -ātŭm, *to hope for, expect*
spēs, spĕī (f.), *hope*
spīnōsŭs, -ă, -ŭm, *thorny*
splendĭdŭs, -ă, -ŭm, *splendid*
stădĭŭm, -ī (n.), *a stade*
stătĭm, *at once, immediately*
stătŭă, -ae (f.), *a statue*
stătŭō, -ĕrĕ, stătŭī, stătūtŭm, *to resolve*
Stilpō, -ōnĭs (m.), *Stilpo*
stĭpendĭŭm, -ī (n.), *pay*
stō, -ārĕ, stĕtī, stătŭm, *to stand, to cost*
strŭō, -ĕrĕ, strŭxī, structŭm, *to build*
stŭdĕō, -ĕrĕ, -ŭī, (no sup.), *to be eager, endeavor*
stŭdĭŭm, -ī (n.), *zeal*
stultĭtĭă, -ae (f.), *folly*
stultŭs, -ă, -ŭm, *foolish*
suādĕō, -ĕrĕ, suāsī, suāsŭm, *to advise, recommend*
sŭbĭgō, -ĕrĕ, subēgī, subactŭm, *to subdue*
sŭbĭtō, *on a sudden*
submergō, -ĕrĕ, submersī, submersŭm, *to plunge*
sŭī, sĭbĭ, sē, *himself, herself, itself*
sŭm, essĕ, fŭī, *to be*

summŭs, -ă, -ŭm, *highest;* summus lacus, *the surface of the lake*
sūmō, -ĕrĕ, sumpsī, sumptŭm, *to take*
sŭpĕr (w. acc.), *over;* sŭpĕr (w. abl.), *concerning*
sŭperbĭă, -ae (f.), *pride*
sŭperbŭs, *rather contemptuously*
sŭperbŭs, -ă, -ŭm, *proud*
sŭpĕrĭŏr, -ŭs, *superior, victorious*
sŭpĕrō, -ārĕ, -āvī, -ātŭm, *to surpass, to conquer*
supplex, -ĭcĭs, *(kneeling) on one's knees*
supplĭcĭŭm, -ī (n.), *execution*
surdŭs, -ă, -ŭm, *deaf*
surgō, -ĕrĕ, surrexī, surrectŭm, *to rise, get up*
suscĭpĭō, -ĕrĕ, suscēpī, susceptŭm, *to undertake*
suspĭcŏr, -ārī, -ātŭs sŭm, *to suspect*
sustĭnĕō, -ērĕ, sustĭnŭī, sustentŭm, *to hold out*
sŭŭs, -ă, -ŭm, *his, her, its, their (own);* sŭī, -ōrŭm (pl. m.), *his men*

T.

tăcĕō,-ērĕ,-ŭī,-ĭtŭm, *to be silent*
tăm, *so*
tămĕn, *however, nevertheless*
tandĕm, *at last, at length, pray*
tangō, -ĕrĕ, tĕtĭgī, tactŭm, *to touch*
Tantălŭs, -ī (m.), *Tantalus*
tantŭm, *only*
tantŭs, -ă, -ŭm, *so great*
Tărentīnī, -ōrŭm, (pl. m.), *the Tarentines*
Tarquĭnĭŭs, -ī (m.), *Tarquin, king of the Romans*
Taurĭcŭs, -ă, -ŭm, *Tauric*
Tĕlĕmăchŭs, -ī (m.), *Telemach*
Tellŭs, -ī (m.), *Tellus*
tempestās, -ātĭs (f.), *a storm, tempest*
templŭm, -ī (n.), *a temple*
tempŭs, -ŏrĭs (n.), *time*
tendō, -ĕrĕ, tĕtendī, tensŭm, *to stretch out*
Tĕnĕdŭs, -ī (f.), *Tenedos*

— 158 —

tĕnĕŏ, -ĕrĕ, -ŭī, -tŭm, to hold, keep
tentŏ, -ārĕ, -āvī, -ātŭm, to try, attempt
tĕr, three times
tergŭm, -ī (n.), the back
terrā, -ae (f.), the earth, land
terrĕŏ, -ērĕ, -ŭī, -ĭtŭm, to frighten
tertĭŭs, -ā, -ŭm, the third
testĭs, - (m. & f.), a witness
Teucĕr, -rī (m.), Teucer
Teutŏburgĭensĭs, -ĕ, Teutoburgian
Thēbānŭs, -ī (m.), a Theban
Thēseus, Thēsĕī, (m.), Theseus
Thĕtĭs, -ĭdĭs (f.), Thetis, mother of Achilles
Thŏās, -antĭs (m.), Thoas
Tĭbĕrĭs, - (m.), the Tiber
tĭmĕŏ, -ērĕ, -ŭī, (no sup.), to fear
Tĭtŭs, -ī (m.), Titus
tollŏ, -ĕrĕ, sustŭlī, sublātŭm, to take up, to take away
Tŏmўrĭs, - (f.), Tomyris, a Scythian queen
tormentŭm, -ī (n.), torture
Torquātŭs, -ī (m.), Torquatus
torrĕŏ, -ērĕ, torrŭī, tostŭm, to roast
tōtŭs, -ā, -ŭm, whole, all
tractŏ, -ārĕ, -āvī, -ātŭm, to treat
trādŏ, -ĕrĕ, trādĭdī, trādĭtŭm, to hand down, deliver
trăhŏ, -ĕrĕ, traxī, tractŭm, to draw, drag
trājĭcĭŏ, -ĕrĕ, trājēcī, trājectŭm, to ship over
tranquillŭs, -ā, -ŭm, calm, tranquil
transĕŏ, -īrĕ, transĭī, transĭtŭm, to cross
transfĕrŏ, -rĕ, transtŭlī, translātŭm, to transfer
transfĭgŏ, -ĕrĕ, transfĭxī, transfĭxŭm, to stab
transĭtŭs, -ūs (m.), a passage
trĕcentī, -ae, -ā, three hundred
trĭbŭŏ, -ĕrĕ, trĭbŭī, trĭbūtŭm, to give, confer on; fidem tribuĕre, to trust; sibi culpam tribuĕre, to put the blame upon one's self
tristĭs, -ĕ, sad

Trōjā, -ae (f.), the city of Troy
Trōjānŭs, -ā, -ŭm, Trojan
trŭcīdŏ, -ārĕ, -āvī, -ātŭm, to slay
tū, thou, you
tŭm, then
tŭmultŭs, -ūs (m.), a tumult
turbā, -ae (f.), a crowd
turbŏ, -ārĕ, -āvī, -ātŭm, to disturb, trouble
turpĭs, -ĕ, shameful, disgraceful
turrĭs, - (f.), a tower
tūtŭs, -ā, -ŭm, safe, secure
tŭŭs, -ā, -ŭm, thy, your; tŭā, -ōrŭm, your property

U.

ŭbī, where [punish
ulcīscŏr, -ī, ultŭs sŭm, to avenge; to
Ūlixēs, -ĭs (m.), Ulysses
ullŭs, -ā, -ŭm, any, any one
ultĭmŭs, -ā, -ŭm, last
ŭmĕrŭs, -ī (m.), the shoulder; also written: hŭmĕrŭs
ūnĭversŭs, -ā, -ŭm, all (together), whole
ūnŭs, -ā, -ŭm, one, alone, only
urbs, -ĭs (f.), a city
urgĕŏ, -ērĕ, ursī, (no sup.), to press
usquĕ ăd (w. acc.), until, up to
ūsŭs, -ūs (m.), use
ŭt, as, like; ŭt (w. subj.), in order that, so that; ŭt nōn, so that not
ŭtĕr, -rĭs (m.), a leathern sack
ŭtĕr, -ră, -rŭm, which (of two)? who?
ŭterquĕ, ŭtraquĕ, ŭtrumquĕ, both
ūtĭlĭs, -ĕ, useful
ŭtĭnăm, O that, I wish that
ūtŏr, -ī, ūsŭs sŭm, to use, employ; lēgĭbŭs ūtī, to obey the laws; felicĭtāte uti, to enjoy happiness
utrimquĕ, on both sides
uxŏr, -ōrĭs (f.), a wife, consort

V.

valdē, very, very much
vălē, farewell
vălĕŏ, -ērĕ, -ŭī, -ĭtŭm, to avail; multum valēre, to be very powerful

vălĕtūdŏ, -ĭnĭs (f.), *health*
vallĭs, - (f.), *a valley*
vānŭs, -ă, -ŭm, *vain*
Vārŭs -ī (m.), *Varus*
văs, -ĭs (n.); pl. văsă, -ōrŭm (n.), *a vessel*
vastŏ, -ārĕ, -āvī, -ātŭm, *to lay waste, demolish*
vātēs, -ĭs (m.), *a prophet*
vectīgăl, -ālĭs (n.), *tax, income*
vĕhŏ,-ĕrĕ, vexī, vectŭm, *to carry;* vĕhī, *to drive, ride;* navi vehi, *to sail*
vĕl, *or*
vēnātŏr, -ōrĭs (m.), *a hunter*
vĕnēnŭm, -ī (n.), *poison*
vĕnĭă, -ae (f.), *permission, pardon*
vĕnĭŏ, -īrĕ, vēnī, ventŭm, *to come*
vēnŏr, -ārī, -ātŭs sŭm, *to hunt*
ventĕr, -rĭs (m.). *the belly*
ventŭs, -ī (m.), *wind*
Vĕnŭs, -ĕrĭs (f.), *the goddess Venus*
vēr, vērĭs (n.), *spring*
verbĕr, -ĭs (n.), *a blow*
verbĕrŏ, -ārĕ, -āvī, -ātŭm, *to flog*
verbŭm, -ī (n.), *a word*
verĕŏr, -ērī, -ĭtŭs sŭm, *to fear*
vertŏ, -ĕrĕ, vertī, versŭm, *to turn;* in fugam vertĕre, *to put to flight*
vērŭs, -ă, -ŭm, *true, real*
vespĕr, -ī (m.), *evening*
vespĕrī, *in the evening*
vestĕr, -ră, -ŭm, *your*
vestĭs, - (f.), *a dress, clothing*
vĕtŏ, -ārĕ, vĕtŭī, vĕtĭtŭm, *to forbid*
Vĕtŭrĭă, -ae (f.), *Veturia*
vĕtŭs, -ĕrĭs, *old*
vĭă, -ae (f.), *a way, road*
vĭcissĭtūdŏ, -ĭnĭs (f.), *vicissitude*
victŏr, -ōrĭs (m.), *a conqueror; victorious*

victōrĭă, -ae (f.), *a victory*
victŭs, -ūs (m.), *mode of living;* facīlis victus, *a good income*
vīcŭs, -ī (m.), *a village*
vĭdĕŏ, -ērĕ, vĭdī, vĭsŭm. *to see*
vĭdĕŏr, -ērī, vĭsŭs sŭm, *to seem, appear*
vīgintī, *twenty*
vincĭŏ, -īrĕ, vinxī, vinctŭm, *to bind*
vincŏ, -ĕrĕ, vīcī, victŭm, *to defeat*
vincŭlŭm, -ī (n.), *a bond*
vīnŭm, -ī (n.), *wine*
vĭŏlŏ, -ārĕ, -āvī, -ātŭm, *to violate, break (a law)*
vĭr, -ī (m.), *a man, husband*
virgŏ,-ĭnĭs (f.), *a girl, a maid, virgin*
virtŭs, -ūtĭs (f.), *virtue, valor*
vīs (without gen.), (f.), *force, power;* vī, *violently;* magna vis, *a great quantity*
vītă, -ae (f.), *life*
vīvŏ, -ĕrĕ, vixī, victŭm, *to live*
vīvŭs, -ă, -ŭm, *living, alive*
vix, *hardly*
vŏcŏ, -ārĕ, -āvī, -ātŭm, *to call, name, summon*
vŏlŏ, vellĕ, vŏlŭī, (no sup.), *to be willing, wish for, like, want*
Volscī, -ōrŭm (pl. m.), *the Volsci*
Vŏlumnĭă, -ae (f.), *Volumnia*
vŏluntās, -ātĭs (f.), *the will, a wish*
vox, vōcĭs (f.), *a voice;* vocem edĕre, *to utter a cry*
vulnĕrŏ, -ārĕ, -āvī, -ātŭm, *to wound*
vulnŭs, -ĕrĭs (n.), *a wound*
vultŭs,-ūs (m.), *the face, countenance*

Z.

Zeuxĭs, - (m.), *Zeuxis, a famous Grecian painter*

STEIGER'S French Series.

AHN'S French Primer. By Dr. P. HENN. Boards $0.25. (Great care has been bestowed upon the typographical execution of this little book, the perplexing difficulty of the *silent* letters being alleviated by the use of distinguishing outline and hairline type.

AHN'S French Reading Charts. 20 Plates with Hand-book for Teachers. By Dr. P. HENN. $1.00. (These Wall Charts are printed in very large type, the *silent* letters being shown by outline type cut expressly for the purpose.)

The same. The 20 Plates mounted on 10 Boards. $3.75 net. Mounted on 10 boards and varnished. $5.00 net.

(AHN'S *French Primer* and *French Reading Charts* may be advantageously used as an introductory course to *any French Grammar*.)

AHN'S Practical and Easy Method of Learning the French Language. By Dr. P. HENN. First Course. (Comprising a fundamental Treatise on French Pronunciation, French and English Exercises, Paradigms, and Vocabularies.) Boards $0.40.

*Key to same. Boards $0.25 net.

AHN'S Practical and Easy Method of Learning the French Language. By Dr. P. HENN. Second Course. (Comprising a Series of French and English Exercises, Conversations, Elements of French Grammar with Index, and full Vocabularies. Boards $0.60.

*Key to same. Boards $0.25 net.

AHN'S Practical and Easy Method of Learning the French Language. By Dr. P. HENN. First and Second Courses, bound together. Half Roan $1.00.

AHN'S Elements of French Grammar. By Dr. P. HENN. Being the Second Part of *AHN-HENN'S Practical and Easy Method of Learning the French Language.* —Second Course— printed separately. Boards $0.35

AHN'S First French Reader. With Foot-notes and Vocabulary. By Dr. P. HENN. Boards $0.60; Half Roan $0.80.

AHN'S First French Reader. With Notes and Vocabulary. By Dr. P. HENN. Boards $0.60; Half Roan $0.80.

These two editions of one and the same book differ solely in the typographical arrangement of Text and Notes. In the latter the Notes are given separately on the pages following the 75 pieces of Text; in the former each page has at its bottom exactly so much of the Notes as is needed to explain the French Text above. In respect to Vocabulary, etc., both editions are alike.

Key to AHN'S First French Reader. By Dr. P. HENN. Boards $0.30 net.

AHN'S Second French Reader. With Foot-notes and Vocabulary. By Dr. P. HENN. Boards $0.80; Half Roan $1.00.

AHN'S Second French Reader. With Notes and Vocabulary. By Dr. P. HENN. Boards $0.80; Half Roan $1.00.

Key to AHN'S Second French Reader. By Dr. P. HENN. Bds $0.40 net.

AHN'S French Dialogues. Dramatic Selections with Notes. Number One. (Specially suitable for young ladies.) Boards $0.30; Cloth $0.40.

AHN'S French Dialogues. Dramatic Selections with Notes. Number Two. (Specially suitable for young gentlemen.) Boards $0.25; Cloth $0.35.

AHN'S French Dialogues. Dramatic Selections with Notes. Number Three. (Specially suitable for young ladies.) Boards $0.30; Cloth $0.40.

Additional volumes of this Series of *French Dialogues*, which fully meet the requirements of advanced students are in press, and will shortly be published.

AHN'S Manual of French Conversation. In press.

AHN'S French Letter-writer. In press.

Collegiate Course.

C. A. SCHLEGEL. *A French Grammar.* For beginners. Half Roan $1.50.

C. A. SCHLEGEL. *A Classical French Reader.* With Notes and Vocabulary. Half Roan $1.20.

[* These *Keys* will be supplied to teachers only upon their direct application to the publishers.]

E. Steiger & Co., 25 Park Place, **New York.**

STEIGER'S Latin Series.

AHN'S Practical and Easy Latin Method. With Latin-English and English-Latin Vocabularies. By Dr. P. HENN. Half Roan, $1.80

Also separately:

AHN'S First Latin Book.* (Rules and Exercises mainly on *Nominal* Inflection). By Dr. P. HENN. Boards, $0.60; Cloth, $0.70

AHN'S Second Latin Book.* (Rules and Exercises mainly on *Verbal* Inflection.) By Dr. P. HENN. Boards, $0.80; Cloth, $0.90

AHN'S Third Latin Book.* (Rules and Exercises on *Syntax* and Latin Composition.) By Dr. P. HENN. Boards, $0.80; Cloth, $0.90

AHN'S Latin Grammar. By Dr. P. HENN. With References to the Exercises in the *First, Second,* and *Third Latin Books.* Boards, $0.80; Cloth, $0.90

AHN'S New Latin Manual. Grammar, Exercises, and Vocabularies. By Dr. P. HENN. Half Roan, $2.00

Also separately:

—— —— First Course. Boards, $0.60; Cloth, $0.70

—— —— Second Course. Boards, $0.80; Cloth, $0.90

—— —— Third Course. Boards, $0.80; Cloth, $0.90

(This is *AHN-HENN'S Latin Grammar*, with part of the Exercises from the *First, Second,* and *Third Books*, arranged under the corresponding rules.)

AHN'S Complete Latin Syntax. By Dr. P. HENN. Half Roan, $

This *Syntax* is very complete; it states every matter clearly, and in connection with an extensive collection of exercises under the title:

AHN'S Latin Prose Composition. By Dr. P. HENN. Boards, $

is calculated to meet all the requirements even for a six years' collegiate course in Latin. These two books can be profitably used in connection with the above mentioned *AHN-HENN* or any other Latin Course.

AHN-HENN'S First Latin Reader. (*De septem regibus Romanorum*, from LIVY.) With Notes, Vocabulary, and References. (To be used, the second year, with the *Second Latin Book.*) Boards, $0.70; Cloth, $0.80

AHN-HENN'S Second Latin Reader (Selections from JUSTINUS, CÆSAR, CICERO, and PHÆDRUS.) With Notes, Vocabulary, and References. (To be used, the third year, with the *Third Latin Book.*) Boards, $0.80; Cloth, $0.90

These two *Latin Readers*, bound together in one volume. Half Roan, $1.50

AHN'S Short Latin Course. By Dr. P. HENN. Containing: I. Essentials of Latin Grammar. II. Parallel Exercises, with Vocabularies. III. Reading Lessons, with Vocabulary. Half Roan, $1.20

Also separately:

—— —— Number One. Boards, $0.60; Cloth, $0.70

—— —— Number Two. Boards, $0.60; Cloth, $0.70

(This book is intended for a one year's or a two years' course in Latin for those who cannot devote more time to its study.)

AHN'S Latin Delectus. Graded Selections from Latin Authors. With Notes and Vocabulary. Boards, $

AHN'S Latin Vocabulary for Beginners. Methodical and Etymological. With a Collection of Latin Proverbs and Quotations. By Dr. P. HENN. (To be used with the *First* and *Second Latin Books*, independently.) Boards, $0.60; Cloth, $0

AHN'S Latin Wall Charts. By Dr. P. HENN. 22 Plates, in Sheets, $1.50, mounted on 22 Boards, $6.00. (To be used in connection with any Latin Series.)

* The *Keys* to the *First, Second,* and *Third Latin Books* (price $0.40 net, each), intended as aids in dictation exercises, etc., will be supplied to teachers only upon their direct application to the publishers.

☞ Latin Texts, without Notes, at very low prices. ☜
(Teubner's Editions.)

Caesar. — Catullus. — Cicero. — Cornelius Nepos. — Curtius Rufus. — Horatius. — Juvenalis. — Livius. — Lucretius. — Ovidius. — Persius. — Phædrus. — Plautus. — Plinius. — Quintilianus. — Sallustius. — Tacitus. — Terentius. — Vergilius.

For prices of these and of the other Latin books published by Teubner, see STEIGER'S CATALOGUE.

A New Dictionary of the Latin and English Languages. (Latin-English and English-Latin.) With an Appendix of Latin Geographical, Historical and Mythological Proper Names. 16mo. Cloth, $0.85

www.ingramcontent.com/pod-product-compliance
Lightning Source LLC
Chambersburg PA
CBHW020305170426
43202CB00008B/500